Two Germans in
the Civil War

Two Germans in the Civil War

The Diary of John Daeuble

and the Letters of Gottfried Rentschler,

6th Kentucky Volunteer Infantry

Edited and Translated by
Joseph R. Reinhart

Voices of the Civil War
Peter S. Carmichael, Series Editor

The University of Tennessee Press / Knoxville

The Voices of the Civil War series makes available a variety of primary source materials that illuminate issues on the battlefield, the homefront, and the western front, as well as other aspects of this historic era. The series contextualizes the personal accounts within the framework of the latest scholarship and expands established knowledge by offering new perspectives, new materials, and new voices.

Library of Congress Cataloging-in-Publication Data

Two Germans in the Civil War: the diary of John Daeuble and the letters of Gottfried Rentschler, 6th Kentucky Volunteer Infantry / edited and translated by Joseph R. Reinhart.—1st ed.
p. cm.—(Voices of the Civil War)
Includes bibliographical references (p.) and index.
ISBN 1-57233-279-4 (cl.: alk. paper)
   1. Kentucky—History—Civil War, 1861–1865—Regimental histories.
   2. Kentucky—History—Civil War, 1861–1865—Participation, German American.
   3. United States. Army. Kentucky Infantry Regiment, 6th (1861–1864)
   4. Daeuble, John, 1839–1864—Diaries.
   5. Rentschler, Gottfried, 1827–1897—Correspondence.
   6. German Americans—Kentucky—Diaries.
   7. German Americans—Kentucky—Correspondence.
   8. United States—History—Civil War, 1861–1865—Regimental histories.
   9. United States—History—Civil War, 1861–1865—Participation, German American.
   10. United States—History—Civil War, 1861–1865—Personal narratives.
   I. Daeuble, John, 1839–1864.
   II. Rentschler, Gottfried, 1827–1897.
   III. Reinhart, Joseph R.
   IV. Voices of the Civil War series.
E509.56th .T96 2004
973.7'3'092331—dc22   2003021289

For Virginia

Contents

Illustrations

꒱

Foreword

While on a boat floating down the Tennessee River, the head musician of the 6th Kentucky's brigade thought he smelled Limburger cheese. The heavy aroma brought back pleasant memories of his native Germany. He demanded to know which of his comrades was hiding the brick of cheese in his haversack, but the commissary had never issued such a "delicacy," despite the fact that a sizeable contingent of the 6th Kentucky, U.S., came from Germany. A soldier standing near the bandmaster quickly discovered the source of the pungent odor, exclaiming to his friend: "Mr. . . . you are sitting on a stand bearing a corpse!" When the musician jumped up, the stenciling on the box revealed that he had been sitting on a casket containing a dead Confederate whose remains had been decaying inside the box for eight days. Gottfried Rentschler, who reported this incident to the *Louisville Anzeiger,* concluded: "Then you can see how everything is pure deception. One cannot trust his own nose."

Gottfried Rentschler relayed this story to amuse his readers, but he also wanted them to understand that truth was nearly impossible to find in war, even when every instinct and impulse led one to believe otherwise. As a member of the 6th Kentucky, Rentschler was mystified by the contradictory behavior of both sides. Union soldiers desired the loyalty of Southerners, but they often wrecked civilian property out of a spirit of wanton cruelty. Confederates often showed less restraint; they committed horrible atrocities against Unionist civilians. Rentschler spoke to an East

Tennessee woman who was accosted by her son's killer, a Confederate cavalryman under General Joseph Wheeler. When she refused to believe that her son had been killed, the Confederate trooper reached into his pocket, pulled out the eyes of the dead man, and threw them on the table, saying: "Here, if you do not believe me here are the eyes of the son of a bitch." Senseless brutality sickened Rentschler, as did the breakdown in social mores. He was horrified by the number of women in East Tennessee who turned to prostitution so that they could buy bread to feed their families. He also noticed a breakdown in morals among his fellow soldiers, some of whom frequently seduced runaway female slaves. The most jarring contradiction Rentschler encountered was the prejudice of his comrades. No matter how brave Germans were in battle, no matter how hard they pushed themselves on the march, "Dutch" soldiers, as they were called, were viewed with suspicion. It was inconceivable to Rentschler that a man's patriotism could be questioned because of his ethnic background. An officer of abolitionist sympathies, whose thin liberalism quickly cracked as soon as he confronted "foreigners," told Rentschler that Germans did not sufficiently value the country and should not be allowed to enlist in the army.

Rentschler's wartime letters contradict the ridiculous but popular opinion in the Union Army that Germans were cowardly scoundrels by nature. A comrade of Rentschler's, John Daeuble, kept a wartime diary that also counters the stereotype of the unreliable, plodding German soldier. His descriptions of the fighting around Chattanooga and during the Atlanta Campaign attest to the tenacity of the German rank and file. While Daeuble's journal chronicles the military actions of the 6th Kentucky, providing the framework for *Two Germans in the Civil War*, Rentschler's writings are the heart and soul of this volume. The dreary and dangerous life of soldiering did not obscure the deeper questions of war. Rentschler penetrated the conflict's hypocrisy and cruelty to discover one indisputable truth: he was giving his life to a cause that possessed a transcendent purpose. He knew that the fate of liberty and the future of the nation rested on his bayonet. Rentschler predicted that any man who stayed at home and criticized the war effort as a wicked failure would eventually suffer unbearable humiliation for his seditious behavior. He imagined the day would come when many would "turn red" with embarrassment when "the scarred veteran next to him calls out rejoicefully, 'I have been there.'" The man who shirked his duty could only respond to this undeniable fact by saying, "'I was not there, when my fatherland stood in flames; I was not there when those brave men extinguished the fire with their hearts' blood.'" Rentschler issued a final reprimand to those men who refused to join: "Shame on you, . . . your soul smells of cheese." But Rentschler and Daeuble, like so many of their German companions, knew that they had done their duty and that they had served their adopted country faithfully.

Peter S. Carmichael
University of North Carolina at Greensboro

Acknowledgments

Many people have helped in the preparation of this book.

First, I would like to thank the late Gustave A. Daeuble III, who generously allowed me unlimited access to John Daeuble's diaries and narratives and provided a photograph of John for use in preparing this book, as well as in my comprehensive history of the 6th Kentucky that was published in December 2000.

Second, I am grateful to the persons responsible for preserving copies of the *Täglicher Louisville Anzeiger* newspaper, and especially the Filson Historical Society where the original copies are archived, and also available on microfilm.

A special note of thanks is due to Harvey Sollinger, Erna and Joel Gwinn, Eberhard and Ruth Reichmann, and Mia Spudat, all of whom responded promptly to my requests for help in translating certain difficult phrases and idioms from German into English.

I want to express my gratitude to the late Eric Losey who read a copy of the manuscript, pointed out errors, and provided useful suggestions for improvements. However, any errors in this book are solely my responsibility.

I extend thanks to June Hensley, who originally typed my handwritten translations, and also to Earl. J. Hess, Giles Hoyt, Dick Skidmore, and Brandon Slone. Finally, I want to thank my wife, Virginia, for her love, moral support, and the installation of critical software on my computer.

A Note about Translation and Editing

John Daeuble's diary entries and Gottfried Rentschler's letters have been translated into English by the editor.

John Daeuble mostly used commas for punctuation, creating lengthy run-on sentences, and he did not use paragraphs (probably to conserve space). When the native German wrote an English word he always capitalized the initial letter. For the convenience of the modern reader the editor has added some punctuation and paragraphing, replaced some commas with periods, and added capitalization at the beginning of sentences. English words written by Daeuble remain capitalized, and words he underlined appear in italics.

When the meaning of a word or phrase was not clear, letters and/or words were added using square brackets [ ], and names he misspelled or persons he misidentified were corrected using square brackets [ ]. Illegible words were identified by a question mark in square brackets [?]. Finally, a date heading has been inserted above each of Daeuble's daily entries.

Unlike Daeuble's diary entries, Rentschler's letters were generally well punctuated and also paragraphed. Nevertheless, for the convenience of the modern reader some of Gottfried Rentschler's sentences were divided into separate sentences for clarity, and some commas added or deleted. Also some paragraphs were combined or divided. Square brackets were used in the same manner as described above.

Angled brackets < > have been employed in a few letters to indicate where Rentschler is paraphrasing rather than quoting the words he says are taken from the work cited.

Quotations from writings of individuals other than Daeuble and Rentschler are presented as originally written in English, with the original punctuation and misspelling retained, except in a few cases, where punctuation has been added for clarity, and square brackets [ ] added to correct misspelled names, and to explain words or phrases that were not clear. Underlined words appear in italics.

Rather than completely separating John Daeuble's diary entries from Gottfried Rentschler's letters, the editor has preceded each of Rentschler's letters with Daeuble's entries for the corresponding periods. The editor believes that placing their writings about the same events in close proximity facilitates a better understanding of the events without detracting from the individuality of each man. The diary entries are clearly distinguishable from the letters, so a reader can easily read only the diary entries and skip over the letters or vice-versa.

Introduction

I

The diary of John Daeuble and the letters of Gottfried Rentschler presented in this work are unique and provide a fresh and much needed contribution to Civil War literature. The uniqueness of Daeuble's and Rentschler's accounts is twofold. First, they were originally penned by Germans in their native language and, second, the pair served in a Union regiment organized in the border state of Kentucky. There is a scarcity of diaries and letters written by Germans who fought in the Civil War and also of firsthand accounts of soldiers from the Bluegrass State, severely restricting scholarly study, analysis, and understanding of these groups of participants in the nation's greatest conflict.

While a very limited number of diaries and letters of Germans and Kentuckians are scattered around the country in libraries and archives, and some have been published in periodicals in previous years, they can be justly described as few and far between. The situation with respect to books is even bleaker. For example, exclusive of this work, the editor could locate only ten Civil War diaries or collections of letters written by native Germans that have been published in English in book form, and half of these consist entirely or almost entirely of mundane items like miles marched, the weather, road conditions, food, casualties, etc. Only a handful of the these books, such as *Letters of Frederic C. Winkler (1862–1865)* (1963), *Your True Marcus: The Civil War Letters of a Jewish Colonel* (1985), and *Lone Star and Double Eagle: Civil War Letters of a*

German-Texas Family (1982), contain comments about issues such as motivation for enlisting, slavery and emancipation, ethnic prejudices, government policies, and changed opinions as the war progressed. (See Appendix A for a listing of the ten books.) Additionally, just three memoirs and one autobiography were found: *Memoirs of the Confederate War for Independence* (1867), *The Reminiscences of Carl Schurz* (1907–8), *Twenty Months in Captivity: Memoir of a Union Officer in Confederate Prisons* (1987), and Carl Schurz's *Autobiography* (1961).[1] This is remarkable considering that around two hundred thousand German immigrants served in the Union army during the conflict and Germans fought in all the major battles and many of the minor ones. Germans fought for the Confederacy, too, but their number was relatively small. The lack of primary sources is not any better with respect to Kentucky's men in blue during the conflict.[2]

The editor believes that one of the principal reasons why so few diaries and letters authored by Germans have been preserved is because most were written in German, and fewer and fewer descendents (and archivists) could read and understand them. Another contributing factor to the scarcity of these valuable documents surely is the anti-German sentiments and hostility created by World War I, when over half the states banned the teaching of German in schools, and German books and newspapers were destroyed, followed by more anti-German sentiment related to World War II. The fact that few of today's Civil War historians and writers can understand German severely limits research and publication in this area.

Comprehensive secondary sources about the German element in the War Between the States are also scarce. In fact, until William C. Burton's *Melting Pot Soldiers: The Union's Ethnic Regiments* appeared in 1988, Ella Lonn's *Foreigners in the Union Army and Navy* (1951) stood alone in focusing any significant attention on the large number of Germans who fought to preserve the Union.[3] Because Lonn's study of Germans in blue was the only book of its kind, it was accepted as authoritative for many years. However, historians now use it with caution, because as Burton reveals in his preface to *Melting Pot Soldiers:* "Lonn accepted nineteenth century views of 'race,' and her descriptions were stereotyped and as filiopietistic as the most ardent champions of ethnic separation. While her work remains invaluable as a source of information—despite errors and omissions—its lack of critical analysis, reduces its value for understanding the subject."[4]

As to Germans, Ella Lonn concluded that they: "gave to the [Union] army a conservative stabilizing force. . . . The mass of German soldiers were patient, philosophical, plodding men . . . and were withal industrious and thrifty. They yielded respect to authority and were, therefore, well disciplined, persevering, and inspired by some idealism; . . . They were somewhat slow in response but were stable and solid in battle; they learned, in fact, to do some skillful fighting. Leisurely in their mental processes, they had a passion for thoroughness in the details of warfare as in everything."[5] Bell Irvin Wiley, in his noted study *The Life of Billy Yank: The Common Soldier of the Union* (1952), gave a somewhat similar but less detailed description of Germans and cited Lonn's work as a source.[6] The description quoted above, in one form or another, has also been used in much more recent works. Upon examination, one can see the stereotyping in Lonn's characterizations. For example, her description of the "mass of German soldiers" as "plodding" and "somewhat slow in response" does not appear to be supported by any credible body of evidence, nor can the statements that the mass was "philosophical" and "Leisurely in their mental processes." Some were and some were not.

Historian and author Earl J. Hess who has studied and written about Germans in the Civil War also believes Lonn's work has flaws, and notes:

> She has a tendency to rely too heavily on obscure German language
> publications, written by German-Americans, adulatory of the
> Germans who fought in the Civil War. She also has a tendency to rely
> on old national stereotypes that don't hold water. While one might
> find a kernel of truth in them, they are not really useful in under-
> standing groups of people. Ultimately, people are people, whether
> they are Germans or Americans, some are plodding, some are sharp,
> some brave and some cowardly. The same is true for members of
> all nations.[7]

Ella Lonn's study of foreigners in the Union ranks was preceded by her study entitled *Foreigners in the Confederacy* published in 1940. Deficiencies in records kept her from arriving at a reliable number of foreigners in Confederate service but she readily concluded that the Irish were by far the largest component, followed by the Germans. Considering that the South's German-born population in 1860 aggregated only seventy-two thousand men, women, and children, compared to one million three hundred thousand Germans in the North, the number of

Germans in Confederate military service was a very small fraction of the number who served the Union.[8] *Foreigners in the Confederacy* contains some of the same type of flaws and merits as her later work on foreigners who fought for the Union.

An English-language translation of one of Ella Lonn's secondary sources—Wilhelm Kaufmann's *Die Deutschen im Amerikanischen Buergerkrieg* (1911), originally published by R. Oldenbourg in Munich and Berlin—was released in 1999. The English language edition, translated by Steven Rowan, is entitled *The Germans in the American Civil War.*[9] Unfortunately, Kaufmann's narrative, like Lonn's, is dated; it contains quite a few factual errors, and reflects the bias of its German-born author, illustrating the need for a modern, well-researched comprehensive history of Germans in the Civil War.

II

Twenty-one-year-old John Daeuble and thirty-three-year-old Gottfried Rentschler were living in Louisville, Kentucky, when they answered the call of their adopted country to take up arms to help preserve the Union. Both men enlisted in what was supposed to become the 1st German Kentucky Regiment; however, they ended up in the 6th Kentucky Volunteer Infantry Regiment—a mixed unit containing four German-speaking companies and six companies comprised mostly of native Kentuckians.[10] Daeuble and Rentschler were among an estimated 177,000 to 216,000 Germans who served in the Union army and 2,000 who fought in Kentucky's volunteer units.[11]

JOHN DAEUBLE

John Daeuble chronicled his army service in several diaries and wrote narratives consisting principally of his diary entries for December 30, 1861, thru February 18, 1863.[12] The diary entries following this introduction comprise his last diary. These special documents were in the possession of Gustave A. Daeuble III (1929–2001), a descendant of John's brother Louis, and no portion had previously been translated into English nor had they been read for at least two generations because the family members, like most Americans, could not read German. Thanks to the generosity of Gus Daeuble and his family, John Daeuble's diaries and narratives are now in the manuscript collection of the Filson Historical Society, Louisville, Kentucky. The editor's translation of John's narrative for December 30, 1861, to February 18, 1863, is also located there for use by interested parties.

The young immigrant's writings provide a running account of many of his experiences in one of the Bluegrass State's finest fighting regiments; he recorded what he saw and experienced, and much of it was not pretty. Hunger, thirst, long exhausting marches in scorching heat and clouds of dust or in freezing cold and snow or sleet, sickness, deaths of friends and comrades, bravery, anger, mischief, cruelty, sorrow over his parents' dire straits, anxiety under fire, and his growing premonition of death, all emerge from the now brittle pages he left behind.

Born on December 28, 1839, in the small village of Mühlheim am Bach in the Kingdom of Württemberg, John Daeuble was the tenth of thirteen children born to Johann Ludwig Daeuble (Ludwig) and Anna Maria Binder Daeuble. Sadly, ten of John's siblings died in their infancy, and only he, his older brother Louis (born in 1828), and his older sister Maria Magdalena (born in 1833) survived. John Daeuble's father first saw the light of day in Mühlheim am Bach in 1805 and was the eighth of nine children. Ludwig was a miller and also served on the village council. The Daeuble family roots ran deep in Mühlheim am Bach—at least back to1740 when John's great-great-grandfather Johannes Daeuble was born there—so, it was surely traumatic for the family to leave for America.[13]

John Daeuble's father and sister departed for America first, perhaps to find a place to settle and/or earn enough money to pay the passage for the rest of the family. Ludwig and Maria Magdalena arrived at the port of New York on August 12, 1853, and settled in Louisville.[14] Anna Maria and her sons emigrated almost a year later and arrived at the port of New Orleans, Louisiana, on June 2, 1854, aboard the *Athens,* which had embarked from the French port of Havre.[15] Anna Maria and her sons most likely traveled to Louisville by steamboat on the Mississippi and Ohio rivers.

It is not known for certain why the Daeuble family immigrated to the United States or chose to settle in Louisville; however, as to the former, the purpose was most likely to seek a better life, and as to the latter, the growing Ohio River city's German-born population had risen to an estimated eighteen thousand persons by 1852, reflecting its ability to attract German immigrants. Unfortunately, by the time the Daeuble

FIG. 1. *John Daeuble, Company E, 6th Kentucky Volunteer Infantry. Courtesy of Mrs. Gustave A. Daeuble III.*

family reunited in Louisville, a growing nativist movement had emerged there (and elsewhere in the United States), whose aim was to protect the so-called rights of Protestant American-born male voters, and anti-Catholic and anti-foreigner feelings were escalating. Election day rioting in Louisville in August 1855 left twenty-two people dead (mostly Germans and Irish), and by 1860 the city's German-born population had decreased to only thirteen thousand. Although the Daeuble family was not Catholic, its members and other Germans were still subject to the strong prejudices of the time.[16]

Both John Daeuble and his brother worked as painters, and family oral history states that John was a talented artist.[17] John's father worked as a wood sawyer for a while, but by 1857 had become physically disabled by rheumatism and possibly a hernia.[18] John's brother married in 1855 and his sister wed in 1856, so most or all of the responsibility for their parents' support fell on John, who still lived with them. Neither John nor his parents owned any real property and, according to U.S. Census records, his father owned personal property worth only $100 in 1860. After entering the army John sent almost all his army pay to his parents, keeping very little for himself.[19]

Although he received little formal education after his arrival in America at age fifteen, John Daeuble learned English and, based on the writing in his diaries and notebooks, he received a basic education in his native land. His diaries and notebooks contain poems written in both German and English, and indicate he read English-language publications such as *Harper's Weekly,* local newspapers, and at least one book. When not hurriedly jotting down diary entries in the field, his handwriting reflects the fine touch of an artist.[20] John was a nice-looking man and possessed a likeable personality. Of medium build, he stood five feet, nine inches tall, had blue eyes, black hair, and was fair complexioned.[21] Pvt. Gottfried Rentschler praised him in one of his letters as "the favorite" in the regiment and "just as true and competent in the service, as he was charming in private life."[22]

John Daeuble mustered into the 6th Kentucky as a private on December 24, 1861, at Camp Sigel near Louisville. The dutiful infantry-man was promoted to corporal in February 1862, to sergeant on May 23, 1862, and to first sergeant on August 4, 1863. He fought at Shiloh and Stones River (where he was severely wounded in his foot) in Tennessee; suffered through the campaigns to seize Corinth, Mississippi, and repel the Confederate army from Kentucky in the summer and fall of 1862; and battled at Chickamauga in Georgia, prior to the battles around Chattanooga, where his last diary commences.

GOTTFRIED RENTSCHLER

Gottfried Rentschler's correspondence was discovered in microfilmed copies of the Democratic German-language newspaper, the *Täglicher Louisville Anzeiger (Louisville Anzeiger),* located at the Filson Historical Society, Louisville, Kentucky. The first of his twenty-four letters is dated November 27, 1863, and the last bears the date of September 3, 1864.

Rentschler's letters kept Germans in Louisville informed of happenings at the front, particularly with respect to his regiment and brigade. The Germans in the 6th Kentucky came principally from Louisville, so there was much interest in Rentschler's letters covering movements, living conditions, battles, casualties, ethnic prejudices, and more. The letters also contain his comments about army officers (both favorable and derogatory), tirades against corruption both within and without the army, humorous and tragic events, and more.

Gottfried Rentschler was born June 8, 1827, in Grömbach, located on the eastern edge of the beautiful and wide-ranging Black Forest, and about fifteen miles north-northwest of John Daeuble's birthplace of Mühlheim am Bach. He was the second youngest of the eight children of Johann Jacob Rentschler (1780–1845), a laborer, and Catharina Bross Rentschler (1787–1870). Johann Jacob was born in the small village of Grömbach, while Catharina's birthplace was the nearby village of Kälberbronn.[23]

Bright and studious, Gottfried received a good education with emphasis on the art of teaching. He immigrated to the United States in 1852 and temporarily settled in Owen County, Indiana, where his older brother Michael, his mother, and Michael's wife and children lived. Michael, his wife, and his mother had emigrated from Germany sometime between 1845 and 1848, and after a stay in Wheeling, Virginia (now West Virginia), moved to Owen County, Indiana. Gottfried subsequently moved to New York and taught there for two years before moving to Wheeling. He married Paulina Vogel on July 24, 1854, in Wheeling, and after teaching there for several years Gottfried and Paulina moved to Louisville, where he was residing at the start of the war.[24]

At five-foot, eleven inches tall, Gottfried was several inches taller than the average German who served in the Union army. He may have been heavy, because at age sixty-six he weighed two hundred forty pounds.[25] No other information about his appearance is available. The erudite German's letters reveal an outgoing, sometimes volatile, highly educated, clever, and talented man who flavored his correspondence with references to historic European rulers, military leaders, writers, the Bible, fables, and jokes. His sense of humor was sometimes dark, and at times he was irreverent toward authority figures. On occasion he was sentimental and poetic, at other times he exuded sorrow for the civilians caught up in the ravages of war, and a few times he spewed fire and brimstone from his pen—making his correspondence highly informative and sometimes entertaining.

Like the large majority of the officers and men of the 6th Kentucky, Gottfried mustered in on December 24, 1861, at Camp Sigel, near Louisville. Originally a private in Company E, he was soon promoted to quartermaster sergeant, but on June 10, 1862, was demoted to private for disobeying an order. Exactly one year after being busted to private, Gottfried was assigned as a clerk in Brig. Gen. William B. Hazen's headquarters. (The 6th had served in William B. Hazen's brigade since January 1862.) Because of his duties as quartermaster sergeant, Rentschler probably did not fight in the battle of Shiloh, but likely fought in the ranks at Stones River and in skirmishes in Kentucky after the battle of Perryville. The learned private's assignment as a clerk may have kept him out of the battles at Chickamauga and subsequent battles, except for Missionary Ridge where everyone in the regiment but the surgeons and musicians participated in the historic charge.[26]

The diary and letters following this introduction cover the important Battles around Chattanooga (October and November 1863), four months of hard service in East Tennessee (December 1863 to May 1864), and the crucial and grueling Atlanta campaign (May to September 1864).

III

Although Kentucky was a slave state, it had strong ties to both the North and South at the beginning of the Civil War, and its people were deeply divided over the major issues that led to the outbreak of hostilities. Nevertheless, most Kentuckians favored remaining in the Union but were against war with the seceded states. In May 1861 the state's legislature attempted to keep the Bluegrass State out of the war by adopting a policy of strict neutrality; however, Unionists won a large majority of the seats in the House and Senate in the August 1861 elections and, on September 20, after Confederate troops had occupied several strategic positions within Kentucky's borders, the legislature declared for the Union.[27] Five days later a call was made for 41,500 volunteers to drive the Confederate invaders from the state.[28] This first call raised 29,203 troops for the Union army, and the state eventually provided an estimated 90,000–100,000 armed men for the Union cause, including about 13,000 militiamen and 23,000 African

Americans.[29] Practically all of Kentucky's 27,000 Germans overwhelmingly supported the Union and an estimated 2,000 of them fought in the Federal army.[30] On the other hand, somewhere between 25,000 and 40,000 Kentuckians served in the Confederate army—evidencing the sharp division within this important border state. Some of Kentucky's Germans served in the Southern army but their number was a tiny fraction of the number of the state's Germans in the Federal army.[31]

As mentioned earlier, Daeuble and Rentschler originally enrolled in what they believed would be an all-German regiment, but instead mustered into a mixed unit. This change resulted from the fact that the 1st German's organizers fell far short of enrolling enough men to complete their regiment, and they decided to voluntarily consolidate with two other incomplete organizations, rather than letting the state's adjutant general choose their merger partner(s) and appoint the regiment's officers. The failure to form the German regiment was not due to lack of support for the Union, but rather the size of the German-born population of Louisville and competition for military-aged Germans by at least eight other organizations including cavalry and artillery units.[32]

The new regiment combined five companies controlled by Col. Walter C. Whitaker, a fiery lawyer, farmer, and state senator from Shelbyville in Shelby County; three companies of German-born men originally recruited for the 1st German Kentucky Regiment and headed by Maj. William N. Hailman, a Louisville high school professor; and two companies commanded by Maj. John R. Pirtle, a Louisville doctor. Colonel Whitaker's men were almost all Kentucky natives and farmers, and the large majority were residents of Henry, Oldham, and Shelby counties (his senatorial district). Major Hailman's German volunteers were principally from Louisville in Jefferson County and had urban occupations. Major Pirtle's companies—a German company from Louisville and a company from Kenton County containing native Kentuckians and more than a score of English- and Irish-born men, plus other nationalities—had mustered in on September 9, 1861, at Camp Joe Holt in Indiana (opposite Louisville) and were in excess of the ten companies needed for the 5th Kentucky Volunteer Infantry Regiment. Walter C. Whitaker was elected colonel of the new regiment, George T. Cotton of Woodford County (a friend of Whitaker's) was elected lieutenant colonel, and William N. Hailman became the regiment's major. Major Pirtle left the regiment because he was not elected its major.[33]

Colonel Whitaker had recruited his companies through personal contacts, advertising notices, meetings, and rallies, and probably offered captaincies to friends or acquaintances on the condition that they enroll enough men for a company. At public events the impassioned and energetic Unionist delivered many rousing and patriotic speeches—referring to flag, country, preservation of the Union, and the need to quell the rebellion.[34]

The 1st German's organizers had used the same methods as Whitaker, including the usual stirring appeal that the country was in danger and patriotic men must hurry and take up arms to defend the Union. But like leaders organizing German regiments in other states, they also stressed ethnic pride and the advantages of serving in a German regiment. For example, an appeal published in the *Louisville Anzeiger* on October 11, 1861, boasted: "Whenever and wherever the Germans have participated in the holy war of justice against injustice, they have always proven their innate talent to be exceptional warriors, and become covered with glory when the opportunity presented itself. Certainly Kentucky's Germans want to have a part in this glory . . . and follow their brave brothers [in other states] and help drive out these thieving hordes." At a large recruiting rally at Schwind's Tavern, Philipp Tomppert, a German-born Unionist and city council member, admonished Germans not to remain uninvolved and thus shamed by their countrymen in the other loyal states.[35]

Language, too, was an important selling point the recruiters used to entice men to join the 1st German. Instructions and verbal communications would be in their native tongue, so even men who did not understand English could serve. Only the officers needed to be able to communicate in English. Recruiters also emphasized that mixing Germans, Irish, and the American-born together had resulted in problems, and formation of a wholly German unit would attract more attention to Germans and better demonstrate that they loved their adopted country and were as patriotic as old stock Americans and should be accepted by them.[36]

The 1st German's organizers were not the only ones who wanted to have a separate regiment. Shortly after the consolidation, Kentucky-born Pvt. Alfred Sampson complained in a letter to his mother that there seemed to be a factional feeling between the German and American soldiers. "They can't understand one another. They seem suspicious of each other. I am afraid it will be the case all through the army. I think it would be better to have them separate."[37] Sampson's feelings were surely common among his American-born comrades, because the consolidation of the German companies with the others was merely a marriage of convenience for the parties involved. Colonel Whitaker had no love for foreigners. He named his recruiting camp after President Millard Fillmore, a one-time candidate of the American or nativist "Know Nothing" Party, and belonged to that party when he was elected to the Kentucky Senate in 1857.[38] Hailman's men believed they would be in an all-German regiment, not a minority in a mixed regiment. Although prejudicial feelings waned some as these groups fought together, they still remained.

The 6th Kentucky Infantry assembled at Camp Sigel (the 1st German's camp) near Louisville in mid-November 1861, and after about six weeks of training and the muster in of the regiment's final seven companies on December 24, 1861, moved to Camp Wickliffe in Larue County, Kentucky (about sixty miles south of Louisville), where it was assigned to the 19th Brigade commanded by Col. William B. Hazen, a highly competent West Point graduate and veteran Indian fighter who forged his troops into one of the toughest brigades in the Union's western armies. The 6th and the rest of its division left Camp Wickliffe on February 14, 1862, and headed for enemy territory. The "Old 6th Kaintuck" (as some later called the regiment) went on to forge a record second to none of the other regiments its state furnished to the Union, and is listed among William F. Fox's "300 fighting regiments" of the Union army.[39] (See Appendix B for a brief history of the 6th Kentucky.)

Prior to the period covered by John Daeuble's diary and Gottfried Rentschler's letters, the unit fought at Shiloh, Stones River, and Chickamauga, and participated in the capture of Corinth, Mississippi, and the campaign to repel the confederate invasion of Kentucky in 1862. After the Army of the Cumberland's defeat at the battle of Chickamauga on September 19–20, 1863,[40] it retreated to Chattanooga, Tennessee, where the Confederate Army of Tennessee began a siege by occupying the west bank of the Tennessee River, Lookout Mountain, and Missionary Ridge; and the Federals suffered severely from a lack of food and supplies. Washington ordered reinforcements sent to Chattanooga from the Army of the Tennessee and the Army of the Potomac and, on October 23, Maj. Gen. Ulysses S. Grant arrived in Chattanooga to take charge. Maj. Gen. George H. Thomas, a highly competent Union-loyal Virginian who had been dubbed the "Rock of Chickamauga" for his courageous leadership in that battle, replaced Maj. Gen. William S. Rosecrans as Army of the Cumberland commander.[41]

While at Chattanooga, the Army of the Cumberland was reorganized and General Hazen's brigade became the 2nd Brigade of the 3rd Division of the 4th Corps. Brig. Gen. Thomas J. Wood commanded the division and Maj. Gen. Gordon Granger headed the corps. After the reorganization, Hazen's brigade consisted of the 6th Kentucky and eight other battle-reduced regiments, and aggregated about 2,200 men.[42] It is in Chattanooga that John Daeuble's diary and Gottfried Rentschler's letters begin.

IV

Before pointing out some of the most valuable information provided by Daeuble and Rentschler, it should be noted that neither man specifically mentioned his motivation for joining the Union army; however, it is safe to assume that both were motivated by patriotism and possibly a desire to help show Americans that Germans were good citizens and should be accepted by them as equals. As a painter, John Daeuble was earning much more than the thirteen dollars a month a private received,[43] and Rentschler was well educated and likely earning more than that, and large bounties were not offered until long after the pair was in uniform, so the reason does not appear to have been money.

Most Germans in Louisville were not abolitionists or even Republicans (Lincoln only received ninety-one votes in the entire city of Louisville in the 1860 presidential election),[44] so the reason certainly was not to emancipate slaves—a war aim that was introduced much later in the war. Abolitionists were unpopular in Kentucky to say the least, and in Louisville the Democratic *Louisville Anzeiger* stated on February 17, 1863, that abolitionists and secessionists were *"Zwillingsbrüder"* [" twin brothers"] in splitting the Union.[45]

It is likely that some Germans who served with Daeuble and Rentschler in the 6th Kentucky were abolitionists because they were Forty-eighters. Forty-eighters had pressed for economic and social improvements, civil liberties, and elected parliaments in Germany, and many had fought against monarchial troops in the German Revolution of 1848 (and/or participated in uprisings in 1849). Forced to flee their homeland, an estimated four thousand to ten thousand of these political refugees came to the United States where they quickly became know as radicals, atheists, abolitionists, and enemies of organized religions, especially the Roman Catholic Church and clerics. Although these radicals were a tiny portion of the 960,000 Germans who immigrated to the United States during the 1850s, and Roman Catholics and many other Germans tended to avoid them and did not agree with many of their ideas, native-born Americans tended to associate all Germans with them, broadening the scope of their anti-German sentiments. The Forty-eighters were strongly pro-Union; a large percentage joined the Union army and they raised many recruits for it.[46]

Like many Civil War diarists, John Daeuble mainly chronicled day-to-day events and conditions and focused almost entirely on the physical side of the war. Even though he omitted comments about the major issues of the war and other personal details often of particular interest to historians, the combination of his more mundane narrative with Gottfried Rentschler's flowery language provides a good juxtaposed view of the war and a fuller account of the events of the period. Of special interest should be Daeuble's description of his experiences immediately preceding and during his brigade's daring amphibious assault at Brown's Ferry near Chattanooga, for which there are few, if any, published contemporary primary sources written by enlisted men, and his entries regarding his growing depression and painful premonition of death after the onset of the Atlanta campaign. This grueling campaign, called by some "the hundred days under fire," wore especially hard on the combatants because of constant contact with the enemy, and dejection and depression among the front-line troops were not at all uncommon.[47]

John's anxiety and fatalism probably resulted from a combination of continuing exposure to danger and death and the cumulative effects of the hardships and privations he suffered during the preceding eight months.[48] He noted on May 15, 1864, after participating in a short-lived but costly failed attack: "We had day or night neither quiet nor rest and lay or crouched behind the fortifications. We could not cook or eat." Four days later he entered in his diary: "Each day brought to us sad hours and weariness with life." His mood plummeted even further later in the month and he confided in his diary: "If a bullet is meant for me, it will hit me . . . God have mercy, protect and comfort my parents. . . . My heart is bleeding in its own misery, when I think of my poor parents." Although suffering from great emotional pain and fully expecting to be killed soon, the sergeant summoned up his courage and continued the campaign with his comrades, rather than straggling or fleeing to the rear.

Unlike John Daeuble's diary, Gottfried Rentschler's letters were intended for the public to read and while they include information about marches, battles, and camps, they also reveal his interesting personality, education, intelligence, interests, likes, dislikes, prejudices, and feelings about both the Rebels and the men in his own army. Gottfried Rentschler served as a private for most of his enlistment, but his position as a clerk in Brig. Gen. William B. Hazen's brigade headquarters gave him access to information and people not freely available to an ordinary enlisted man serving in the line, so his correspondence includes a wider range of subjects than might be expected from a soldier of the lowest rank. Additionally, the inquisitive, self-described "gabber," whose advanced level of education put him in a class much higher than the average man in the ranks, met and conversed with a variety of persons outside his own regiment, including field officers, nativists, abolitionist officers, Sanitary Commission officials, captured Rebels, and both Union-loyal and secessionist civilians. Rentschler's recorded experiences, observations, insights, and strong opinions provide an important primary source originated by a well-educated German immigrant who risked his life for his adopted country. Following are some highlights from his letters.

Prejudices against Germans were a fact of life in the army and became one of the most frustrating aspects of the war for Gottfried and many of his fellow Germans.[49] The prejudices manifested themselves through both words and deeds, and Rentschler revealed that during a conversation with abolitionist officers in March 1864, one told him "Germans had no business to bear arms and become soldiers, because they value the country so little just like the Negro." This statement surely insulted and angered him. As to biased actions, after giving a couple of flagrant examples, he noted: "As a rule, the German has to wade through the mud, while the American walks on the dry road." Then he added: "The German is a 'Dutch soldier' and as a 'Dutchman' he is, if not despised, is disrespected, and not regarded or treated as an equal."[50]

Importantly, while complaining about the anti-German prejudices of Americans, Gottfried revealed his own biased opinion and professed:

> . . . the German soldier is generally far more faithful, conscientious
> and zealous than the native-born American. This is part of the
> German nature, which is our reason to be proud of our nation.
> One more thing: The German soldier is obedient and loyal to duty
> without regard to reward or punishment. The American generally
> considers, only reward, or—The Guard-House. This is caused by
> the national education on either side, in the broadest sense of
> the word.[51]

Then, he warned: "Because of the situation as mentioned, you may possibly draw the conclusion that the mixing of Germans and Americans
in the army may be beneficial to both parties, but such conclusion is
in error."[52] Apparently Gottfried believed that some Germans thought
that if they showed their superiority to the Americans, the Americans
would learn from them and, therefore, accept them as equals. Such an
attitude of superiority, however, would have the opposite effect. As
William C. Burton has noted: "Exaggerated claims of ethnic prowess led
both to unfilled expectations and jealousy on the part of native-born
Americans."[53]

Regardless of the fact that old stock Americans and Germans each
believed they were superior to the other group and also other ethnic
groups, they apparently had no problem closing ranks within their own
corps on the issue of whether they were better than another corps. For
example, Gottfried reported that the soldiers of his 4th Corps had developed a strong dislike for the 23rd Corps (Army of the Ohio), with which
his division had been operating in East Tennessee. He admitted he could
not give a principal reason for this feeling, but "the feeling had been
formed by so many little incidents." He wanted to return to the Army of
the Cumberland and declared: "Our hearts will not lighten . . . until we
have Knoxville behind our back and Lookout Mountain in our face."
Capt. Henry Richards of the 93rd Ohio agreed and wrote in a letter to his
family: "I am fast becoming disgusted with the situation here."[54]
Rentschler's preceding statements support William C. Burton's observation that: "The perception that the stranger, the foreigner, is both different and inferior, is a regular part of the human condition."[55] So Gottfried
was similar to his American counterparts in this way.

Early in 1864, when the Union army began enrolling blacks from
Kentucky as soldiers, Rentschler sided with the vast majority of white
Kentuckians who were strongly against this action, and he stated in a

letter written in March: "I had a discussion once with a party of abolitionist officers about the employment of Negroes as soldiers and uttered
my disapproval." Rentschler's own negative feeling toward abolitionists
surfaced when he wrote on May 1, 1864, that if "the gentlemen in
Washington . . . do not take my advice, then it is their own fault if the
abolitionists one day throw a plantation full of niggers in their face." The
foregoing, combined with jokes he tells about them and words he uses
to describe Negroes, reveal his agreement with most white Americans of
the time on the question of Negro equality—that they were not equal.[56]

Regardless of his religious training to "love thy neighbor," he held
only contempt for Southern secessionists, be they man or woman. He
believed Southerners were ignorant ("Intelligence, even in the simplest
form does not seem to be found its way into this part of the country"),
and some of the women he saw ". . . have sunk far under other people . . .
[and] the war has produced an indescribable moral decline in the female
sex of the South." On the other hand, he praises the Unionist men and
women of East Tennessee (who were in the majority in that part of the
state), is sorrowful over their often harsh treatment by the Confederates
while they controlled the region, and fondly remarks: "I have found that
in relation to warmth, the East Tennesseans are equal to the Swabian
[his] people. God bless and protect these warm people from the Rebel
devils in the future."[57]

Interestingly, after Gottfried described the miseries that the war had
inflicted upon the poor farmers and their families in East Tennessee
(their homes had been destroyed, their fields lay fallow, they had no seed
and no draft animals), he pointed out a perceived difference between
Americans and Germans of the time, concluding that: "The misery of
these people would be bottomless if the Americans themselves felt
bound to the soil with heart and soul in the same degree as the Germans.
Fortunately, the American has a lighter spirit and his home is where he
finds the most plentiful bread." Minetta Altgelt Goyne, translator and
editor of *Lone Star and Double Eagle,* made a similar observation: "The
Anglo-American had always shown a willingness to pick up his domicile
when conditions became too trying. The German, on the other hand,
was little inclined toward the nomadic life, and was in fact, conspicuous
for his stability as a landowner."[58]

The lack of voluntary enlistments by men at home and the government's reluctance to conscript men to fill up the army was a sore point

with those already in uniform, and in early January 1864, when it appeared to Gottfried that the army's efforts to reenlist soldiers whose enlistments were nearing expiration was going slowly, the soldier-correspondent explained to the *Anzeiger*'s readers that the morale of the troops was good:

> and they are prepared to hold out until the Rebellion's last rib is broken and its last heartbeat; but they have tallied that besides them still about one million young men from 18–20 years old are sitting at home doing nothing for the grand cause. They say "First, let the young men sitting at home come out and carry their share of the load, send volunteers and, if there are none, enough conscripts to fill out the ranks . . . then we would be glad to stay to the last man." . . . Everyone knows our soldiers out here, and they know that is the reason they do not enlist.[59]

Coincidentally, a soldier from the 9th Ohio (a German regiment from Cincinnati) who was identified only by initials, affirmed the preceding statement in a letter he wrote to the *Louisville Anzeiger* from Chattanooga on January 30, 1864:

> To date, only one man from our regiment has gone to the Veteran Volunteers Corps, and this will probably be all they receive from us. The opinion out here in our army is quite different. But we are all one in this: "That so long as not every young man in the North able to bear arms, who enjoys the protection and benefits of our government, takes up arms in order to do something for the cause of the Union, we will also sit back for a long time and criticize battles and campaigns from behind beer tables. However, when they are all out and a decisive blow is to be dealt, we would gladly be prepared to volunteer again with them [and] to take up arms as at the outbreak of the war. Therefore come out here you men in the North and the support will not be distant!"[60]

In Rentschler's own regiment (the 6th Kentucky) only forty-one men reenlisted and only two of them were Germans. In addition to feeling they had done their part while those at home had not, changed war aims (emancipation) probably influenced a number of the native Kentuckians not to extend their enlistments, while the prejudicial treatment experienced by the Germans also probably had some impact on their decision. William C. Burton pointed out that the "feeling of biased treatment shows in the low rate of reenlistment in the veteran regiments by ethnics," so it is reasonable to assume it influenced the decisions of some Germans in mixed regiments.[61]

Many Americans felt that the conflict had become a rich man's war and Gottfried agreed. The native German chastised civilians who were getting rich off the war at the expense of the government, the soldiers, and their families—contractors, manufacturers, suppliers, and vendors who either overcharged the army or soldiers, or who furnished shoddy goods and equipment. "At the top stand the contractors," he declared, ". . . then come the sutlers and bakers. When they become rich quickly, it happens, likewise, through overcharging whereby they deliver to the poor soldier his needs only for sinful prices." As to cheats who advertised in newspapers and did not deliver the merchandise the soldier had paid for in advance, Gottfried swore: "God damn these swindlers!"[62] The provoked Swabian criticized fellow Germans as well, including a baker named John Dohn who scolded Rentschler for mentioning bakers among the profiteers because most were Germans.[63]

Finally, Gottfried held out little hope that the South would sue for peace because he believed they would never agree to give up slavery—an issue Lincoln and his cabinet would not yield on, so the Rebels would have to be brutally beaten into submission. "Our enemy is desperate, desperate to the point of insanity," he wrote in early March 1864. By late July the enemy was still resisting savagely and he wrote: "As all Rebel prisoners here agree, as does everyone agree, the Rebels will not stop fighting as long as they can assemble a company"—a statement that gave little hope to his fellow Germans in Louisville that the war would end soon. However, he believed that the only way the Union could be defeated was through internal corruption and not force of arms.

Here then are rare documents—the wartime writings of German Americans from a border state. Their unit was in the middle of the war in the west and their comments add much to what we know. They also do so from a different perspective as well. Their accounts reveal a great deal about soldier life, but also class, racial, and ethnic matters. It is a special story, one that allows the reader to enter the world of two foreign-born men who laid their lives on the line for their adopted country, even though most native-born Americans treated them like second-class citizens.

CHAPTER ONE

The Battles around Chattanooga

First Sgt. John Daeuble began his diary entries at Chattanooga on October 26, 1863, just one day before his brigade attacked and drove off enemy troops posted at Brown's Ferry (located west of the city on the Tennessee River). This attack was the first offensive action undertaken to break the enemy siege that had the Army of the Cumberland on the brink of starvation; it was especially notable because pontoon boats were used as landing craft for the attacking force. Subsequent battles at Orchard Knob on November 23, 1863, Lookout Mountain on November 24, 1863, and Missionary Ridge on November 25, 1863, finally broke the strangling Confederate siege of Chattanooga—the city known as the gateway to the South.[1]

OCTOBER 26–27

On the evening of 26 October the general talk in the camp was that we would leave our camp the following night, but at what hour or where to was a mystery to us. The advance post of our brigade which consisted for the month of October of the 1st Ohio, 6th Ohio, 41st Ohio, 93rd [Ohio], 124th Ohio, 5th Ky., 6th Ky., 23rd Ky. and 6th Ind.,[2] was relieved by others, and they came back to camp. Cartridges were drawn, every soldier was provided with 60 of them. Night brought keen expectations and all of us returned to our quarters. On the previous day each company received the order to prepare a listing of the most capable men, together with the

1

required number of officers and non-commissioned officers. We provided [from] Co.[mpany] E, 12 privates, 1 off.[icer] and 3 non-commissioned officers, together with a corporal. Comp.[any] G, Comp[any] C and Comp[any] I together provided 25 men and 1 captain.[3] During the day of the 26th a second list was demanded, which gave the remainder not in the first list of named soldiers and officers, supposedly they were to be drilled, but afterwards that was shown to be incorrect. After dismissal that evening it was ordered that everybody be ready to march at any time. Next we were advised no blankets, baggage, and then a little later [the] time for breaking camp was put at 12 midnight. The night was moonlit and suited for a night march. About 9 o'clock the remaining troops, called the Invalid Corps,[4] received orders to depart immediately with bag and baggage. Detachments of the different regiments in our brigade came together, only a third consisted of off.[icers] and non-coms [noncommissioned officers]. We stayed in our camp for ½ hour, the same at the brigade headquarters and in Chattanooga. We left our tents standing in camp. We then marched from Chattanooga along the river where we reached a pontoon bridge ¼ mile beyond Chattanooga, and we crossed over it to [Moccasin Point].[5] The road was very poor because of the earlier rains. We entered the forest, where in many places the mud ran over our shoes. We must have been 2 miles away from our camp when we made a halt in the woods and spent the rest of the night right there. Next morning 45 minutes before sunrise we set off again, [and] men were handed axes and spades. We moved forward very carefully, and reached the predetermined crossing point at daybreak. Those [men] we had left in camp the previous evening started their marching at 12 midnight with rifles and cartridge boxes. They boarded pontoons on the river near Chattanooga [and] all other baggage and even the tents were left behind in the camp, together with the sick and men not capable of duty. There were 45 [50] pontoons each containing 35 [27] men [and two flatboats holding about 50 men each].[6] They moved leisurely down river, to the foot of Lookout Mountain which extends into the river at this point, where the river is only 12 to 15 yards wide. The enemy outposts fired on them several times, but because it was foggy on the river, and our men merely steered and left them drift downstream the enemy was unable to recognize anything and left them alone. They reached Brown's Ferry at the same time as us. They climbed the hill Sandy's Hill[7] and we crossed over the river in their pontoons. The enemy had not expected this sudden attack, and they pulled their men together in order to present some

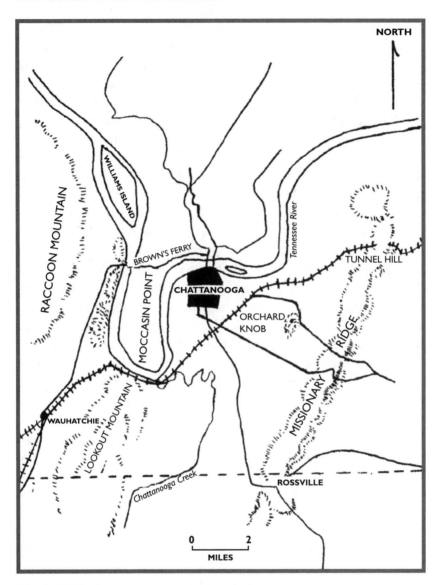

MAP 1. *Chattanooga area.*

resistance. The bullets whistled past us as we crossed the river. Two men were killed during the crossing in the pontoons. For each pontoon there were 25 men who had to be ferried across as quickly as possible. The enemy, only small in number, fired on us from the top of the hill. We then climbed the steep hill, and as we reached the hilltop, the enemy withdrew. When our men had reached the top of the other hill the enemy tried to get ahead of them and to reach the same hilltop; however, after climbing up to halfway, they were repulsed by our men and driven down. We were called back from the hill that we had climbed earlier amid passing and hissing gunfire. Other units marched up and took possession of the hill. One sergeant of Comp.[any] B from our regiment was killed [captured];[8] altogether there were 5 killed, 21 wounded, and 9 missing or taken prisoner from our Brigade. We had, compared to the others, before [their] arrival, to stand up to more difficulties, although we were called Invalid Corp[s]. Below in the ravine on the road where two hills divide we had to throw up fortifications. The enemy brought up two cannon, and began to bombard us. Since we had thrown up [only] a light breastwork, we proceeded up the other hill, where the regiments of our brigade were located. They also had thrown up fortifications, and still continued to fell trees. Opposite us, below in the valley, stood the enemy, whom we clearly saw as before. They had 2 cannon together with a Regiment for support, which was the 34 Ala. [4th Alabama]. The infantry on both sides remained quiet; however, they continued to fire shells towards us. Part of them buried in the hill in front of us. They sent most over our regiment and they roared from 5 to 30 feet over us and burst in the air over the river. They had their cannon also directed, in order to hinder our people who were building the pontoon bridge, which was started immediately after the troops were shipped over, however, their shells did not reach them. The bridge was completed towards evening then our batteries were brought over and set up in the valley.

The enemy kept up his bombardment for two hours, whereupon he then moved back to the Lookout mountain around 2 o'clock. Left of us, [Brigadier] General [Walter C.] Whitaker[9] bombarded the Lookout [Mountain]. During the enemy cannonade we lay flat on the earth behind the crest of the hill and fortifications, where we had to wait out the enemy's ineffective shooting. According to statements of the few residents of the valley, 2 days before, the enemy had a strong brigade located on this same place from which 2 Regts were recalled.[10] A brigade on this hill could have kept off more than a Division, which the enemy did not expect. Otherwise he would have planned better, in order to stymie our plan. We had the same day not the slightest more to eat. Then about 8 o'clock in the evening we drew only ¼ rations for 2 days, which we could have eaten up at one mealtime.

FIG. 2. *Hazen's Troops landing at Brown's Ferry. Harper's Weekly.*

OCTOBER 28–29

On the morning of the 28th it was very foggy. It began to rain after daybreak but stopped again around 9 o'clock. A man from each company
was sent to the camp in order to bring blankets back with them.
Brig. Genl. Whitaker and the enemy on Lookout undertook a mutual
cannonading. Every man in our company came on service in our regiment, [and] those not assigned to other work had to pull 13½ pound[11]
cannon of the 2nd Ill. Battery, which [battery] had belonged to our
brigade since October, up a hill with a rope. The rest of the regiments
pulled 3 more further up to the top of the hill and fortified them. The
enemy who was occupied with the bombardment of Fort Whitaker[12]
turned his attention one time westerly, where he saw troops move up
and directed his fire on the said troops. We saw the troops in the distance advance in the flank march with a skirmish line in front. Because
they came towards us from the enemy's area, we were in general belief it
was the enemy. Our general [Brig. Gen. William B. Hazen] was of course
familiar with these troops' movements, but the soldiers and the majority of the officers were in doubt whether it was friend or enemy. When
the troops were still ¼ mile distant, one recognized our flag with the
naked eye. The officers could not distinguish more with their spy glasses than we with the naked eye, until the named were recognizably near,
[and] with eager eyes we gave the troops our attention which only
shortly before had filled us with misgivings, but now made us feel all the
better. [Major] General [Oliver O.] Howard (who only had one arm)
from 11th Army Corps rode in front with his staff,[13] He turned off the
road and came to us on the hill where we saw him in person. [Major]
General [Joseph] Hooker[14] came up with his staff, which rode along the
road, and in a short time spoke with General Hazen and praised him for
capturing this position. The divisions of [Maj. Gen. Carl] Schurz and
[Maj. Gen. Daniel] Butterfield [Brig. Gen. Adolph von Steinwehr]
encamped down in the valley.[15] The fencing located there disappeared
suddenly and their canvas houses [tents] appeared in the valley; shortly
thereafter lovely music sounded all of which made a stimulating impression on us. The 12th Army Corps was still back between Bridgeport
[Alabama] and this place and the river route was free of the enemy and
boats could run without interference. Around midnight the enemy
made an attack out at Hooker's troops' outposts [at Wauhatchie],

[and] it developed into a general battle, with cannonading intermingled. This nighttime battle by moonlight lasted until about 3 o'clock in the morning. Our brigade remained quiet in our assumed position. There were no shots fired by us. The newly arrived troops which had camped below in the valley, marched immediately to the scene, they took two fortifications from the enemy, lost however 400 dead and wounded men.[16]

OCTOBER 29

On the morning of the 29th mutual cannonading opened between [General] Whitaker and the enemy on the Lookout. The same morning Genl. Whitaker advanced with 2 Regt.[s of] his Brigade to join us.

OCTOBER 30

On the 30th, 7 men from our Comp[any] were ordered to work the whole day in the rain and with ¼ rations. In the afternoon of the same day each company was given a sheet of paper on which we had to make out muster rolls. I made Muster Rolls out in the rain using a bayonet to draw lines and [a] pencil as [a] pen. Several times drops of water fell on the pages, I was forced to stop several times. It rained until 9 o'clock at night [and] we could barely maintain a sparse [camp]fire. When it ended a terrible storm arose, [and] the fire was fanned by the wind which blew the fire 15–20 steps away [and] chased the few [men] situated there. Officers' tents were blown down by the storm. This storm raged for ½ hour, then it abated some, but that night the weather stayed windy. The weather held some, and was colder,

OCTOBER 31

Around 10 o'clock the next morning, the 31st, the sun appeared again. At noon we had an inspection down in the valley and then climbed up and down the steep hill. Around 10 o'clock at night, we drew ¼ rations for 2 days, which were divided out immediately after receipt.

NOVEMBER 1

The 1st of November a troop detachment arrived again in the Lookout Valley. The enemy bombarded them from the Lookout Mountain. In the evening we left the mountain Sandy Hill, We proceeded to the valley and a camping place was already dug out for us. Had to suffer wretchedly with the hunger; several times the pickets received two cobs [ears of] corn as rations. With each day corn was roasted and eaten which barely curbed the hunger and which we were right happy to receive.

NOVEMBER 2

On the morning of the 2nd Nov. two men from each Comp.[any] were sent to go over the river into Whitaker's abandoned camp to get boards. They returned because the [pontoon] bridge was broken by tree trunks thrown into the river by the enemy. At this time the Orderly Sergt. in our regiment was called to Major [Richard] Whitaker's[17] Hd. [Head] Quarter[s], then an order from Brig.[ade] Hd. [Headquarters] was read to us about the building of winter quarters that should be 8 foot wide, 10 foot long and 6 foot high, and each 6 men must proceed to work on a house of the designated size. The building of such began immediately. Trees were cut and fence bolts [rails] taken, it did not take long, so stood nice log cabins with shingled roofs. We had not the slightest more to eat. Cornmeal was distributed to us from Brig[ade] Hd. [Head] Quarters, which each regiment in the Brig.[ade] received, and each man received ¾ cup, from which we made soup. The night of the 4th to the 5th our regiment came on picket with the 93rd Ohio and were posted up along the hill abandoned by us. The enemy on Lookout Mountain had a glowing fire that looked like fencing or wooden breastworks had been set on fire.

NOVEMBER 5

After daybreak on the 5th when our regiment came back into camp again it began to rain; however, the men worked on their wood huts uninterruptedly. The majority had already erected them and equipped [them] with fireplaces in the nicest order. At noon we received orders to march off from there about 2 o'clock in the afternoon to our old camp [at Chattanooga], which was an annoyance for everyone who had built their huts to abandon them again. It rained continuously, [and] when we left our new camp around the aforementioned time the mud and water ran over our shoes in some places. The ground was very slick and slippery, also we had to wait a long time in order to cross the two pontoon bridges at Brown's Ferry and Chattanooga. We reached our camp by nightfall. There on the morning of this same day our tents had been taken down and loaded on the wagon, which in concept was to bring to us our things left back in camp. Of course our woodwork was immediately taken by the surrounding troops, and when we arrived we found not the slightest more. The ground was wet and nothing remained but

FIG. 3. *Major Richard T. Whitaker, 6th Kentucky Volunteer Infantry. Courtesy of the Filson Historical Society.*

for us to lay in the muck. Next day we improved our camp again. The 6 Nov. Comp.[any] B went to [Brigadier] General [Thomas J.] Wood as Provost Guard.[18]

NOVEMBER 7

The 7th Nov. we believed our camp had to be moved to Fort Palmer,[19] however 3 other regiments came there, whereupon we improved our camps using the boards abandoned by the departed Regiments which were distributed to each Company in the Regt.

NOVEMBER 10–11

The 10th and 11th I made out payrolls together with clothing bills[20] for 4 months, July, Aug., Sept., Oct.

NOVEMBER 13

On the 13 Nov., shortly after noon, 2 soldiers, one from 44th Ill and the other from the 88th Ill, were shot to death because of Desertion in front of the enemy. A division was present. During this time, the paymaster reached us and we were paid in the afternoon for 4 months and the clothing [cost] deducted and made good.

NOVEMBER 14

On the morning of the 14 [th] it rained [and] we had to make a ditch 1 foot wide and 1 foot deep along[side] our quarters. At daybreak our Regiment came on picket [and] around noon our Brigade was turned out, when 3 soldiers were drummed out of the Brigade, one because of cowardice 41st Ohio, one because of Desertion, 124th Ohio, and one because of desertion 15th Missouri,[21] who had his head shaved and his clothes taken off his body, and also will be sent to the prison at Nashville.

NOVEMBER 16

In the afternoon of the 16th we had to clean up a drill ground. The whole Brigade took part in this, also each man drew a loaf of bread early the same evening.

NOVEMBER 17

In the morning of the 17th we heard a violent continuous cannonade for ¼ hour, which was 5 or 6 miles distant above Chattanooga [near] Chickamauga Landing. We saw the flash of the cannon that they fired. We drilled for the first time by our camp at Chattanooga. The Regt. counted barely 34 privates and several Sergt. [Sergeants] and officers [because] the others were all on duty and already absent from camp 4–5 days.

NOVEMBER 18

There was cannonading in the morning of the 18th and rifle fire heard below the Lookout Mountain.

NOVEMBER 20–21

The 20th Nov. around 1 o'clock in the afternoon we received orders to make ready to march off toward the enemy. It was misty weather and rained at times, therefore we were not drilled. In the evening we drew rations for 1 day together with 60 cartridges, so that each man had 100 pieces on his person. At dress parade in the evening about 5 o'clock inspection was held and an order read before us that we on the next following morning would leave our camp and come before the enemy. Our fire should be directed on them again, [and] each man who is absent from the regiment should be treated as a deserter in front of the enemy. No soldier should help carry the wounded away. The same evening after it became dark, still different positions were taken by our army, which was signaled shortly before departure. In the evening 8 o'clock, we received orders again to deposit 40 cartridges per man at the Q.M. [Quartermaster] Department. Around 10 o'clock at night it began to rain and rained continuously until daybreak when on the 21st it newly began again.

NOVEMBER 22

In the night on the 22nd the weather cleared up, the Batteries in Fort Wood[22] opened their fire on the enemy, part of which appeared to be in motion. In the afternoon we drew our 100 cartridges again. Toward nightfall [Brigadier] General [Adolph von] Steinwehr of Genl Hooker's troops arrived and camped next to us. We drew in the evening [at] 8 o'clock only ¼ rations for 2 days.

NOVEMBER 23

23rd at daybreak our regiment and the Louisville Legion came on picket. About 2 o'clock in the afternoon our Brigade and Division advanced.
Our regiment and the Legion were the skirmishers from our Brigade.
Several steps from our advanced post line the firing began. We drove the
enemy back at the double-quick. The 41st Ohio took a whole regiment
prisoner 150–200 men, the 28th Ala., with their flag.[23] Our regiment
received 6 lightly wounded.[24] The 41st Ohio had suffered there some 80
men killed and wounded. They had on average more dead than we at [the
battle of] Chickamauga.[25] Our division was supposed to have taken 300
prisoners.[26] Afterwards we pursued the enemy [unknown word] 1½ miles
to within ¼ mile of the camp and halted.[27] In the evening the enemy
unleashed a fearsome cannonade on us from Mis.[sionary] Ridge. Shells
roared 4 feet over my head and buried themselves in the ground several

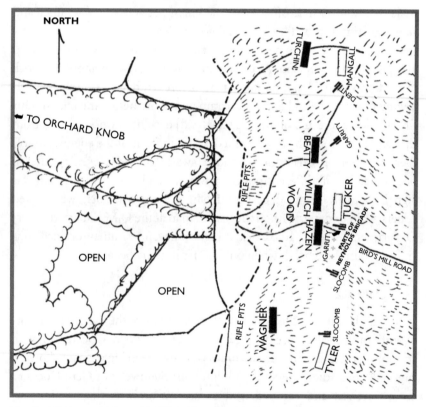

MAP 2. *Missionary Ridge—4:50 P.M., November 25, 1863.*

yards behind me. Our troops threw up fortifications, when again one shell or more were again fired by them, so the officer called loudly, ["]Lay down boys.["] During the night the fortifications on the hillock were fully completed. Our regiment and the L.[ouisville] Legion stayed on picket until 1 o'clock in the night when we were then relieved. We took our position behind the captured fortifications of the Rebels and cooked ourselves some coffee. After we had rested about ½ hour, we were disturbed again and had to fill fortifications with brushwood. Afterwards shovels and picks came, then we made the front of the Rebel fortifications to our rear. We dug a trench on the other side where it appeared as a double fortification.

NOVEMBER 24

On the morning of the 24th it was foggy weather and rained from time to time. The Batteries from Fort Wood, earlier [General Braxton] Bragg under the enemy,[28] [along] with a battery to the right of us from [Maj. Gen. Philip H.] Sheridan's division,[29] opened fire toward the enemy on Missionary Ridge. During the night the weather improved. On Lookout Mountain there was a heavy cannonade the whole day and one saw the flash of the rifles in the night. They fired mutually until near midnight. The enemy was located on the peak of Lookout Mountain and our men [were] on the first rocky terrain below the height.[30] Before midnight our Major [Whitaker] received orders to be prepared to advance at daybreak. The moon was ¾ dark.

NOVEMBER 25

And on the 25th each man drew 100 cartridges and expected a movement at any moment. The enemy moved mostly on the [our] left wing along the Missionary Ridge. Our cannonade began about 9 o'clock. The weather was cold. Around noon the enemy maintained a strong cannon fire on us. The 25th about noon [Lt.] Melcher[31] came to the Regt. Around 4 o'clock in the afternoon, the Brig.[ade] formed in a double line. The advance was blown. Our Regt. was in the left wing of the Brig.[ade] in the first line. The enemy directed a terrible cannon fire on us. We only had orders to go to the foot of the mountain to draw the enemy's attention from [our] left wing. We stormed the hill however without orders, a terrible cross fire from cannon was directed on us. When we reached the

FIG. 4. *Union Troops reaching the crest of Missionary Ridge.* Harper's Pictorial History of the Civil War.

foot of the hill the leaded rain of the musket balls came hissing at us. Our Brig.[ade] captured 18 cannon and the division, in total, 41 pieces. A general Hurrah cheer occurred along our lines after the assault and conquest of the hill and greeted our Generals. Before midnight we still threw up fortifications.[32]

NOVEMBER 26

The 26th we saw in the distance a large amount of smoke rising from fires that the enemy had set in order to destroy bridges and the like. There was a bombardment again in front of [Major] General [William T.] Sherman on the left wing. Around 10 o'clock in the morning 35 shots were fired from Fort Wood as a salute, which proclaimed the great victory of Missionary Ridge. The weather was clear but cool. In the afternoon part of the troops from the left wing marched to their camp at Chattanooga, around the same time glorious music resounded to us on the left wing of our Div[ision]. In the evening I went to the camp 3 miles away. We had marching orders to march off the following morning to proceed to the support of [Maj. Gen. Ambrose E.] Burnside at Knoxville, after I again arrived at the camp on the Missionary [Ridge], it was sounded to leave. Our division left the hill and returned to the previous camp. The marching order was called off because Burnside had repulsed the enemy [General James] Longstreet by Knoxville.[33] About 9 o'clock we reached the camp and before noon we heard heavy cannonading in front. In the afternoon we received Marching Orders to depart the following morning with 60 cartridges and 4 days rations. In the evening was a dress parade.

NOVEMBER 27

On the 27th we were given the highest praise in an order by our Division Com.[mander] Wood for our bravery [on] the 25th.

■   ■   ■

Pvt. *Gottfried Rentschler's first letter published in the* Louisville Anzeiger *was dated November 27, 1863, and briefly covers the battles around Chattanooga and the casualties incurred by the 6th Kentucky and the rest of its brigade on November 23 and 25, 1863.*

LETTER 1

Published December 7, 1863
Written Chattanooga, November 27, 1863

Dear Editor:

Enclosed, I send to you a list of the dead, wounded and missing in our brigade, consisting of 9 regiments, which at the beginning of the battle numbered 2,200 officers and soldiers.[34] The list will show you that the total casualties amounted to about 25 percent. Missionary Ridge was solely and only taken through the courage of its soldiers, not through the skillfulness of any of its generals. The order stated that our troops should only seize the position of the breastworks at the foot of the mountain range. However, when they came into these works, they realized quick enough that everyone would meet certain death there, therefore they stormed up the mountain in spite of a terrible cannon and small-arms fire and arrived at the right time on the top of the ridge in order to support Sherman and to capture a large number of cannons, rifles and prisoners. The victory was a complete one.[35]

We are under marching orders. [Lt. Gen. James] Longstreet has probably united with [General Braxton] Bragg by this time and in quite a short time another one will, and according to all appearances there will be a fight just as bloody as the last.[36] Lookout Mountain is free from the Rebels. In the *[Louisville] Anzeiger*[37] of the 13th of Nov. I read [Maj. Gen. Joseph] Hooker took Lookout Mountain and restored the connection with Bridgeport above Chattanooga.[38] This is not correct. Lookout was first taken on the 24th of November and, in fact, by [Maj. Henry W.] Slocum[39] and the 1st Division of the 4th Corps after a very bloody battle.[40] The way to Bridgeport (which lies below Knoxville) was opened by Hazen's brigade through an excellent, successful night expedition on the 27th of November [October] and not by Hooker. Hazen's brigade has acquired unfading laurels. A correct description, perhaps the only correct description of this expedition, you can find in a certain number of the "Cleveland Herald."

Casualties in the 2nd Brigade, 3rd Division of the 4th Army Corps from the 23rd through the 25th of November 1863.

Regiment	Dead Officers	Dead Soldiers	Wounded Officers	Wounded Soldiers	Missing Officers	Missing Soldiers	Total Officers	Total Soldiers	Total
1st Ohio	1	10	4	64	0	0	5	74	79
6th Ohio	1	5	2	26	0	5	3	36	39
41st Ohio	1	17	5	65	0	0	6	82	88
93rd Ohio	1	19	4	64	0	0	5	83	88
124th Ohio	1	5	3	18	0	2	4	25	29
5th Ky.	2	8	6	46	0	0	8	54	62
6th Ky.	0	0	1	22	0	0	1	22	23
23rd Ky.	0	9	2	34	0	0	2	43	45
6th Ind.	0	13	3	60	0	0	3	73	76
Total	7	86	30	399	0	7	37	492	529

I do not want to give details about the last battle, I do not have time for that, and details will reach you from many sources.

Respectful greetings,
G. Rentschler

CHAPTER TWO

To Knoxville and Blain's Cross Roads

John Daeuble and his comrades in the 6th Kentucky did not get to relax after their victory at Missionary Ridge because their division was sent to Knoxville as part of a force to assist General Ambrose Burnside's army, which was threatened by Lt. Gen. James Longstreet's corps. Although John Daeuble and his comrades did not engage in any fighting they suffered terribly from shortages of food, adequate clothing, shelter, and extremely adverse winter weather for an extended period of time. Near the end of December, the War Department began an effort to get soldiers to extend their enlistments in exchange for a large bounty and a thirty-day furlough. However, it met with little enthusiasm among Major Whitaker's Kentuckians.

NOVEMBER 28

During the night of 27 to 28 it rained, also that day if a man had over 40 cartridges he had to turn them in together with the rest of the rifles to the Q.M. [Quartermaster]. We marched off from our camp towards 2 o'clock in the afternoon.[1] The majority left their tents back in camp. We lingered sometimes at the beginning of the march, afterwards going forward in the morass was hard. The sky was cloudy [and] occasionally it rained a little. Our Regt. and the 6th Ohio formed a Battalion. Our regiment was divided into 3 Comp[anies].[2] After five miles march we bivouacked in the woods next to the Knoxville Railroad.[3] A woman wailed fearsomely when we passed her house. She said the Yankees came only to kill the poor people, they also had shot her husband (Rebel) dead.

November 29

The 29th at daybreak we proceeded on the march again. We were forced to make long halts several times because the rain had made the route impassable in several places without making improvements with tree trunks and brushwood. A pontoon bridge was built over the Chicka-mauga Creek at the mouth of the Tennessee River, then we crossed over. Towards evening after covering 15 miles on the march we reached the little country town of Harrison and located our camp next to the same. It was very cold weather.

November 30

At daybreak on the 30th we marched off again in the morning. The water in our canteens was frozen into ice. There was ice on the road and [other] places 1 inch thick ice. The road had a large number of depressions filled with mud and water around which we had to make detours every time. Towards 4 o'clock in the afternoon [after] some 16 miles march we reached Georgetown where mostly Union people lived, who welcomed us with joy and flags.[4] We camped 6 miles from there at nightfall 1 mile from the High Wassie [Hiwassee] river. We were supposed to receive beef in the evening but the cattle had run away.

December 1

The 1st of December in the afternoon we drew rations for 3 days. The crackers were located in Barrels. We barely had time to divide out the rations when we marched off. Towards 3 o'clock arrived at the Highwassie [Hiwassee] River which is a tributary of the Ten[n]essee River. We lingered there a long time, because our brigade sent 4 boat loads [across]. We and the 6th Ohio were last. It was already night when we embarked. We marched still ¾ mile uphill and down dale, where we made a halt and encamped. We made fires from fence bolts [rails]. Our Regt. was ordered on picket, we groped around in the darkness in the woods and set up our posts [and] during the night a drunken soldier of the 6th Ohio came out to us on picket, who ran in front making a dis-turbance, [so] that we could not sleep. He came to us with the flag of our

Regiment, the 6th, which he had taken away from the flag carrier after he was fast asleep. He received two hits on the head from our men. We could not sleep a wink the whole night. The advance post had set fire to a dead tree, which fell during the night, we believed cut down by them. There was a Platoon [gun]fire, which got our attention for the moment.

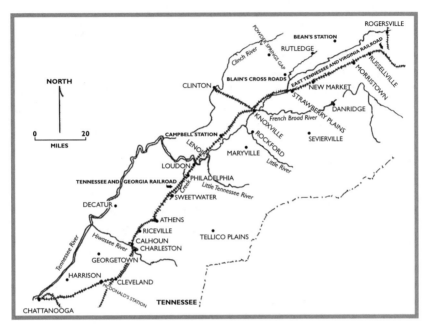

MAP 3. *Theater of operations—December 1863 to April 1864.*

DECEMBER 2

At daybreak the 2nd Dec. We marched off again. Our march was fraught with much difficulty, because mud and water lay in the depressions in the road. We reached the little city Decatur after 13 miles march and advanced from there still 7 miles, then we camped by a river. We marched very fast in the course of which many of the soldiers fell behind.

DECEMBER 3

The 3rd Dec. we marched off again. The road was terrible through a quagmire. During the night we reached the little city Sweet Water [Sweetwater after an] 18 M[ile] march. We had to spend a good hour standing around because only one man behind the other could cross over the river [creek] Sweetwater on a tree trunk. There was a complete jumble in the

Regiments [and] it was another half hour until we pitched camp. Every man was full of anger. A prolonged fuss was raised over the delay of the troops. It was after 10 o'clock before we established permanent night camp.

December 4

The 4th December we marched off again and made many detours because of the mud and water in the roads. In the morning before we marched off 6–8 men from each Regt. were ordered to forage [for food]. We covered 18 miles the same day and camped about 4 o'clock in the evening. In the evening [about] 9 o'clock after we had already started to rest we drew 3 Tin Cupsfull [of] cornmeal and other things mixed in and for two days horrible salt cured meat that was distributed by the foragers.

December 5

On the morning of the 5 we marched off before daybreak. Our Regiment and Brigade were in front. After 3 miles march we reached the Big [Little] Tennessee River where we crossed over on a bridge that had been erected from boards and tree trunks. Reached the other side. We passed through the little city of Morgantown [Morganton] which was almost totally abandoned and demolished. We passed there a part of [Maj. Gen. William T.] Sherman's troops and made a halt here in an open field.[5] After about 10–15 minutes we marched off again and made another halt one mile from there. Our Comp.[any] was stationed on picket. After 2 hours we marched off again. We advanced about 14 miles and camped after nightfall in the woods. The weather was misty the whole day, [but] cleared up again in the evening. Around 9 o'clock we drew cornmeal again and meat from sheep. Our company had only one sheep, the rest of the Co[mpanies] from the Regiment wanted none because no one had any crackers to go with it.

December 6

The 6th Dec. we marched off again at daybreak and reached the little city of Marysville [Maryville] after 3 miles march, which might have been a nice little city, but now quite demolished and mostly abandoned. After 10 miles march we made a halt in the woods next to Flint Creek.

December 7

The 7th Dec. we marched off again and crossed over the Flint. After a 5 mile March we reached the Little Tenn[essee] River [Little River] at Rockford. After we crossed there we were still 10 miles from Knoxville. We camped at nightfall in the woods 2 miles from Knoxville. In the evening about 9 o'clock we drew only [corn]meal.

December 8

The 8th Dec we remained still, the sky was cloudy and rained from time to time.

December 9

The 9th Dec. before daybreak, our Regiment and the Louisville Legion came on picket.

December 10

The 10th Dec we drew for 2 days 2 cupfuls of ground maiz[e] and ration of awful pork, molasses, some chewing tobacco and salt. In the afternoon we received orders that those soldiers who had torn up shoes that would not endure the march back to Chattanooga are supposed to mend the shoes themselves out of sheepskin. On the day before shoes were ordered but there were none to get here.[6] Shoemaker [Cpl. Engelbert] Emig from our Comp[any E] had to cut moccasins out of sheepskin, which the soldiers could mend their shoes with or cover them with it.[7] Nothing came from it; the majority refrained from it, this nonsense.

December 11

The 11th Dec I took a pass and went to Knoxville which was 2 miles distant from our camp. I walked over the Tennessee River on the Pontoon Bridge. The same day I with a comrade visited the fortifications and scene of the last battle between Burnside and Longstreet [at Fort Sanders].[8] The rise of ground where the Rebels had carried out their attack on our fortifications was covered with blood spots of the enemy. We saw the graves of the slain enemy which were barely covered with 3 or 4 inches of earth. We saw one whose toes as well as his face were left visible. We left there and proceeded again to the city. We passed through it 3–4 times and investigated all over before we could get something to eat. On the morning after arrival in Knoxville I bought 6 little apples and 3 cigars for 50¢. Toward 2 o'clock after many inquiries we ate lunch at Mrs. Lee['s] near [Maj. Gen. John G.] Foster's Hd. [Head] Quarter[s].[9] The food cost 50¢ per man [and we] received several spoonfuls of soup, some cornbread, and sheep's leg, [and] with that we could leave half full. Then about 3 o'clock we proceeded back to the camp.

December 12

The 12th Dec we drew again rations and cornmeal for 3 days and a spoonful of coffee per man. In the late morning had to drill again. Our Battalion numbered 62 men. A number stayed in camp because they had torn up shoes.

December 13

The following night on Sunday [the 13th] it rained continuously. The whole day it was misty weather. The following night it rained very hard we could not get a half hour's sleep the whole night because a continuous noise and fighting occurred in Co.[mpany] A with drunkenness.[10]

December 14

The 14th we were more organized around here.

December 15

The 15th towards noon we received marching orders and shortly thereafter marched off through Knoxville and camped some 2 miles from there. That evening we drew a half spoonful sugar and coffee and 2 little crackers and 2¾ Tin Cup full meal for 2 days, and only 25 cartridges per man.

December 16

The 16th we marched off again before daylight, the road was bad. After 15 miles march we camped by [General] Foster's men [from the] 23rd A.[rmy] C[orps]. Wounded soldiers in ambulances and baggage wagons met us from [General] Burnside's army, which the first-mentioned [large ink smear] Knoxville, and baggage wagons back in the rear, and it rained the following night without stop until daybreak.[11] We were all fully soaked through to the skin. The same for our Blankets and Haversacks.

December 17

The 17th around 10 o'clock we marched off again and moved Camp 2 miles from there on the extreme left wing. Our Regt and the Louisville Legion immediately came on picket, where we fortified during the day and worked until 9 o'clock at night. A section from our Battery also came and fortified.[12] Our regiment camped by a GraveYard. The weather was terribly windy and cold. We camped in Richland Valley between two large mountains, the nearest behind us were the Clinch Mountains and the other House Mountain.

December 18

The 18th in the late morning the fortifications were finished. It was windy and cold also.

December 19

The 19th one could not sleep at night also we now had nothing to eat.

December 21

The 21st it was nice weather. In the afternoon the Reenlistment order appeared.[13] No one was inclined in the beginning to do that.

December 22

The 22nd the Section [of] Artillery located near us was replaced by another battery.[14]

December 23

The 23rd we drew again 3 rations [of] coffee, crackers and cornmeal, which in bread was full rations. At nightfall we drew sugar and bacon. Each company received 2 loaves of old baked bread which had to be distributed and [was] hardly edible. Each man in our Company received bread the size of a walnut. Each morning at Rollcall we had to appear with cartridge boxes.

December 24

The 24 Dec. Major Whitaker issued the Reenlistment Order to us. We were formed in line. On the right wing heard a half-hour cannonade. The cavalry that was located in our front was ordered back.

December 26

The 26th it rained almost the whole day.

December 27

The 27th it was windy and rained day and night. In the evening after dark an order came from Brig.[ade] Hd. [Head] Quarters which put before us an offer of $402[15] bounty for reenlistment of veteran soldiers until 5 January[,] and who joins again after the 5th receives only the usual Bounty of 100 doll[ars].

December 28

The 28th our regiment came on picket.

December 29

The 29th we moved our camp several hundred yards farther right down in the valley on an open place on a little hillock.

December 31

The 31st December I wrote up 3 muster rolls for Co. E, C and G on sheets of writing paper with [a] pencil. The previous night it rained continuously with fearsome wind.

    In the evening at darkness the 31st our Major [Whitaker] held an inspection in the hardest rain. It rained until towards midnight then terrible wind and cold set in. The 31st we heard in the distance the thunder of cannon, a salute fired in Knoxville.

■ ■ ■

Gottfried *Rentschler marched to Knoxville and Blain's Cross Roads with the 6th Kentucky but was ordered back to Chattanooga "to perform other duties" shortly after Christmas Day 1863. His second letter to the* Anzeiger *focuses on the army's foraging for provisions and the terrible suffering of the residents of East Tennessee—a region where the majority of residents were Unionists, but which was controlled by the Confederacy until Burnside arrived in September 1863.*

LETTER 2

Published January 9, 1864
Written from 4th Army Corps, Chattanooga, January 1, 1864

Dear Mr. [George Philip] Doern,

I just came back from Knoxville where 2 divisions of the 4th Army Corps under [Major] General [Gordon] Granger were called to temporarily reinforce the Army of the Ohio.[16] The march there provided interesting details, such that I could not keep from giving you a short description.

On November 26 the regiments of both divisions (Wood's and Sheridan's) received orders to make preparations to march off to Knoxville at any minute. The hour of departure was twice stipulated and twice changed. The third marching order issued was for the 28th, at 1 P.M., and was carried out. The troops were in a very precarious condition. On the 23rd and 25th of November they were in the fights at Missionary Ridge; and before that they had barely received half-rations for a long time, and inadequate or not sufficient enough rations for a winter march of 113 miles—as far as the distance to Knoxville from here—clothes were inadequate; missing were mainly overcoats and blankets. On the night of November 26 they were led back from the battlefield to their old camps in and around Chattanooga, and on the 27th were busy with the preparations for their march. Each regiment was allowed one wagon to transport provisions and the necessary articles for the officers and headquarters. The men carried on their bodies all their belongings, including flour, half-rations and sixty cartridges per man.

The purpose of this march was, as is well known, to reinforce Foster [Burnside] at Knoxville, who would be severely attacked by Longstreet.[17] According to the promise of the top generals,[18] within ten days (counting from 28 November), we had to get him out of this mess and supply him with provisions. We learned several days after we marched off that Foster [Burnside] knew how to help himself, and Longstreet received a bloody warning.[19] Some provisions for our troops were sent ahead by boat up the Tennessee River; however, it was distributed on the way and was sufficient for only a couple of days. When this was gone, the need began in the literal sense of the word. The army, if two divisions can be called that, had to feed itself. Whoever witnessed this self-feeding will understand fully the words of [General Albrecht von] Wallenstein when he wrote his "emperor," "I cannot feed twenty-thousand soldiers, but I will find ways to feed fifty thousand."[20]

General Orders were sent to the regiments in order to give this self-nourishment an orderly process. The contents: From each regiment, each day, 5 men under an officer should pick out near or distant farmhouses lying on the way to "press" provisions for their regiment; for each regiment, a wagon for holding provisions and a horse or mule for each man and officer of each party sent out should be "pressed" from the farmer; they should leave receipts filled out with the details and political status of the proprietor; report each evening to the relevant brigade commissary, and the total food will be distributed evenly to the regiments; each not-too-distant farmhouse and its outbuildings will be rummaged through according to size; the chickens and geese are to be taken from the resident; horses, mules, oxen, cows, calves, sheep, mainly everything that was useful to move or to carry or that could be prepared for nourishment should be taken. It did not stop with 5 men per regiment; by the dozen, the soldiers went out of the ranks in order to hunt down something edible. It was a disgusting chase. The screams of hunted and chased-down chickens and geese often drowned out the thousand steps of the troops and clatter of the wagons following on the dry streets.

In order to find the real truth about civilization in our much-praised country, I followed a forage party into the yard of a large farmhouse. Here's a true picture:—the farmhouse in question was directly on the road on which we moved and had several connected outbuildings. When I entered the courtyard a five-man party was already busy loading salted pork on an ox-drawn farm wagon. Dozens of soldiers who had broken out of the ranks stormed over the fences and chased after the chickens. At the corner of the house a boy about 16 years old caught a young cock, which he in the company of an older soldier had chased for a long time. The latter questioned the first about his right to the cock. The latter declared he had made the cock lame with a stone he had thrown, and by all rights the prize was his. The younger one argued—from words it came to violence, and the older [one] tired; at which time the younger one forcefully ripped the cock away. A third soldier, a comrade of the younger, intervened. The older one gave the hen up for lost and grimly chased another. The victorious younger one looked at his hard-won poultry with an affectionate look, already whetting his teeth for the tasty snack. A soldier hurried out of one of the nearby buildings with a tin cup full of molasses, which he was trying to put into his canteen. The day was cold, and the molasses was thick and not fluid enough to flow through the narrow neck of the canteen. He therefore shook it, and half of it covered his hands and clothes.

The owner of the house appeared—an old man. "Sir," he said, "they will not take everything from me? Leave me only a little in order to be able to live. I have, besides my family, twenty Negroes to feed, and I am myself, as you can see, a cripple." "When I am finished here," replied the officer of the forage party; who just then was busy loading two barrels of molasses. "When I am finished here, we want to speak a word together." In the meantime, a soldier came out of nearby building with a hand full of honey. The honey was crammed into his tin cup and he was licking his hand. A second soldier had a slab of bacon impaled on his bayonet; another is doubly pleased with a pack full of sausages; about a dozen ran over the courtyard chasing chickens; another asks the Negro of the house who was standing there, if there were any green apples, eggs or butter in it. The scared Negro answered yes and pointed out the place where the requested items were located. The soldier ran into the house to get the apples, eggs and butter, etc.; and again asked the old man—nothing helps—in a fast business-like manner the soldiers pressed on with their work. No one found time to answer the old man. Then an officer came rushing along with a drawn revolver! It was General [Gordon] Granger. He put a quick end to this chaos, and read the forage officer the riot act in a strong voice.

I had seen enough, and as the eternal Jew in the parable asked the devil, "Satan, how late is it in eternity?" So I asked myself silently, "How late is it in civilization?" and trotted sullenly down the street. Had the old man, who was a secessionist, afterward learned how the meal that had been taken from him caused the whole regiment pain, he would have at least had some satisfaction. His meal was the so-called "sick wheat," and after the men ate the fried bread prepared from it (prepared without salt or lard), they vomited it in misery and lost not only the meal but also the previous day's half-ration. The man received receipts for the items taken. However, they had absolutely no value to him. The receipts showed not only what was taken from him; but also that he was a Rebel, and thus no reimbursement could be claimed as long as he could not prove his loyalty. This picture is fit to test your feelings for justice. Of course, want excused much. The ministers of the church say that want is the fire through which our souls are tested, which I as a German-American would translate like this!: "Only in need does a gentleman show his true color." I do not want to pass judgment in this matter; but leave contemplation and application to those who have not as much to do, and think as a soldier in the field. The troops were only sparsely provided with provisions through this forage system. One wagon is not capable of supplying a regiment in these circumstances. Further, not once could this wagon be filled.

The country people had nothing but meat and corn, and only in small quantities. The previous troops, namely the Rebels, who had moved over this same road 14 days before had taken away almost everything. And so we finally came to Knoxville, almost starved after a 10-day march. The shoes, which were already worn-out, were completely torn up on the march, and in order not to have to go barefooted, the men made themselves moccasins from hides or sandals from the same material.[21]

We were camped one and one-half miles from Knoxville for about 8 days. Then we had to march on our bad soles about 20 miles further. Eight miles from Blain's Bluff Cross Roads Station[22] our troops threw up breastworks, because Longstreet's rear guard was near to our camp; and small skirmishes occurred on the right wing (we were on the left). After remaining there 8 days, I received a General Order to return here to perform other duties. This march to Knoxville and beyond again showed us right before our eyes convincing proof of the grave ravages of the war. The small, market-towns and little towns are devastated, and are deserted. The prettiest buildings are burnt down or demolished and, thus, the Secessionists pay tribute. I have spoken with many secessionists. All wish ardently for peace, but only peace under the condition that their demands are accepted, i.e., with slavery the South will make peace. The furious rage which one could read on the faces of the Rebels a short-time ago has changed for many to quiet despair, with others, resignation. Many have nothing more to lose than their lives, which half of these are also prepared to sacrifice for their erroneous opinion.

The loss to the property owners is enormous. If one received only one cent for each fence rail already burned during this winter, the whole of Jefferson Street[23] in Louisville could be covered in Gold Dollars; in addition, with the value of the burnt and demolished houses, all of Louisville's streets could be paved; and considering the value of all movable and immovable devastated property, the entire city of Louisville could be covered with gold; but this is the truth.

The two divisions mentioned above have not returned yet.

The "higher authorities" have tried to incorporate the whole 4th Army Corps into the Army of the Ohio; however, the officers and men have no desire for that. They want to remain in the Army of the Cumberland in which they have proven their capabilities so often.[24]

Today, after so many days of rain, it is so cold here that in an enclosed heated room (11 A.M.) I must hold the pen to the fire a full two minutes, in order to make the frozen ink flow.[25] The Rebellion changes, as it appears, even the climate.

In the hope that the year 1864 will bring us peace; and with it, as much as possible, the domestic tranquillity of which we have been deprived for so long; and also that death will not have caused irreplaceable losses.

> Greetings, Respectfully,
> Your servant,
> G. Rentschler

■　■　■

The outside temperature in East Tennessee dropped to twenty degrees below zero on New Year's Day 1864, so it is understandable that John Daeuble's first entry for the new year describes the freezing cold weather.

JANUARY 1 AND 2, 1864

The 1 January 1864 it was so cold that the water in containers next to the fire froze. Two days, the 31st and 1st, we had not the least [to eat] and we drew nothing. We suffered much hunger. The evening of the 30th was the last time we drew rations. Sergt. [Sgt. Louis H.] Brauser and [Pvt. George Friedrich] Dittrich went into the country and brought back for 4 dollars

Shorts [shortening], [and] meal, each man got 2½ Tin Cup full.[26] [First] Lt. [Lorenz] Amon gave us 5 dollars money due us from 1st Lieut. [John] Sensbach.[27] The 1st and 2nd it was terribly cold and windy. We suffered hunger and at night no one could sleep. Also the fire gave us no warmth because the wind blew too strong.

Fig. 5. *Brig. Gen. William B. Hazen, commander of the 2nd Brigade, 3rd Division, 4th Corps. Ron Beifuss Collection at U.S. Army Military History Institute.*

January 3

The afternoon of the 3rd an order from General Hazen about reenlistment was read aloud to us again by Major Whitaker. 2 men out of the Regt. enrolled themselves.[28]

January 4

The 4th it rained lightly and continuously. Several from our Regt. signed up as Veteran Volunteers. In the afternoon an Order came from Brig.[ade] Hd. [Head] Quarter[s] that the ammunition per man must be reported. The order stated we would march off in 2 or 3 days toward the enemy.

January 5

The 5th Jan our regiment came on outpost. The previous night it was stormy, it rained from time to time. The 5th it was cold and stayed windy. They re-enlisted some more. The number in total of the Regt in the evening was 21 men. The 41st Ohio marched off about noon. All except 7 men had re-enlisted.

January 6

The 6th it snowed late in the morning. The Section of the Battery left their place and Fort.

January 7 to 8

During the night of the 7th to the 8th it snowed a 2-inch deep snow.

January 11

The 11th we left our camp in the afternoon. We pitched camp in the woods next to the Brig.[ade] Hd. [Head] Quarters. The snow still lay frozen on the ground.

■   ■   ■

Separated from his regiment, Gottfried Rentschler focused on newspaper coverage of the war, the weather, and the Commissary Department.

LETTER 3

Published January 16, 1864
Written from 6th Kentucky Regiment, Chattanooga, January 10, 1864

Dear Editor:

Several newspapers complained the last time about the lack of war coverage. I am quite surprised about this complaint because the correspondents of the different newspapers feel it is not true. Many newspapers have dozens in the field. Do they find no material of the correspondents worthwhile? Impossible. There is enough material available because our different armies are in constant motion, like the surface of the sea; and each second has their special piece of news. These movements could be covered down to the smallest detail and it would be worth the effort. The reading public may not be taught anything, but they would be entertained.[29] However, each general and colonel and each individual regiment has his, or its, own correspondents, in order to broadcast into the country credit and praise of the officer or regiment.[30] As a result, one reads of so many General-Heroes and Hero-Generals against whom Hannibal and Scipio are merely small fry.[31] Who knows the all-pervading power of the press in this country, knows, also, why it is so. Only the daily, trite laudations and the rose-tinted reports will eventually find the same fate as that donkey in the fable, in which a clever person dyed it green and exclaimed that it was a naturally green donkey; so that everyone from near and far ran together to stare with amazement at the marvelous animal. The crafty person earned much money, but only for two days; because already by the third, the people had become used to the green donkey and no one looked at it anymore. Whether the man was as smart as many of our correspondents and dyed that donkey blue to again delight people, the fable does not say.[32]

Here I praise the little Swabian[33] organ-builder's helper Pfeffer, whose feet had the problem that they sweated very much and gave off a very unedifying odor. One pretty summer day, a village schoolmaster who did not know this, and who was a big lover of Limburger cheese, happened to sit next to the organ-builder's helper, Pfeffer, in the inn. He smelled something strong and, after our village schoolmaster had taken a few good sniffs, he asked, with a sense of well-being, "Mr. Pfeffer have you eaten cheese?" "No," said Pfeffer. "Mr. Schoolmaster, my feet stink." That's it uncolored.[34]

Apropos!—Because I speak of Limburger cheese, a little mishap that happened to our brigade's music-band director some weeks ago occurs to me. He traveled in the company of a companion on a boat from here to Bridgeport and grew tired from standing. He sat on an object without looking at it closely beforehand; while his companion, with a travelling bag in his hand, remained standing next to him. The director sniffed several times, one right after the other, and asked his acquaintance: "Where do you have your Limburger cheese?" He looked up, surprised, because Limburger cheese had not been available in his region for a long time; and asked where the cheese is supposed to be. The director said his nose told him that he must have a brick of cheese in his travel bag. The acquaintance quickly got an idea. Mr. . . . you are sitting on a stand bearing a corpse! The director jumped up frightened. The address on the box told him that it had contained a dead Rebel for eight days. Then you can see how everything is pure deception. One cannot trust his own nose.[35]

Almost all chaplains have left the Army of the Cumberland. I have not seen one for a long time. Whether they ran out of seeds, or whether they themselves could not find more fields to sow; or whether their sheep have matured in this wasteland, and shepherds are no longer necessary; or whether they are worth a shepherd; I really do not know.[36]

It is severely cold here.[37] The day before yesterday the boat brought about 100 Rebel prisoners from Louden.[38] One of them was sickly and poorly clothed. He froze on the boat. The Rebels for the most part are poorly clothed. They freeze pitifully. The better or well clothed of them have bought the clothes themselves or have been provided them from home. Our troops are also not clothed warm enough for the harsh winter and the severe strain. There has been, up-to-now, insufficient quantities delivered by the government. Our soldiers only want to receive the most essential items, because the price of clothes has been greatly increased since the beginning of the war; say 40 to 70 percent, and without a concurrent increase in the annual amount allowed for clothing. A soldier may draw $42 a year for clothing; if he draws more, the excess amount is deducted from his pay. Forty-two dollars a year is not sufficient for a man who lays in the cold the entire year.[39]

Also, our troops in and around Knoxville suffer from a lack of provisions. There is a lack of necessary means of transportation in order to supply the army adequately.

Until recently, what the troops were not provided in kind, or could not be provided, was paid in money by the government under the name "company savings." These "savings," however, will not be paid out in the future. The "General Commissary of Subsistence" has explained that there are no "savings," if the companies do not draw, what they cannot have, because it is not available. "Savings" is now understood as only the amount for provisions which were not drawn, if full provisions could have been drawn. In this event, the provisions not drawn will be considered as sold to the commissary by the company and is supposed to be paid in cash. This sounds ridiculous, because for as long as I can remember, the troops have never received full rations, as mentioned in the Regulations; they could not have, for the simple reason that all the articles were never in the commissary at the same time. In accordance with these regulations, the troops may receive as little provisions as the officialdom finds necessary or possible, without giving reimbursement for the permitted, but at the time not available and, therefore, not drawn items. Each company drew, in proportion to their strength, $10 to $40 monthly in "savings," with which money several of the needs of the men could be satisfied. The withholding of these savings is unjust. Our brigade commander, General William B. Hazen, who is just as fair as he is strong, gave his Commissary Orders to distribute the "company savings" in the future. Incidentally, I doubt a favorable outcome.[40]

In comparison, several improvements in other things in the Provision Commissary Department have been made since the beginning of the war. For example, initially, each regiment's Quartermaster drew provisions for the entire regiment, and distributed them to the companies and sold them to the officers. This has long since ceased. Now the provisions are distributed by the Brigade Commissary Agent to the individual companies and sold to the officers. As I recently learned from a reliable source, the Brigade Commissary Department is supposed to shrink, and for each division only one commissary agent be permitted, who will distribute directly to the individual companies and sell to the officers. This will be a second significant improvement of the same point; because the shorter the way is by which the provisions directly reach the men and officers of the company, the fewer delays on the way. Because the troops only received half-rations most of the time, General Wood issued the order that the commissary should not sell the officers more than half-rations, because they had to set a good example to the troops and share in the deprivation. You may gather here that Uncle Sam can still learn something if he gets older and stays alert.[41]

I cannot tell you exactly how the reenlistment in our regiment goes. Our brigade is still above Knoxville, expecting a battle at any hour, and I have only meager news about it.[42]

Day before yesterday the 41st Ohio arrived here; which, with the exception of 8 men, has enlisted again. That regiment will stay here perhaps a week, in order to make the necessary preparation to travel home. They have 30 days leave, and after that they will have to fill out their ranks again with conscripts or volunteers and return. The 41st Ohio is without doubt the best regiment in our brigade, perhaps in the division. It was recruited by General Hazen and commanded by him for a time.[43] The soldiers of this regiment are pleased with the thought that they are going home again after enduring so many extraordinary dangers and hardships, and after being absent from their homes for so long. The happiness of these men can perhaps hardly be better described than a Negro woman described her happiness when she was asked at her conversion ("revelation" it is called by the quite religious), to explain how she actually feels when she is so happy. She said, "She can't actually describe it; but I feel just like I had a fiddle in my belly." And the same with the 41sters.

The 28th Kentucky has likewise enlisted as a regiment again. They are expected here in the morning, in order to go home.[44]

The 6th Kentucky has not yet reenlisted.

Respectfully,
G. Rentschler

CHAPTER THREE

To Dandridge and Lenoir

On January 14, 1864, John Daeuble, the 6th Kentucky, and its division left Blain's Cross Roads for Dandridge, Tennessee, where forage was expected to be available.

JANUARY 12

The 12th our Regiment came on outpost[.]

JANUARY 13

The 13th we had our huts erected[;] towards 8 o'clock in the evening we received marching orders, we drew only 3 little crackers for each man around 7 o'clock.

JANUARY 14

The 14th we marched off from the camp, and reached Strawberry Plains after 8 miles march[,] where we crossed over the Holston River on a newly built Railroad Bridge[,] where the convalescents from our Co.[mpany] came to us[:] Capt. Frank,[1] Aug.[ust] Eversberg,[2] Ch.[arles] Grunewald.[3] In the morning it was frozen hard and noon when it thawed out it became terribly muddy[,] we marched 18 miles and were quite weakened because we also had nothing to eat[.]

■ ■ ■

Word that the 6th Kentucky and its division were departing Blain's Cross
Roads had not reached Private Rentschler when he wrote his next letter in
which he discusses the supply situation at Chattanooga, transportation difficulties in East Tennessee, and the reason many soldiers did not extend
their enlistments.

LETTER 4

Published January 20, 1864
Written Chattanooga, January 14, 1864

Dear Editor,

Finally the railroad from here to Bridgeport and Stevenson has
opened again.[4] It was a happy time, because the people and animals suffered unspeakably from lack of nourishment, etc. Horses and mules
starved by the thousands. Those still living are only skeletons. The soldiers would have been pleased to spend the few dollars a month they
receive to purchase the necessary food; however, there was nothing to
have in this desert. No store has been open in Chattanooga for a long
time, other than a clothing store with officers' clothes; and it had and still
has horrible prices. We have received, through the reopened railroad, the
wished for means of transportation; and it will not be much longer
before we are abundantly provided with everything.[5] For that reason, the
first time the train's whistle sounded in our ears it was like the trumpets
of angels announcing new and better times. For a period of time, only
government goods will be transported.

The Army of the Cumberland will be provided with everything that
is needed for a successful spring campaign. This will happen as quickly
as possible because Grant burns with desire to advance.[6] What they say
in "high official circles" about this projected campaign is neither advisable nor appropriate to disclose to the public at this time. Enough, we
expect a momentous and, in the highest measure, a happy new year

The two divisions of the 4th Army Corps, Wood's and Sheridan's, are
still near Blain's Cross Road's Station. The communication with them is
very difficult because of the low water level of the Tennessee River.[7] Only
a small boat can travel from here to Loudon; that, of course, is, by-far,
not sufficient to supply the army located in and around Knoxville with

the necessities, and that is the only way in which it can be accomplished. That the troops themselves, as a result of these severe circumstances, have very hard times should be easy to understand. However, if one believes that this stifles the warrior's courage or the good humor in them; you are wrong. The good humor in a soldier is not so easy to kill. Hundreds of wild, practical jokes are played each day; and I would tell you many amusing little stories, if room would permit.

The reenlistment of the veterans in the Army of the Cumberland is going slowly, as is being reported by many correspondents, and is supposed to be the case in other armies. The reason is not that the troops are tired of the soldier's life and demand to go home; this is only the case with one in a hundred. The troops' morale is good at present, and they are prepared to hold out until the rebellion's last rib is broken and its last heartbeat; but they also have tallied that, besides them, still about one million young men from 18 to 22-years old are sitting at home doing nothing for the grand cause. They say, "First let the young men sitting at home come out and carry their share of the load; send volunteers and, if there are none, enough conscripts to fill out our ranks that have been thinned through iron, lead, and sickness; then we would gladly stay to the last man."

At home, behind the stove, it's certainly comfortable: There, they chase not only regiments, no, whole divisions through buttonholes; and break the neck of the whole South with a yardstick; and the guys who fall faint when they hear a fly swat, because they take it for a slap, criticize whole armies;—when, however, the call "to arms" is sent to them, they crawl into their fathers' shirt pockets or hide under the counter; when it comes loud they remain, forcing themselves to make a disparaging smile, and pity "the stupidity" of those grasping the arms. Everyone knows our soldiers out here, and they know that this is the main reason if they do not reenlist.[8]

As is well known, the regimental organization stays if ¾ of its present men reenlist. That the officers all make an effort to achieve this ¾, in order to keep their own places, is natural. The soldiers, however, have learned something while wearing their blue jackets. Some tried to win veterans in several regiments through promises. They [the soldiers], however, know from experience, how the idle promises usually turn out, and do not believe them; almost all remember that after their first enlistment, instead of fulfilling the promises they reduced us to beggary. Those who reenlist do it out of love for their country and, as well, for the love of freedom.

However, I will close. I have already said more than I wanted, because I wanted to say, in brief, that this afternoon about 3 o'clock the first railroad train arrived here from Bridgeport; but "so it goes," as my grandmother tended to say, "when one runs into a gabber."

> Respectfully,
> Your Servant
> G. Rentschler

Trailer. [Major] General Thomas has released an order that two men from each company should receive leave; this means that we will remain here a rather long time.[9]

■ ■ ■

Lieutenant General Longstreet's corps soon began aggressively attacking the advance Federal line near Dandridge and General Granger ordered an unpopular retreat. General Hazen later wrote that the disorganized withdrawal over mud filled roads was "one of the most annoying episodes of my life."[10] Daeuble and his comrades then marched approximately sixty miles southwest to Lenoir, Tennessee, to guard the railroad.

January 15

At daybreak the 15th we marched off again. The Veteran Volunteers, 40 from our Regt, [including Pvt.] John Lang[11] and [Cpl.] August Eversberg out of our Company [E], marched back again to Strawberry Plains with those [re-enlistees] of the Louisville Legion. We marched 7 miles farther in terrible muck and camped outside the little city of Dan[d]ridge which is a tolerable little city and pretty region.[12] The French Broad river flows past nearby. The Blue Ridge Mountains in North Carolina offer the eyes a rich view there. We had nothing to eat for two days long but what we searched for and bought ourselves.

January 16

The 16[th] our Cavalery [Cavalry] maintained fights with the enemy [Longstreet's] outposts together with cannonading.[13] The 6th Indiana, 6th and 5th Ky had to move our camp several hundred yards farther, when we had been settled again, we the above regiments were ordered to the front in the fast step and marched in terrible muck almost 3 miles, the enemy and our Cavalery [Cavalry] bombarded each other. We halted in a cornfield where it was terribly muddy by a battery, which we had to support. At nightfall we marched back again to the previous camp. Around 8 o'clock we drew only beef and 2 little crackers per man.

JANUARY 17 TO 18

The 17th we drew full rations for 2 days. Our supply train arrived from Chattanooga. Our tents and cookware, the mess pans and camp kettles were destroyed the night of the 17th to 18th. The 17th towards evening we had to stand in Line of Battle because the Cavalry maintained a heavy fire with the enemy. At nightfall we proceeded to the Quarters again. About 8 o'clock orders came to us to be ready to march at any moment. What could not be taken with us was burned. ½ 3 [2:30] in the morning the 18th we departed. All was still quiet in the little city of Dan[d]ridge. We marched back the same way we had come. It was terribly muddy and still rained on top of everything. Several shots were exchanged with the Cavly [Cavalry] in the rear. We camped 5 miles from Strawberry Plains after 13 miles march [and] our Regiment and the Louisville Legion came on picket.[14] Toward morning it snowed a 2 inch deep snow.

JANUARY 19

At daybreak the 19th we marched off again and reached Strawberry Plains around noon. The road was hardly passable, the wagons were mostly stuck fast. After the wagon train had passed the bridge, we crossed over the Holston River, towards 3 o'clock, 3 miles from Strawberry Plains we crossed over a Railroad Bridge over the river *Flat Creek,* whereupon we camped next to the same.

JANUARY 20

In the afternoon of the 20th marched 5 miles further towards Knoxville.

JANUARY 21

The 21st we marched off again at daybreak and after 8 miles march reached Knoxville and crossed over the Holston River, where we encamped one mile from there. The 23rd we marched off again in the late afternoon and crossed over the Holston River by Knoxville again. We advanced 8 miles in an arduous march. We ran into a one mile detour because we were located on the road leading to Kingston and not located on the one to Lenoire [Lenoir] and from there had to proceed on the other road.

January 24

The 24th we marched off again at daybreak. We advanced 15 miles and encamped at darkness in the Winter Quarters which were built by [General] Burnside['s troops at Lenoir]. The 124th Ohio was stationed 10 miles from Knoxville and the 6th Ohio 14 miles from Knoxville on the Mudroad.[15] We had nothing to eat the whole day, [but] after arrival we got a Tin Cup full of cornmeal per man.

January 26

The 26th our regiment was ordered on picket however returned to our camp at noon. We had to move our camp several hundred yards farther to a hill by the Holston river and leave behind the well constructed Winter Quarters of Burnsides troops, which angered us not a little.[16]

January 29

The 29th two cannon came to us on the hill where we camped. Out of the 1st Ohio only 2 strong companies had re-enlisted and received orders to travel home. Also we received 1 little loaf of bread that was baked from Sick Wheat and which made us terribly sick.

■ ■ ■

Gottfried Rentschler was still on special duty in Chattanooga on January 29, 1864.

Letter 5

Published February 3, 1864
Written Chattanooga, January 29, 1864

Dear Mr. Editor!

Bragg has left our front [at Chattanooga]; as is generally assured, he has retreated from Dalton to Atlanta.[17] Also, Longstreet is quiet. Our brigade had been ordered back to Marysville [Maryville], a little town on the Tennessee, six miles from London [Loudon], where it will go into winter quarters.[18] Grant cannot advance until the railroad from here to Knoxville has been made usable.[19] Little or nothing will happen before the 1st of April. Commissary and quartermaster stores are plentiful here. The soldiers live in *floribus*,[20] and the famished donkeys are being fed. The sutlers have supplied the market again fully with everything and, therefore, here, in Chattanooga and the near-by areas, everything is in good order.[21]

Relations of the soldiers of the 6th Ky., receive the news that the regiment will be mustered out on September 24th. A short-time ago a full register came from Washington to the Department Headquarters, in which the muster-out day for each regiment of the Army of the Cumberland was listed.[22]

From the 6th Ky., 50 men;[23] from the 5th Ky. (Louisville Legion) 85; and from the 23rd Ky. nearly all, have re-enlisted. All arrived here 8 days ago from Knoxville and will stay here at least 14 days to finish up the muster rolls and get paid. Each man mustered-out and-in receives 200 dollars cash, i.e., $100 bounty for the first enlistment, $26 pay for November and December, $13 as a month's advance payment and about $60 of the new bounty.[24] It was to them the tidings that they should receive a warm reception in Louisville and heartily enjoy themselves with it. I do not believe, however, they will come to Louisville before 3 weeks; consequently, there remains enough time to make arrangements for a public reception.

While I am writing this I received a copy of an order from Gen. Thomas stating that all officers and soldiers of the 2nd and 3rd divisions of the 4th Army Corps should set out for Knoxville without delay, with baggage and everything, and all property belonging to the divisions, in order to unite with them. We will depart from here tomorrow. You will receive my next writing from Knoxville or Marysville [Maryville][25] with, I hope, more news that I can share with you. It is well established: 1st, that we go into winter quarters in-and-around Knoxville (our brigade in Marysville [Loudon]), and 2nd, that the 4th Army Corps is allocated to the Army of the Ohio. However, the 1st Division, [Brig. Gen. Richard W.] (Johnson's) has marching orders.[26]

Respectfully
Your servant
G. Rentschler

■ ■ ■

On January 30, 1864, Hazen's brigade reassembled at Lenoir, Tennessee.

January 30

The 30th 2 Companies of the 6th Ind. which were 90 men strong marched off from us at the same time the 1st Ohio, the 124th Ohio and 6th Ohio arrived by us (together with cannon) which were back by the R.[ail] Road Station [and] which we left back there on our march here.

January 31

The 31st [Brig. Gen. August] Willich together with 2 Veteran Regiments came over the river.

February 1

The 1st February they all[27] came back from Loudon again, we had orders to be ready (toward morning the wind blew very strong whereupon a short rain followed, during the day it cleared up. In the evening the talk was that we would leave our camp at 2–3 o'clock in the morning.

February 2

Right after daybreak we left our camp and marched toward Knoxville and had advanced 2 ½ miles and [had] started again just after a rest when [1st] Lt. [John L.] Chilton[28] brought the happy message to turn back. We marched south back to our old camping place back to our huts. In the evening after dark a terrible storm arose. We had to hold onto our tent poles, so the wind would not knock them down, it lasted over ½ hour, during the night it was very cold.

February 3

The 3rd Feb. drill began again also had to move the 2 cannon up the hill again.

February 7

The 7[th] on Sunday we held a Brigade Inspection Review.

FEBRUARY 8

On the 8th the start was made digging earthworks around our camp.

FEBRUARY 11

The 11th our wagon arrived from Chattanooga. The [company's] books were all wet because the wagon overturned in the Ten[n]essee River at Loudon.

■ ■ ■

In his sixth letter, Private Rentschler shared details of his trip from Chattanooga to Lenoir and gave some examples of the cruelty inflicted on Union people by Confederate soldiers during their occupation of East Tennessee.

LETTER 6

Published February 23, 1864
Written from Camp at Lenoir's, Tennessee, February 12, 1864
Departure from Chattanooga—Wire Fences—War Cruelty—Atrocities by Guerrillas—Starvation of the South Impossible—Willich and Hazen Now in Command of Wood's Division

Dear Editor:

On February 4, the wagon trains of the 2nd and 3rd Divisions of the 4th Army Corps left Chattanooga with 235 wagons and about 1,200 men; mostly recruits and recovered convalescents. A General Order to take all mules, even those which were only capable of pulling an empty wagon, made us fear a slow and uncomfortable trip. However, the weather was absolutely beautiful and the paths were excellent; consequently the trip here was the most pleasant that each participant had had since they had been in Uncle Sam's [United States] Army. We barely made six miles the first day and camped on the Chickamauga River [Creek].[29]

I noticed at several places that the farmers fenced-in their land with wire for two reasons. The first reason is that wood is rare there. The forests were burned out by the troops.[30] The second reason is that the wire fence is not burnable by the troops. They stay secure from destruction by the troops. A splendid phenomenon may make the wire fences dangerous. When the lightning strikes them it rages in circles around the properties, sometimes like the fire pool in [Johann von] Goethe's Faust [*Faust: A Tragedy*].[31]

On February 5, we came through Harrison, which had been almost totally destroyed. We made 15 miles and spent the night on the plantation of the notorious Capt. [William] Snow. This bloodhound gathered up and bound the Union men in his neighborhood; and through his guerrillas had them driven onto his plantation, with fixed-bayonets, in order to harvest his crops. After they had done this, he took them to Knoxville and sold them to a recruiting officer for $30 per man. Eight days earlier, before we passed by there, he came with a party of his guerrillas into his home area and began to hunt up the Union men living in the surrounding area. They caught some, tied them up, and shot three of them. The rest were tied to trees and beaten. I have all this from eyewitnesses.[32]

On the 6th we came through Georgetown, a small town that had little damage; and camped overnight on the farm of Major Baird of the 3rd Tennessee Cav. Regt.[33] There, many of the country people in the neighborhood sought us out and gave an account of how dreadfully they had suffered from the Rebels. When [Maj. Gen. Joseph] Wheeler[34] made the last invasion in the area, one of his soldiers, by the name of Roberts,[35] went into the house of a certain Carter (the Carters consist of a very large family in East Tennessee and are all very good Union people) and shot Robert Carter, a young man, poked his eyes out, shoved them into his pocket, and went to his mother, to whom he said that he had killed Bob Carter. She said, "You did not do that." He pulled the eyes out of his pocket and threw them on the table saying: "Here, if you do not believe me here are the eyes of the son of a bitch."[36] This is only one of the numerous atrocities. Here and there the Southern barbarians have most certainly received their rewards for their cruelty as, e.g., the Sesech who hideously beat an old man whose son was a lieutenant in a Tennessee regiment. When the lieutenant went to Knoxville with his regiment and came through his home area, and learned who committed this atrocity on his old father, he went into the house of the Sesech, pulled him into the street, and shot a bullet through his head.[37]

On the 7th we came through Charleston on the Hiawassee [Hiwassee] River. Charleston had about 100 houses, all of which were totally ruined with the exception of a few. The little town had no inhabitants.

[Col. Eli] Long's cavalry[38] brigade remains there in order to guard the railroad bridge that presently is being built over the Hiwassee River and it will be finished in a few days. Our train crossed the river on a pontoon bridge.[39]

On the 8th we moved through Riceville, a little village in a splendid valley. Nothing had been destroyed there and the residents had not fled. At 3 P.M. we reached Athens, one of the prettiest country towns I have seen. The city has nothing further as all fences have been destroyed. We camped a mile from Athens. In the evening, a party of us went back into the town to the house of Mr. Keith, a wealthy Union-man (almost all residents of Athens are loyal). He entertained us with music, Rhine wine and tobacco-chewing ladies. This may be the place to say that all the women in East Tennessee chew tobacco and "dippen," a bad-habit which makes the prettiest ladies unappealing.[40]

We came through Sweetwater on the 9th. The name does not suit it anymore because the water in this little town became real bitter because of our troops.[41] In all of Sweetwater is only one Union man, a doctor.[42]

On the 10th our way led us through Philadelphia, a little town that does not contain one tidy house, and through Loudon on the Tennessee River. Loudon is the most miserable little town that I have seen in my life. No neat people live there anymore. The whole place is filled up with Southern women who have sunk far under other people. Allow me to say here, that the war has produced an indescribable moral decline in the female sex of the South. Thousands indulge themselves in vice in order to earn the necessary bread.[43]

While crossing the Tennessee River a little accident occurred. A wagon of the 6th Ky. Regiment and its two mules plunged into the river; one of the mules drowned, and the other was rescued with much trouble. Captain [William] Frank's[44] and Lieutenant [Lorenz] Amon's effects, which were on the wagon, received a baptism, and either they or someone else said, "Amen"; which consequently cannot be Benediction according to theological concepts. All the less when many a "Sacrament" escapes the lips of the godfather.

On the 11th we reached our brigade at this place. Lenoir is named after the owner of the place where our troops are stationed and the camp was christened after him, as has been the railroad station for a long time. Lenoir has a large cotton factory here, is an Arch Secesh [Secessionist], and allowed Union people here to be beaten, and recently swore the Oath of Loyalty in order to protect his property.[45]

Fig. 6. *Brig. Gen. Thomas J. Wood, commander of the 3rd Division, 4th Corps. Jerry Ringer Collection at U.S. Army Military History Institute.*

The whole way from Chattanooga to here led through a very pretty and fertile area. The farmers everywhere say that they sow their fields and want crops very much. They raise all hope that they will not be visited by Rebel troops again.

The bridge over the Tennessee at Loudon is still not finished; that is, at the same place. All the essential materials will be prepared in Knoxville, so that when finished there, the bridge merely needs to be erected in order to be used; which should happen in about 14 days.[46] As soon as this bridge is finished, trains can travel uninterrupted from Knoxville to Nashville, because the road is in place everywhere, except at the bridges at Charleston and at Loudon.

Our division (Wood's) is scattered around here. As stated above, our (the 2nd) brigade is located 5 miles from Loudon on the railroad at Lenoir Station. The 1st ([Brig. Gen. August] Willich's) and 3rd ([Brig. Gen.

Samuel] Beatty's)[47] are located in Maryville, 18 miles from here. [General] Wood has gone home, and therefore Willich and General Hazen are in command of the division.[48]

The troops must remain ready to march. [General] Foster[49] has issued an order that officers and soldiers who received a leave, but have not yet left, can not use it for the time being. Everyone has to stay here, because the dance[50] could start at any moment and our army has been weakened by the ongoing Veterans Leave.

Longstreet is located in Sevierville about 40 miles from here.[51] His outposts come to blows with ours very often. In a few days, when I can give my attention to something other than official writing, I want to write of the disposition of the various Rebel divisions, as well as ours. At the present moment I am too busy.

Most respectful greetings,
Respectfully yours,
G. Rentschler

CHAPTER FOUR

Return to Knoxville

Hazen's brigade and its division finally departed from Lenoir for Knoxville on February 16, and John Daeuble described the cold and wet weather experienced and a reconnaissance to Shooks Gap on February 23–24. The sergeant then moved to a convalescent camp near Knoxville.

FEBRUARY 14 TO 16

The 14th it was misty weather with rain, also we had again provisional Marching Orders. During the night it rained, also the following day. In the evening of the 15th we also received a March Order and left our camp by Lenoire [Lenoir] at daybreak the 16th. We advanced 20 miles. Also our Regt. had to serve as the Rearguard. We set up camp 3 miles from Knoxville near the Holston River. It was bitterly cold, as cold as it had been only one time this winter.[1]

FEBRUARY 17

The 17th we marched ½ mile further back and camped. Our regiment came on outpost.

FEBRUARY 18

The 18th we were relieved. The weather was cold [and] it snowed from time to time.

FEBRUARY 19

The 19th our first Baggage arrived from Lenoire [Lenoir], also we obtained some Rice and Beans, Vinegar and Molasses.

FEBRUARY 20

The 20th we had Brigade Inspection Review 1 mile from our camp.[2]

FEBRUARY 21

The 21st it snowed heavy in the late morning. 8 men from our Co.[mpany] went on work detail and also from each [other] Comp.[any] depending on their size in relation to the Brigade. They made fortifications 5 miles from camp, and 2 miles northerly from Knoxville. They did not arrive in camp until toward 9 o'clock at night and had nothing to eat the whole day.

FEBRUARY 22

The 22nd our Regt. came on outpost. Around noon we received orders to send all extra Baggage to Knoxville, which was immediately taken away. Toward dark our Brigade marched off, our Regt which was on picket was not relieved until around 9 o'clock at night by the 89th Ill of the 1st Brigade. We then marched to Knoxville and crossed over the Holston River and camped one mile from there with our Brigade. It was after 10 o'clock before we could rest. [It] was said that we would set out again around 1 o'clock. One could not sleep because the ground was wet and cold. Shortly after 12 o'clock a brigade from the 23rd A[rmy] C[orps] passed us up, which set off with us around 1 o'clock [A.M.] at night. The way was miserable in places, frozen and slick. We marched 9 miles up to Sheal's [Shooks] Gap[,] which we reached after daybreak.[3] We made a halt there, the enemy scrammed before we arrived.

FEBRUARY 23 TO 24

Around 12 o'clock noon the 23rd we set out on our march back again and reached our camp after an advance of 12 miles by the onset of night, we were all immensely tired, very many stayed back. During the night there was a storm and rained in the morning. The 24th already around 3 o'clock we had Reveille. The order was that we would leave our camp at daybreak with 80 cartridges and 3 days rations. Our Brigade left the camp towards 8 o'clock, I stayed back because I had to finish up the Company C payrolls.

FEBRUARY 25

The 25th the most essential [payrolls] were sent to the people by R.R. [railroad].

FEBRUARY 26

The 26th the Orderly [1st] Sergeants from Cos. [Companies] I, D, and H came back in order to finish the writing of their companies.

FEBRUARY 27

The 27th the payrolls were sent to the Front. I finished the payment list of Co.[mpanies] C and G here in Convalescent camp. The Co.[mpany] Clerks and Orderly Sergeant also.

FEBRUARY 28

The 28th the Convalescents of our Brigade moved to a camp next to the city.

FEBRUARY 29 TO MARCH 1

The 29th it rained and as well on the 1st of March–day and night. Our Regt was paid out at Morristown the 1st of March. Our camp was in a terrible state. Wood was very scarce.

■   ■   ■

Like John Daeuble, Gottfried Rentschler remained in Knoxville while most of his comrades in the 3rd Division marched off to Strawberry Plains and points beyond. Rentschler's letter dated March 1 was so long that the Anzeiger published it in two parts. The native German displayed his sharp sense of humor in several instances and described East Tennessee, drawing in good part from an article written by William G. Brownlow and published in his Unionist newspaper—the Knoxville Whig and Rebel Ventilator.

LETTER 7

Published March 6, 1864
Written Knoxville, March 1, 1864
Departure of the 4th Army Corps from Knoxville—Wretched
Condition of It—Adjutant General's Kindness to a Negro Woman—A
Description of East Tennessee: Character of the Country and Its People;
Earth and Mineral Wealth of the Country

Dear Editor,

The "Anzeiger" informed us that on February 22, Washington's
Birthday, Louisvillians had splendid festivities.[4] Our mouths naturally
watered when we read it; however, we swallowed dry, because with us it
goes as bad as with the Israeli people in the "desert." Our eyes see nothing but "hard tacks" that have nothing in common with the Manna of the
Jews, if it's true that it tastes like sweet bread and honey.[5] Our hard tacks
taste more like terrible baked matzoth. We scarcely have a memory of the
meatpans, of the onions and the garlic in the kitchens and pantries of
our dear mothers and darling wives.[6]

Most of us know well, that Washington's birthday was on the 22nd
of February; but when the 22nd of February was, most do not know. We
have totally lost track of the calendar and, since the chaplain [Capt.
James. J. Johnston] left the field, we often do not even know when it is
Sunday; which, however, has its good aspects. We do not put on our
Sunday-best and, therefore, also do not spoil them.[7]

The officers must think along the same line, and prefer to wear their
old coats rather than have new ones made. Many high officers become
promoted so quickly that they find it too costly a game to obtain one for
their new, higher rank. As is well known, a major has two rows of 7 buttons each on his coat; a lieutenant colonel 8 each; and a colonel 9. A
brigadier general has two rows of 8 buttons, each arranged in sets of two;
a major general 9, each arranged in sets of three.[8] They probably don't
have their coats changed because of the buttonholes, and it often seems
that we see a colonel in a major's coat, or a major general in a brigadier
general's coat; [General] Thomas, himself, only had on a brigadier general's coat in the battle at Mission[ary] Ridge.[9] The fiendish button holes!
It is for that reason that some officers are not paid the proper respect that
their rank demands.

On February 22, all baggage of the brigade was stored in a large house
at Knoxville. Only one wagon-load may remain with each regiment, and

everything must be in position to be ready to depart at any moment. The baggage was not yet half out of the camp when marching orders came. The brigade left in order to make a reconnaissance and went about 10 miles northeast [southeast] of Knoxville; however, they met no Rebels. They had retreated over the Holston River that morning. The brigade came back again on the evening of the 23rd and took a position in their old camp, 3 miles from the city toward Loudon.[10] During the night of the 23rd to the 24th, an order came that the Subsistence Commissary should send a sufficient number of wagons to the depot in Knoxville to draw provisions for the troops. On the 24th the brigade left their camp for the second time in order to go to the front. They went with the 4th Army Corps and other troops belonging to the Army of the Ohio up to Strawberry Plains, 15 miles from Knoxville, at the Holston River. The bridge over the same, which had been unsuccessfully set on fire by our troops in the humiliating Dandridge affair; and subsequently had been fully destroyed by the Rebels, has still not been rebuilt.[11] The railroad is interrupted there as well. The goods being transported to Strawberry Plains by rail will be carried across the river on a boat and again loaded on freight cars. During the night of the 24th to the 25th, the order came to send all the brigade's property stored on the 22nd to the depot in Knoxville without delay, in order to deliver it to the troops by railroad. On the morning of the 25th, however, the order was withdrawn and the property that had been sent to the depot was brought back again. It appears this is supposed to happen at this time every night; likewise on the night of the 25th to the 26th.

For a short time we have had a Negro woman in the headquarters who functions as the officers' cook. When the brigade went to the front, the Negro woman was left behind with all the clerks of the brigade's bureaus and about a 200-man guard and convalescents. The Negro woman was disturbed in her sleep, and she complained about this wicked act to the Adjutant General who had been left behind. He had a warm heart, so that the surrounding ice crust began to melt and the honorable seed of mercy that lay there blossomed; and before similar disturbances took place, he took the Negro woman into his own tent out of noble mercy; where she, up until now, found a secure place by the side of the Adjutant General. This little painting may give a small idea of the morality of the troops and especially the officers, which is laid on the soldier in general orders with the usual closing sentence "and he will be obeyed and respected accordingly."

On the 26th the brigade received orders to prepare to march in order to go to Bristol, Virginia, to where Longstreet is supposed to have pulled back. All the baggage had to be left behind. The brigade will therefore have hard times again, and even more because the route is through a country sucked-dry; and still not enough clothes, provisions, etc., can be brought up from Chattanooga, in order to only equip the army fairly well. A lot of soldiers are almost naked and without shoes.[12] Thank goodness a general order keeps me at Knoxville and I do not have to share in the plight of the troops.[13]

If all goes as it should go, the brigade is supposed to return again in about 20 days; so thinks the commander. I fear, however, that the 4th Army Corps will be sent to Virginia in order to cooperate with the Army of the Potomac, in case they should run out of luck.[14]

There is located in [William G.] Brownlow's "[Knoxville Whig and] Rebel Ventilator"[15] of the 27th of February a description of East Tennessee, in general; and of Knoxville, in particular, which I provide herewith:[16] East Tennessee—as loyal toward the Government as any of the other loyal states;[17] consisting of 31 [30] counties and just as separate from Middle and West Tennessee, as Kentucky is from Virginia. It is a valley that is 300 miles long and varies in width from 50 to 75 miles. It is separated from Kentucky in the north by a range of mountains known as the "Cumberland Mountains," extending westward and southward and lying between the great valley of East Tennessee and the Cumberland River, rising among the mountains in the southeast portion of Kentucky. The Cumberland Mountains belong to the "Appalachian" chain, and extend across the whole length of the great valley of East Tennessee. Over this mountain range, through its dense forests and interminable laurel thickets, about 25,000 Union men from Tennessee have forced their way to Kentucky, Ohio and Indiana; and most have enlisted in the Federal army.[18] They traveled at night and camped during the day; and when they climbed over the eminence they cast a lingering glance back on their beloved homeland, offering their family and friends a troubled adieu.[19]

In the south, East Tennessee is separated from North Carolina and Georgia by the Chilhowee and Iron Mountains, and by the Allegheny Mountain range, extending in a continuous chain from Virginia to Georgia and Alabama. This range of mountains forms a dividing line between Eastern and Western Virginia,[20] and makes East Tennessee and southwest Virginia into almost one country; identical in interest, as they are one in soil, climate and productions; East Tennessee, however, has a more advantageous climate.[21]

(To be continued in next issue)

> Respectfully,
> Your Servant
> G. Rentschler

■   ■   ■

LETTER 7 (Continued)

Published March 8, 1864

The residents of East Tennessee have the same origin as those in Kentucky. The original settlers came mostly from North Carolina and Virginia, and they take second place to none in manly character, energy and loyalty to the Government; <East Kentucky excepted.>[22] There are fewer slaves in East Tennessee than in any other areas of the South [State][23] of equal extent, and, in general, the residents were equal in possessions before the Rebellion broke out here. <With our return, after having been absent for 2 years, we found more slaves than when we left—the Rebels stole them in Kentucky, and bought them in Virginia with worthless money, and brought them here. We found men who owned 3 to 6 slaves who did not have enough credit before the war to have had a horse.>

The natural features of East Tennessee alternate advantageously with mountain, hill and plain; and it possesses within its borders great fertility of the soil, much scenic beauty, and a comfortable, moderate climate. The hills and mountains are wooded up to their peaks with every variety of timber; while on all the rivers and small creeks there are embosomed lovely and fertile valleys of farming land that stood in a high degree of cultivation before the war. <Along the country and mountain roads, and where enemy armies march, destruction and ruin can be seen. The traveler or visitor who comes here now sees the most horrible conditions everywhere, and should not form an opinion about the country as it presently appears to the eyes.>

The climate of East Tennessee is mild, <about middle ways between northern Ohio and the Cotton States. In spite of this, we had two unseasonably cold periods this winter; the first around the New Year; and the

second from the 15th to 20th of February, but we had no snow. Half of the winter is so mild that we do not get any ice that is thick enough to be able to store luxury articles.> The summers are free from that intense oppressive heat of the Gulf States; consequently, many families of the South spend the summer at our valuable mineral spas, of which each county possesses a number.

East Tennessee is not a cotton-producing section; it is grassland and had exported large quantities of horses, donkeys, beef cattle, swine, sheep and poultry to the Atlantic states. Indian corn, wheat, oats and potatoes are the natural products. Apples, peaches, pears and plums are grown in large quantities and are of excellent quality. The finest types of maple sugar, butter and cheese are produced. <For three difficult years the Rebel army has drawn its provisions chiefly from East Tennessee. They took their cavalry horses from here in the first stages of the Rebellion, so that now there are not enough horses available to cultivate the land.>

In one word: East Tennessee is the Switzerland of America.[24] <That is the reason for the desperate efforts of the Rebels to win it back, and also the reason for the reluctance of the dejected Union men to be driven through the land by these more than savage beasts who have chased them for so long already.>

The Holston River runs through the entire valley of East Tennessee, 20 miles south of Knoxville, and is navigable for 9 months of the year with small boats. Its tributaries above Knoxville are Pigeon, French Broad, Chucky and Watauga; with numerous little streams adequate for all sorts of [water-powered] machines. Below Knoxville it receives the Little River, Clinch and Hiawassee [Hiwassee]. There is no better-irrigated land on the continent; and where it is well irrigated, there are also good woodlands. When the war is over this land will become what it has been destined to be by nature—the garden of all the border states.

Gold has been found in considerable quantities. The principal metals are iron, copper, zinc and lead. Coal of excellent quality has been found in the counties bordering on the Cumberland Mountains. The land also yields gypsum, marble, saltpeter, slate and salt. Salt is produced within 25 miles of Knoxville in Anderson County; the works, however, have not been operating due to a lack of capital. <The abundance of iron, coal and water power will attract capital as soon as the war is ended. Thousands in the Federal army have expressed their admiration for the land and they have seen it under the most doubtful conditions.>

Knoxville is the metropolis of East Tennessee and one of the first cities established in the state.[25] The city is situated in the middle of East Tennessee; east and west, as well as south and north. <A railroad from here to Kentucky has to be built within 1 or 2 years. We already have the large railroad that connects us to Nashville. We have a lack of carpenters, shoemakers and mechanics of all types in Knoxville. We need saw mills in order to cut our wood; our pine, walnut, oak, ash and other types. We need planing machines, carpentry workshops and countless other workshops.>

This sketch of East Tennessee is a totally accurate one. Brownlow has forgotten to say, however, that the residents of East Tennessee form the warmest little group that exists in America.[26] Associating with these fine people reminds me of the song, "There's Nothing in the World as Warm as the Swabians." I have found that in relation to warmth, the East Tennesseans are equal to the Swabian people. God bless and protect these warm people from the Rebel devils in the future.

Respectfully
Your servant,
G. Rentschler

CHAPTER FIVE

Still Stuck in East Tennessee

Sergeant Daeuble remained in the convalescent camp near Knoxville until March 31. Meanwhile, the 6th Kentucky operated between New Market and Morristown (south of the Holston River) until March 18, and then crossed the Holston at Strawberry Plains and marched around in the Richland Valley.

MARCH 4

It was very windy the 4th March.

MARCH 5

On the 5th the Convalescents received pay for 2 months.

MARCH 6

Sunday the 6th a soldier [unidentified] was accidentally shot through the upper arm by a pistol.

MARCH 8

The 8th March about 150 of the Convalescents were sent to the Front.

MARCH 9

The 9th March the 100th and 104th Ohio Regt[s]. Provost Guard stationed here went from Knoxville to the Front.

■   ■   ■

*Still separated from his regiment, Private Rentschler had little news to relay
about its daily operations for the first ten days of March, so he reported on
a variety of matters, including—the disgusting odor in Knoxville, dislike
for the Army of the Ohio, and poor food. The sharp-witted savant illustrated his points with humorous little stories or quips. He even poked fun at
Major General Thomas by referring to him as "Fat George." However, he
found no humor in the prejudicial treatment received by German Americans in his own army, and railed against it, while revealing some biases of
his own.*

LETTER 8

Published March 15, 1864
Written Knoxville, March 10, 1864

"The whole world stinks," said the Swabian corporal awakening from his
sleep during which his soldiers rubbed his mustache with all kinds of
garbage. Here in Knoxville we can indeed understand the awful, widespread odors. Here the entire world is full of dead mules and shallowly
buried Rebels; they are spreading an awful odor that will eventually end
up in intolerability until the sun sends down its hot summer rays on this
huge cemetery. All roads from Chattanooga to Knoxville are strewn with
dead horses, mules, cattle, hogs, dogs, etc. Chattanooga and Knoxville
however are actually rotting carcass depots. It is not understandable, how
the people can stand the stink without using snuff, because I nearly suf-
focate [with] my well-padded nose.[1] [William G.] Brownlow has in his
Rebel Ventilator of 5 March an urgent petition to the military officials, to
order a general world cleansing. It is from the most extreme necessity
that this happens, because in the case of omission epidemic must devel-
op, as soon as the warm days come.

Our brigade advanced on 24 Feb. as I shared in my last letter.
Longstreet however is not falling back as quick as we assumed, our
troops found, as it appears, a stone in the way, that they are not able to
jump over, because on 2 March they fell back again and our brigade is
now stationed 10 miles on the other side of Strawberry Plains in New
Market. It was stupid to assume that Longstreet would retreat without
further provocation or leave East Tennessee at all.[2] East Tennessee is also

of inestimable value to the Rebels, that they will not leave, until they are driven out, and Longstreet will say, "there must I also be in the process." The ground of East Tennessee will still receive a good amount of blood to drink, before we have the whole territory in our hands. There is no doubt that the Rebels have put together a numerically stronger army this spring than ever before. To depend on the weakness of the Confederate army for an easy victory is unwise; it is up to us to proceed with caution. We are dealing with a desperate enemy and it is common knowledge that in a state of madness man will rely on his animal instincts. Our enemy is desperate, desperate to the point of insanity.[3]

The 4th Army Corps is wholly disunited. The 1st division is attached to the 14th Army Corps ([Maj. Gen. John M.] Palmer's).[4] The 3rd [2nd] Division lays in and around Loudon, and the 2nd [3rd] Division lays in New Market.[5] We all, from Major General down to the "high private in the rear rank," long with all our might to be back in our old Department of the Cumberland.[6] Our two divisions, however, cannot be taken at the moment from the Army of the Ohio, because without us they will not have enough troops. The highest vigilance is required to prevent an invasion of Kentucky by the Rebels under Longstreet.[7]

The area that is to be covered by the Army of the Ohio is immensely large. The experience that we have had with them up to now leads us to believe that "something is rotten in Denmark."[8] The Department of the Cumberland and the Department of the Ohio are two totally different things. The Department of the Cumberland has up to now written a shining piece of history. A united Department will be led against the enemy, and it will show to the world that until now, and also in the future, an iron will prevails, and it will be crowned with glory and success. With our "Fat George" ([Maj. Gen. George H.] Thomas) at the head we will fight like hell and every tailor will become a hero.[9]

As I have already said several times, so I say again, namely that before the 1st of April little of importance will happen. General Hazen went home on leave on 7 March, which he certainly would not have done were he not sure that quiet winds prevail. He is a man, who would not leave his command so long as a cloud hangs over his soldiers.[10]

Now let me tell you the very latest. With the newly arrived recruits in our brigade came several resigned officers, who have enlisted as privates. That is just as curious, as it is new. However, it is merely curious at the first glance. A little thinking over the thing explains the whole mystery.

These officers have all resigned in order to be discharged as such; however, after they were home a long time something unconquerable drew
them back into the army; it was something irresistible that pulled them
back into the Army. It had become almost second nature for them, a
lover of the wild life as it exists in the army. The second reason that
brought these officers back into the army is probably that they spent all
their savings. Then too, they are too lazy for real work, because the long
time in the army, had accustomed them to idleness. Also, a sutler who
functioned 1½ years as an officer in an Ohio regiment arrived here a few
days ago, he has enlisted as a private. Back home they must get the idea
that the life of a soldier is not quite so pitiful as it seems. After all, there
are a number of high-born people who went to join part of a gypsy troop
or a wandering theater or other groups. Our life in the field has in more
than one respect resemblance with that of the gypsies, etc., why should
not a former Captain or Lieutenant join the different life in the army for
a second time, even as a lower ranked private? Even when it is for the
lofty and holy purposes, such as the continuation of the fatherland and
the liberty of a great nation?! Therefore all are welcome, high and low,
millionaire and beggar, lord and servant![11] Many will turn red [suffer
embarrassment] in later years, when the scarred veteran next to him calls
out rejoicefully, "I have been there" and he must say to himself: "I was not
there, when my fatherland stood in flames; I was not there, when those
brave men extinguished the fire with their hearts' blood." Shame on you,
Kramer, your soul smells of cheese![12]

Lately the troops have been well supplied with provisions; all rations
were not distributed however; also our rations are not always the best,
instead at present, often of the worst kind, and one often hears the
soldiers complain about them, even more, when they know, that the
guilt lies with cheating contractors and irresponsible Subsistence
Commissioners.[13] A soldier went to his colonel, with which he otherwise
stood on a good footing with, and complained about this, that the salted
pork distributed by the commission agent is so miserable, that no ordinary person can eat it. The Colonel said calmingly "Henry, I partake of
the same meat every day, and feel right well with it." "That is all right and
good," replied Henry, "It all depends on what one is used to in his home;
it is impossible for me to eat that meat." The colonel understood the
remark, he blushed, (as much as a colonel is allowed to), he turned right
around and went back into his tent. Did eating the pork cause him some

discomfort?![14] The fresh meat is usually of the leanest kind. The Brigade Commissary always has a good number of cattle on hand, even though they are suffering from a lack of food. Consequently, several of them fall by the wayside when we are moving. And then—when the brigade butcher doles out the meat to the troops, he will have to suffer many a good joke about the meat.[15]

The Sanitary goods[16] are a big blessing for the soldiers and could became a still larger blessing, if they would distribute it more conscientiously, but that will not happen, until the Commission sends out here an honorable and conscientious man with the goods, then the different regiments will have those men to hand out the goods to those for whom they are meant. As long as that does not happen a large part of the goods will remain in the hands of individuals and usually in the hands of those for which they are least intended. Corruption rules everywhere, and the deceit is elevated to a science. Everyone wants to make money and become rich. An old saying rings very true: "Who wants to become rich, falls into temptation and gets roped in." May God help them to get into that situation. If one would rope in all the cheats in the army, and all those with commercial interests, the big ones and the little ones—the entire fleet of ships would have to be ordered to foreign countries in order to look for enough rope in all parts of the world—and rope-making would be the most lucrative trade for the next ten years. Corruption, which has been opened through the war, has become an unlimited field, and it will be the main reason, sooner or later, for our Union to cease to exist.[17]

The treatment or rather mistreatment of the Germans in the army has recently demanded the attention of the German press more than usual. My experience with people close to me enables me to speak competently about this subject. There may be about 600 Germans in my brigade. They make up five all-German companies,[18] the remainder are scattered over the different regiments and companies. If a full company is needed for some easy service, e.g., Provost-Guard, a German company is never taken. If an entire company is required for rough service, e.g., several days or several weeks as Train-Guard, a German company will be ordered whenever possible. As this happens on a company basis, so it happens to individuals in the mixed companies. As a rule, the German has to wade through the mud, while the American walks on the dry road.[19] The German is a "Dutch soldier" and as a "Dutchman" he is, if not despised, is disrespected, and not regarded or treated as an equal.[20]

I had a discussion once with a party of abolitionist officers about the employment of Negroes as soldiers and uttered my disapproval. Their main argument against me was that the Germans had no business to bear arms and become soldiers, because they value the country so little just like the Negro. A colonel once said that he could not understand why so many Germans volunteer so readily for the army, after all, as foreigners they could not be interested in it. This opinion is mainly represented by Americans from the North.[21]

I have already heard many crude jokes made about one of the best known generals of the Union, not because he is not up to his high position, every Know-Nothing will argue the opposite, but rather because he is a German.[22] When I say this lack of respect for the Germans comes mainly from the Free States' Americans, let me state at the same time also the fact, that the Free States' Americans give the Negro, wherever they come in contact with him, much worse treatment than those who belong to the Slave States. In my brigade there are 5 Ohio, 1 Indiana, and 3 Kentucky Regiments. The Kentuckians treat the Negro more humanely, the others treat him like a dog. The former call him Negro, the latter call him Nigger.[23]

Let me return to the German soldiers, and state another fact, i.e., that the German soldier is generally far more faithful, conscientious and zealous than the native-born American. This is part of the German nature, which is our reason to be proud of our nation. One more thing: The German soldier is obedient and loyal to duty without regard to reward or punishment. The American generally considers, only reward, or—The Guard-House. This is caused by the national education on either side, in the broadest sense of the word.[24] Because of the situation as mentioned, you may possibly draw the conclusion that the mixing of Germans and Americans in the Army may be beneficial to both parties, but such conclusion is in error.[25]

For the relatives of soldiers who have the misfortune to be wounded in battle, may the following look at a competent staff doctor serve to instruct you. They say, that up to now at least 20,000 of the wounded soldiers who died could have been saved, if they had undergone amputations.[26]

After the battle of Chickamauga and that on Missionary Ridge I visited several hospitals and heard the decision expressed, that they would prefer to die than have an arm or leg taken off. I know several of them, who died, whom the doctor maintained, would have lived if they had an amputation. Loving women and girls may cover this when they write to their men and sweethearts. Those women who know prefer to see their men buried may take this thing to heart and advise them against an amputation in case such is necessary.[27]

Men who are aware of the heart-felt desire of their shrewish wives, will take revenge and marry some Southern Belle. Such incidents are not exceptional but, to the contrary, they are happening quite frequently. It is proof that some of them are not afraid of the fire, even when they have burnt their fingers.[28]

> Respectful greetings
> Your obedient servant
> G. Rentschler

■ ■ ■

John Daeuble continued with his diary at Knoxville.

MARCH 11

During the night following the 11th it rained continuously until daybreak. On the 11th there was a Convalescent Camp Inspection regarding the sick. Then about the same number as previously were sent to the Front.

MARCH 12

On the 12th the Company Clerks and Orderly Sergeants received orders to stay in order to take care of the writing [record keeping].

MARCH 14 TO 18

The 14th, 15th and 16th it was tremendously cold and windy. Also the 17th and 18th. The 18th I let myself be taken into Knoxville; it cost two dollars and one half $2 ½.

MARCH 20

The 20th of March the written Muster Rolls for Jan and Feb. arrived here from the Front. It was said our division marched off to the Cumberland Gap from Strawberry Plains.[29] Also the 41st Ohio which had re-enlisted arrived here.

MARCH 22 TO 23

The 22nd March it snowed a 6 inch deep snow, which however melted again during the night of the 23rd.

MARCH 25

The 25th it snowed and rained, as well as rain on the following day. Toward 9 o'clock in the evening Lt. [Lorenz] Amon and [Pvt.] John Foerster[30] from our Co.[mpany] arrived here on the trip to Louisville in order to get conscripts for our regiment.[31]

MARCH 26

They departed from here Knoxville about 6 o'clock in the morning the 26 March, the weather was cold.

MARCH 27

The 27th on Easter it was warm.

■   ■   ■

Unhappiness and anger pour forth from Gottfried Rentschler's March 27 letter. He and his fellow members of the Army of the Cumberland disliked serving in the Department of the Ohio and yearned to return to Chattanooga. The soldier-correspondent then railed against graft and corruption, both outside and inside the army, and gamblers, too. "God damn these swindlers," he exclaimed. Finally, he reports the occurrence of orgies between blacks and whites in the army and concludes that "nothing is impossible in the 19th century."

LETTER 9

Published March 31, 1864
Written Knoxville, March 27, 1864
Tension Between the Cumberland and Ohio Armies.—Fruitless Marching Back and Forth—Demoralization and Corruption—Swindling of the Army and the Government—Miscegenation

Dear Editor:

Still in Knoxville, oh we are sick, real sick; sick in the heart and sick in spirit. The sight of Knoxville makes us sick; this city looks like every other city of the theater of war, i.e., it has been robbed of its adornments and makes the same melancholy impression as one of its fruit trees stripped of its blossoms, leaves and twigs, or as an arbor of fruit trees destroyed by storm and hail; and it will require a long spring, with people full of vitality, to restore the ruined and the neglected.[32] That alone is not, or least not solely, what makes us sick at the sight of Knoxville. Our sickness is homesickness! Perhaps some people find this condition laughable, because each soldier, strictly speaking, has no home. The hard earth is his bed in the field and the sky's vault his roof. He will not enjoy the comforting "Good Night" of a loving mother, or the blissful "Good Morning" of a faithful, affectionate wife. The trumpet orders him to sleep; the drum beats his morning greeting, be it in Knoxville, be it in Chattanooga, and we have homesickness; homesickness for the body of troops of which each individual soldier forms a part; homesickness for our department, the Department of the Cumberland, from which we have been separated for more than four months. Our hearts will not lighten, and our pulse will not beat courageously and free, until we have Knoxville behind our backs and Lookout Mountain in our sights. Then at the sight of Lookout Mountain even the plumpest will jump up in the air at least two and three-quarters yards with the risk of breaking his neck with the act.[33] I cannot tell you how miserable the troops of the 4th Army Corps feel as long as they are connected to the Army of the Ohio. There occur so many fruitless quarrels between troops of both groups. A soldier of the 23rd Army Corps asked me recently, almost whining. What is the reason that we of the 4th Corps so hate them, the 23rd [Corps]? I could not give him a good answer on the simple basis that I do not know. We do not really know ourselves why we do not respect the Army of the Ohio. The feeling has arisen through so many little events that its hard to give a solid answer. Since [General] Burnside left the Army [of the Ohio] everything in it has been run very loosely, and the past has featured little praising for it. Our corps, in relation to the Army of the Ohio, may justly be named the Corps of Heroes. Jealously on the one side and disrespect on the other form the main basis for the mutual feuding and hostility.[34]

I refer above exclusively to the jealousy among the soldiers, and it should not be mixed up with jealousy among the officers. The jealousy among the latter I explain as follows: as soon as one receives Shoulder-Straps [becomes an officer] he does not look straight ahead any more, but looks right and left in order to have the insignia of his rank constantly in his eye. The existing stiff neck would be pardonable, but the next consequence is that the officer then becomes addicted to mistrust, so that to him the most natural things lean; and the leaning things, to the contrary, appear all right. This is to the disadvantage of the general state of affairs. This mistrustfulness has, of course, taken on the most dangerous character among the general officers.[35]

On March 22nd we received a cold covering in the form and figure of a 3 to 4 inch deep snowfall. O, how the poor soldiers shivered. It was to us, as painful as a flea on a chilly poodle; however, the next day the sun melted it. Also, on the 25th, we received a second, though not as deep accumulation, but not cold enough to cool down the hottest brow. This was the first snow we saw this winter. We have had rain for several days. The rain will delay the construction of the bridge over the Tennessee by Loudon. The trestle work had been erected but the swollen river tore it down, and when this bridge will be completed, only God knows.[36] The goods transported from Chattanooga to Loudon were unloaded at Loudon, brought over the river on boats and then loaded up again on this side, in order to be brought here by rail.[37]

Our division is presently located in Rutledge. If one draws a line through Strawberry Plains in the direction of north–northeast to south–southwest and thinks of this line as a seashore, then the movement of our army can be compared with the ebb and flow of the sea. There is an everlasting advance and withdrawal from Strawberry Plains without achieving a visible result.[38] I am not there with the division, so I can say nothing about details of the operation. It is my principle to write to you only what I have seen and discovered myself, in order to stay faithful with the truth as much as possible.

Our division commander, General Wood, has since the March 8 order held the division ready to march back to the Army of the Cumberland.[39] The order to march will still have to be delayed a considerable time because the 9th Army Corps, which formed a part of the Army of the Ohio, has since been sent to Annapolis in Maryland and, therefore, our corps cannot be done without up here.[40]

The furloughed veterans come back in mass.[41] They appear, however, not to have learned much good at home. They come back in a demoralized condition and many behave like cattle. However, never mind, the strict, tight reins of subordination will soon make them tame again. In Louisville, they have seen with their own eyes where the problem lies. It is not the soldiers alone who become demoralized through the war. The demoralization corrodes our entire society. At the top stand the contractors. When the contract is established they become unusually rich quickly only through fraud, in which they either sell too expensively to the Administration or deliver bad goods to the troops. Then come the sutlers and the bakers. When they become rich quickly, it happens, likewise, through overcharging; whereby they deliver to the poor soldier his needs only for sinful prices.[42]

In Chattanooga, last fall, the bakers sold a pound of bread for 25 to 60 cents and, in spite of these fantastic prices, found more customers than they could satisfy because we were starving; and in order to live, we had to reach into our pockets. How such a son of a bitch is capable of acquiring such profits, you can see for yourself. The sutlers [civilian vendors] are allowed to charge 75 percent higher than their purchase price, but they take 300 to 1,000 [percent]. Who has to fill the pockets of these swindlers full? The poor soldier. The devil will bless them their profit sooner or later.

The gamblers are another profiting class. I know several privates who win monthly $100 to $500; or better said, send more home by dishonest means. The many curses that weigh heavily on these profits will, in time, deliver a terrible harvest.[43]

Next come the merchants and manufacturers back home. The many advertisements in the New York, Philadelphia, Cincinnati, etc., newspapers show superb business is being done with the armies. Gold watches, silver watches, rings, stickpins, and other valuable gold works are all one dollar per item. Everything is here my lords; inexpensive wares, inexpensive wares, now is the time for the soldiers. Is it necessary to say that all these businesses are frauds on the largest scale? God damn these swindlers![44]

After the merchants and manufacturers at home, comes the Quartermaster and Commissary Departments employees.[45] If they make more than the amount of their monthly pay, then they make it through theft. Another type who make money are the speculators who profit

from horses. All unusual profits of these people are made through deception, through deception of their country. They buy a number of horses,
lead them out the front door of the stable and bring them in the back
door; today they pay $5 to the authorities for a worn-out horse, in the
morning they sell it again to the Government for $125. O Patriotism!

Far be it from me to say that all contractors, sutlers, bakers, merchants,
manufacturers, horse traders and employees in the Quartermaster and
Commissary Departments are deceivers and thieves. I speak here solely of
that class which quickly becomes rich, and refer to only that class; because
in them the fraud shows most of all. There are apart from these, still
many classes who do business with the army; who, likewise, are guilty of
swindling.

In the "[Louisville] Anzeiger" of March 20th, I read a short article
about miscegenation and melaleukation or amalgamation. Why give
common things names that are so darned hard to pronounce? The subject probably is supposed to be sprinkled with sugar, and here especially
the Negro? It is not at all necessary, because our soldiers and officers eat
things plain and it tastes good to them without sugar. Orgies occur
between whites and blacks in the army that are too shameful to be able
to be published.[46] It should not surprise me at all, if a certain remark of
a Negro boy was fulfilled. He interfered in the play of white boys and was
ordered by one of them to leave the playground, whereupon the Negro
boy retorted: "You would be happy to be a Nigger before the war is over."
The 19th century has brought to light nowadays so many wonders, nothing is impossible in the 19th century.

My next letter will be limited exclusively to the operations of our
troops in the field.

Respectful greetings
Your servant
G. Rentschler

■   ■   ■

*Sergeant Daeuble finally rejoined his regiment at Powder Springs Gap on
March 31, and after a few days of tramping around, the division headed
back to the Chattanooga area to reunite with its beloved Army of the
Cumberland.*

MARCH 28

The 28th I bought myself History of the Army of the Cumberland in Knoxville.[47] The book cost me $3.50. Toward the evening we received orders to move to Division Hd. [Head] Quarters. The weather was terribly windy with rain.

MARCH 29

The 29th in the afternoon our Co.[mpany] Desks were driven to the Division Hd. [Head] Quarters. Toward evening the Qr. Mr. [Quartermaster] Dept. and Sergeant Major proceeded there. We stayed at the old campground and had orders to depart at 8 o'clock the next morning for the Front.

MARCH 30

The 30th it snowed. We marched off, [but] had to return again.

MARCH 31

And departed from Knoxville March 31. On the 31st we rode the Railroad up to Strawberry Plains, from there we had to still run 14 miles and arrived by the Regt. at darkness. Late in the night rations were drawn again for 3 days and divided out. During the night it rained rather hard and stopped near noon.

CHAPTER SIX

Return to the Army of the Cumberland

The 6th Kentucky and its brigade conducted their last reconnaissance in East Tennessee during the early days of April, and then departed to rejoin their beloved Army of the Cumberland near Chattanooga, where Maj. Gen. William T. Sherman was concentrating his grand army for one of the greatest offensives of the entire war.[1] John Daeuble continued with his chronicle on April 1, 1864.

APRIL 1

The 1st April the signal blew to pull down the tents. We marched off the 2nd Brigade first from our camp by Powder Springs, next to our camp we had to cross over a creek on a primitive broken log bridge, which claimed a rather long time, because only one man after the other could cross over here. It began to rain and rained continuously the whole afternoon. The road was poor and difficult, and it was even worse in the depressions in the Mud road of which there were not just a few, because most of the time it went uphill and downhill. Water stood in them, which made much trouble for us—wetness and covered with muck. We reached Rudledge [Rutledge] after 4 o'clock (distant from our camp 9 miles) which is a little hamlet of several houses, [and] made camp on a hillock. It stopped raining for a short time, began again however after the onset of night and continued to rain during the night. The 3rd Brigade started its Reconnaissance in Poor Mens [Man's] Valley, and we [the 2nd Brigade in] the Richland Valley.

APRIL 2

After daybreak on the 2nd April we took up our march again. Our Regt and the 5th Ky together with a Squad [of] Cavalry turned off to the right of the little city and took a wretched forest path. A creek flowed a good stretch along it and crossed the path often. We marched 4 miles, where-upon we rested about 2 hours when the cavalry returned again we took up our march again back to the little city Rudledge [Rutledge]. The rest of the regiments in our Brig[ade] also had undertaken a reconnaissance on different roads for 4 miles and returned to Rudledge [Rutledge] again, where we encamped at our previous camp. It began to rain again.

APRIL 3

On the 3rd the weather cleared up and was warm. We marched off around 7 o'clock to the old camp, Camp at Powder Springs, which we reached before noon.

APRIL 4

During the night of the 4th it also rained again. Since my arrival by the Regt. [on] the 31 March, when in camp we had to get up around 4 o'clock, and stand in Line of Battle until it is fully daylight, and Recall blew. The 4th April it rained, as well as on the following night.

APRIL 5

Toward evening on the 5th we received marching orders. It rained dur-ing the day, at times strongly.

APRIL 6

The 6th we marched off from camp, we had to cross over a creek by the camp on a fallen tree trunk. The Baggage of the officers etc. had to be carried over it. The donkey [mule] swam and the empty wagon was pulled through the creek by soldiers with ropes. It was stopped on the other side until all were located on that side. We marched off. The way was wretched because of the previous rain. We had to cross several creeks, which took a long time. After 12 miles march we camped in the woods 2 miles from Strawberry Plains, where [General] Willich's Brigade was still stationed. Our Regiment came on outpost. The weather had cleared up.

APRIL 7

At daybreak the 7th we marched off again [and] we had several stretches of water to cross over which at times caused much disorder. Toward 4 o'clock in the afternoon we marched through Knoxville, and pitched night camp 3 miles from Knoxville at our previous camping place. We had advanced 21 miles. During the night it rained.

APRIL 8

On the 8th April I bought a tobacco pipe for 60¢. Around 1 o'clock we marched off and advanced some 7–8 miles, and pitched night camp.

APRIL 9

During the night of the [8th to the] 9th it rained continuously [and] around ½ 6 o'clock [5:30] in the morning of the 9th we left that place. It rained without stop until near noon. The road and the ground were therefore deep muck and the depressions filled with water. We marched 13 miles and set up camp early afternoon at Lenoire [Lenoir] Station. Each man drew 2 small potatoes from the Sanitary Commission. During the night it rained.

APRIL 10

We marched again at daybreak the 10th, it rained from time to time the whole day. After 6 miles march we reached Loudon. We had to wait there until afternoon until we were taken across the river. In the beginning only a little Flatboat was available which could take on Board a small number of troops together with 2–3 wagons. The weather was very *unfavorably* cold with rain. Our Brigade was the first of the Division, however not all the troops crossed over on the same afternoon. The rest of the troops pitched camp in the morning, after crossing the river we marched through Loudon and pitched camp in an open field 1½ miles from *the same* Loudon. After onset of night we drew whisky the men got a good swallow.

APRIL 11

The 11th the weather improved[,] in the evening the 6th Ohio Regt. brought Q.M. [Quartermaster Harvey R.] Wolfe[2] a cigar [illegible]. We received an Order that in the morning the 12th around 7½ o'clock, we the 5th and 6th Ky would march off from here to the depot in order to travel to Cleveland, Ten[n.] on the railroad.

APRIL 12

We marched off on the 12th about the aforementioned time. During the previous night it had rained [and] the road was terribly muddy. At Loudon we crossed over a creek on a dangerous Foot Log, then we marched through the little city there. The Railroad [train] did not arrive because it was supposed to have run off the track somewhere, so we marched about 3 miles around and over the hills in horrible muck where no little screaming and cursing took place.[3] We camped again on the old place. However all the surrounding troops had departed and we could obtain wood and *forks,* in order to pitch our tents. In the afternoon Orders came that we would march off on the 13th [at] 5½ in the morning. It stormed toward evening, with hail for ¼ hour, and thundered.

APRIL 13

We marched off. It was a cheerful day. After 6 miles march we reached Philadelphia [Tennessee]. We marched 7 miles farther and reached the little city Sweet Water [Sweetwater] and pitched camp 1 mile from the same, (march[ed] 14 miles). Our Regt. was in Front of the Brigade which was at the rear of the division.

APRIL 14

The 14th we marched off again at daybreak. We passed on our march the little country town of *Mossville* some 4–5 miles distant from Athen[s]. About 1½ o'clock we reached Athen[s] and camped near there. Our march was 14 miles that day.

APRIL 15

At daybreak the 15th we took up our march again [and] in the early morning hours we passed through the little city of Athen[s] which is a *cute little country town* and with Railroad service. On our march we also came through the little city of Riceville which is of no consequence and also lays on the Railroad. After 14 miles march we reached *Calhoun* at the Highwassie [Hiwassee] River. We crossed over the same on a Pontoon bridge and on the other side we marched through the little city Charleston. At the last named [place] the buildings were not of significance. We pitched camp here in a Cedar Forest on a hill not far from Charleston. The ground was covered with stones and we had a rough camp.

■ ■ ■

Private Rentschler was in Cleveland, Tennessee, on April 15, waiting for his regiment, so he could rejoin it as it passed through on its way to McDonald's Station. He reported on a recent visit to William G. Brownlow's home in Knoxville, commented on the U.S. Sanitary Commission and a few other subjects, then launched a lengthy and caustic verbal attack on a baker from the 24th Illinois regiment who took issue with statements he previously made about some bakers overcharging for their bread.

LETTER 10

Published April 20, 1864
Written Cleveland, Tennessee, April 15, 1864
A Visit With Parson Brownlow—Swindling—New Baked Aristocrats
A La John Dohn—The Bloodsucker Of The Poor Soldier

Dear Mr. Editor:

On the evening of March 20, following a friendly invitation, I was in [William G.] Brownlow's residence for the first time. The inside of the house is elegant; fine, almost rich carpets and furniture. Brownlow is sick; the 2 years in captivity under the Rebels has undermined his health.[4] Mrs. Brownlow is full of fire and spirit;—once welcomed she treats the stranger as belonging to the family; a real comfortable, and homey feeling "with heart" is created within her midst.[5] The daughter "Sun" [Sue] has an excellent gift for conversation and a full education. Too bad, she was not a boy, she would have been a splendid Secretary of State.[6] In Brownlow's everyone moves freely; you come and go, eat and drink, make music and sing and only a hypochondriac can leave moody. Brownlow is a minister; however, in his house one does not sense the tears, the guilt of sincere sinning, the supplication to Jesus, the heart and soul searching that other ministers project. In the rooms of his home there is an atmosphere of fresh healthy air that makes everything so cozy.

—Colonel [Leonidas] Houk, leader of the 3rd Tennessee Cavalry [Infantry] was one of the guests.[7] He illustrated through several interesting examples the acts of the Rebels. He also pointed out that the East Tennesseans have suffered not a little from the Union troops. His own country house was burned down by Union troops. Brownlow's property in Knoxville was not damaged by the Rebels; on the other hand, the Union troops tore down his outbuildings and fences and used them as firewood.[8] There were many complaints about the lax discipline of the Army of the Ohio. Mrs. Brownlow illustrated the strange spirit of the present time with the story of a lieutenant of the 100th Ohio Regiment, who married a Negro woman, to the great amusement of the ladies of Knoxville.[9]

In my last letter, when I spoke of the returning veterans, I forgot to mention, that in the 41st Ohio Regiment all non-commissioned officers, who did not re-enlist, have been demoted to private. So, therefore, a man, who was perhaps a sergeant for 30 months and had performed his duty in every respect, is demoted like a criminal, merely because he perhaps faced the most pressing family circumstances.[10] Something like that you can find only in a country, where looking for warm hearts one can only find the cold stone of [Wilhelm] Hauff's Black Forest Michael[11] or—a bag of money.—The order from the War Department to move non-re-enlistees of a veteran regiment to a different regiment, has rightly been withdrawn.[12]

[Major] General [Gordon] Granger goes to Washington, where he will take over another command.[13] General [Oliver O.] Howard[14] has taken over (Granger's) Command (the 4th Corps). On the 6th of this M[onth], the 4th Army Corps was released by [Major] General [John M.] Schofield. [Brig. Gen. Thomas J.] Wood's division is on the way here, where I have preceded them by railroad. A division of our corps remains stationed in London [Loudon], the other 2 divisions come here for the present.[15]

The bridge over the Tennessee River by London [Loudon] is nearly finished. During our first look at the bridge, we saw a worker fall under it. He drowned. The bridge is 80 feet high and built by civilians, mostly Rebel deserters.[16]

On the way here, I made the comment, that only very little farmland is cultivated. The cause of it is, the fences are missing.[17]

Guerillas linger in the area, yesterday 11 of our soldiers were captured by them.[18]

Capt. [Isaac N.] Johnston[19] of the 6th Ky. Regiment came back a few days ago. He escaped with many officers from Libby Prison [in Richmond, Virginia] and was [a] chief engineer while digging the tunnel, through which they escaped. He will write and publish a history of the affair. Captain Johnston says the imprisoned soldiers suffer unspeakably, but the lot of the captured officers in Libby Prison is bearable, because they are allowed to buy food and clothing or receive it from home. As soon as I receive a copy of his story, I will translate the most interesting parts and send them to you.[20]

In London [Loudon] I paid a visit to the agent of the Sanitary Commission and his department. This Commission is the most charitable organization in the world. The agent says, however, as confirmation of my remark in one of my correspondences, that of the packages sent to him, half were broken into and their contents stolen, before they reached him. I have his permission to publish this. He mentions, however, that the soldiers are not shortchanged, because they are the ones who are stealing the contents of the packages.[21]

Finally, I consider it my duty to give a short reply to Mr. John Dohn's Epistle in the Anzeiger of April 1st.[22] The bakers have sold their bread for from 25–60 cents per pound. Captain [William] Frank[23] of the 6th Ky. Regt., bought loaves last fall in Chattanooga for 5 cents each. He weighed the loaves, they weighed not quite 2 ounces each, which would make it about 40 to 50 cents per pound. The complaints about the bakers were so commonplace that the Inspector-General of our brigade felt forced to present the matter to the Department Headquarters. He said in his official report, that the bakers sell a pound of bread for "25 cents to 60 cents;" I have read that official report and Mr. John Dohn can also read it, if he will write to [Major] General George H.] Thomas.[24] Our Inspector-General will issue a General-order that the bakers may take only 6 or 7 cents per pound, and a baker, who does not obey the order, will be sent away by the General-Provost Marshall of Chattanooga.[25] Day before yesterday I paid 50 cents for 2 pounds of bread in London [Loudon]. How Mr. John Dohn has the gall to complain about the publication of this fact, is not understandable to me, and he would have acted more intelligently, if he had put his fingers into a baking mold, instead of an inkpot. Mr. John Dohn should remember, that he once was a baker for the 24th Ill. Regiment and I can give him the names of very respectable men, who say, Mr. John Dohn has taken few good wishes, probably, however, a great deal of curses, as he was persuaded to quit his function as baker for the regiment.[26] Whether Mr. John Dohn sold his bread last fall for 25 cents for 3 pounds, I do not know; in comparison I know, that Dohn did not set up his bakery in Chattanooga, but on the other side of the Tennessee River and well-informed men told me that Mr. John Dohn did not dare to come to Chattanooga; Why? He will know best himself. Mr. John Dohn thinks I should not have anything to say against the army bakers, because most of them are Germans. If Mr. John Dohn wants to take the trouble to search out the word "swindler" in the conversational lexicon or dictionary, he will find, that the definition of the word by no means makes a distinction between German or English swindlers; if he wants to obscure the sins of the German swindlers with the word "fraternity," "then he only proves that his mind is not worth a farthing.

Mr. John Dohn also found himself persuaded to set himself up as protector of the sutler. In reply I give him herewith a part of an official letter of a general to [Major] General Rosecrans. "Upon investigating the affairs of the sutlers of the brigade, I discovered that by a system of permits a class of merchandise has found its way into camp, consisting of Canned Fruits, Canned Berries, Cordials, Bitters and various disguises for the vending of spirituous liquors and not unfrequently liquors themselves, greatly beyond the list of articles authorized by law. These articles were sold at FABULOUS prices—."[27]

And now I want to give the price of a few articles. In Knoxville the sutler sells a pint of whisky for 3 dollars, a drink for 50 cents, 10 drinks per pint, in this manner they get 1000 to 1600 dollars per barrel. I have received 3 ounces of coffee for 25 cents in Knoxville. Another sutler sold totally spoiled grocery-cheese for a dollar per pound, a cigar for 25 cents, a pair of boots for 12 dollars (I saw his [the sutler's] bill, he paid 4 dollars for the pair). If there was space, I could give thousands of examples that prove the truth of my statement "that many sutlers take 300 to 1000 percent profit." Mr. John Dohn has as, an "intelligent" baker probably read of the assembly, that was held in New York for the protection of the women workers, and which informed them that the best women workers with a machine cannot earn more than 20 to 30 cents per day.[28] Mr. John Dohn must know, that most women workers are soldiers' wives and soldiers' daughters, as opposed to their employers who are for the most part contractors, or suppliers of the contractors and sutlers. Is the word "scoundrel" exaggerated when applied to such cads? Is it enough to merely give to them the name? Should they not become strung up at the closest tree, which is strong enough, to bear them and their heavy sins? If Mr. John Dohn wants to inquire a little in Louisville, he may find similar examples, and if Mr. John Dohn would think and consider that out here every piece of apparel is supplied to the soldiers by the quartermaster, and the soldiers can only look at it and ask spontaneously: How many tears of sorrow did a soldier's wife sew into this garment? So he will grasp, that we soldiers can think only with anger about the money-making class.

Also Mr. John Dohn includes a lance for the veterans.[29] Too bad that he stumbled with it and turned a very ridiculous somersault. Just put your imagination to work and visualize a wolf, that has sucked out all the blood from a sheep, and afterwards, with the blood inside, and after wiping his snout, he rolls his eyes upward to heaven, and he praises the innocence, the gentleness, and the patience, and all the good qualities of a sheep;—I would say "The weather should slay the wolf"—what would you say, Mr. John Dohn? Of course, you may not say much, because I can not picture you so stupid, that you would not find a certain relationship between the wolves with the ex-army bakers and sutlers.

Finally, just a little advice for Mr. John Dohn: The *Anzeiger,* the [Louisville] *Volksblatt*[30] and almost all the most-read newspapers will deliver to the soldiers for half the subscription price, as generally, the press, German as well as English, acts more for the soldier than any other institution. I have still read of no baker who delivers bread to the soldiers for half the usual price,—they are smarter and bring their sheep under cover when the time appears right. This is my last word "on this subject."

It gives me great pleasure to be able to say that I know sutlers and army bakers who sell at very reasonable prices and are a large benefit for the soldiers

G. Rentschler

■ ■ ■

John Daeuble and his comrades arrived at McDonald's Station on April 16, 1864, where they prepared for the upcoming campaign that hopefully would destroy the South's Army of Tennessee and plunge like a dagger into the heartland of the Confederacy.

April 16

Around the usual time that we previously started, we marched again on the morning of the 16th. We passed through Charleston after 11 miles march we reached *Cleveland,* Tenn. which is a nice little city of rather good size. We camped 6 miles from there next to the Chattanooga R.R [at our] Camp near McDaniel's [McDonald's] Station. After we had pitched camp, our Regt. was ordered on picket.

April 18

During the night of the [17th to] 18th it rained. Toward 10 o'clock in the morning troops from another Brigade practiced target shooting, etc. not far distant from our camp. We believed at first it was the enemy who attacked our outpost because it was outside or distant from the lines and hence we formed a Skirmish Line. Toward evening we changed our camp several hundred yards farther distant, and encamped according to regulations. Also our Brig Gen Hazen arrived from leave.[31]

April 19

The 19[th] we spent time cleaning our camp, it was very windy and cold. Co.[mpany] H from our Regt went to Gen[era]l Hazen as Provost Guard.[32]

April 20

The 20th drills started again 3 times a day. In the morning Company and Battalion Drill and in the afternoon Brigade Drill.

April 21

Capt. Frank went off on the 21st on 2 days leave to Chattanooga in order to buy clothes.

April 22

The 22nd a Brigade of fresh troops passed by here, which were destined to Loudon to relieve the troops of [Maj. Gen. Philip H.] Sheridan's [former] Division.[33]

April 23

The 23rd our Regt came on outpost.

April 27

The 27th at nightfall we received vague marching orders.

April 28

The 28th I gave my rifle to [Pvt.] Henry Webert[34] by order of Capt. [William] Frank.

April 29

On the 29th we had Division Review in front of the camp on an open field already partly cultivated with grain, some grew wild, [Major] General [Oliver O.] Howard was present together with two women on horseback. It was cheerful weather but terrible to march, it was very dusty in the newly cultivated fields. About 9 o'clock we departed from the camp and arrived there again after 12 o'clock. [Cpl.] August Eversberg and [Pvt.] John Lang together with other Veterans from our Regiment had again returned to the Regt and Company.

April 30

The 30th April our Regiment came on outpost. We had to make out the payrolls again because the Veterans were classified differently.

■ ■ ■

Private Rentschler's eleventh letter was published in two parts by the Louisville Anzeiger. The Württemberg native began his letter by eloquently expressing the wonderful feeling that spring brings, and touched on the obstacles the army faced, the terribly depleted condition of his own regiment,

the miseries suffered by the civilians in East Tennessee, and the raging debate
in the North over whether to continue the war. In typical Rentschler style, he
uses a humorous little story brought from Germany to illustrate the difficult
task someone would have trying to reconcile the opposing sides.

LETTER 11

Published May 4, 1864
Written McDonald's Station, Five Miles from Cleveland, Tennessee,
May 1, 1864
May—Thoughts in the Field.—Still Not Ready to Launch Attack—The
4th Army Corps in Cleveland.—The 5th and 6th Kentucky Regiments.[35]

"May has come." It is abundant with newly awakened life. What rich-
ness of blooms and flowers and decorous leaves are contained in these
three simple words?! The breast of the young man expands; his thoughts
represent the ideal. Loving seizes and embraces his existence and is the
focal point of all his May philosophy.—Love.—Charm swells the bosoms
of the girls. Laughing, they catch the scent of the first garland of flowers of
the year in order to crown their musing foreheads to please him; because
May has also aroused the tender feelings in her, and love radiates out of the
mirror of her soul. It is something different with us old people.[36] "The May
of life blooms only once and not again, to us it has faded," and "to us nothing is left but the faded bouquet of the past"; however, the wilted bouquet
of the past receives a lighter color with each spring and with special ten-
derness we press our "old one" to the heart on a May morning; pressing to
her the springtime kiss on her often nibbled lips and, if however not
through words, through eyes asking: "Remember still—?"[37]

A quite peculiar feeling stirs the soldier in the field in May. It is a
strained and pressing yearning that takes hold of him, "to make foot-
prints on the mountains" in order to hike over them to her; the one not
seen for a long time; who has been missed for so long, but nevertheless,
a warm and tender sweetheart. Poor Soldier! Perhaps that blooming tree
will cover your grave with its fallen blooms, because today or tomorrow
the drum calls you into the bloody battle and you have lived and loved!
Be calm, "You slumber only a short while," and all your love follows you
to the everlasting May Day.[38]

We out here are just as surprised as those at home that our Army yet
stays still, in spite of the progress of the season. The basis for the above-

written lays in the simple words, "We are not ready"; or we were not, at least, until now.[39] I have very good grounds to believe that at the present the Rebels are greater in number than us.[40] Assuming, however, that they have barely the same numbers as we, they still have a big advantage over us; because they do not have such a colossally long line to occupy.[41] They can concentrate their troops at any favorable point. It brings no danger to them to leave open any one subordinate part of their country. We could hardly have an advantage by making use of a gap if we would find no armed enemy. We would only distance ourselves from our depots, without compensation, in enemy country. We must be where the armed enemy appears. We must keep sufficient possession of this whole line. The Rebels could win in our district through force.[42] The essential issue is a fundamental disbursing of our strength, and requires that we place more troops in the field. Why the government does not feel confident to proceed in earnest with the conscription, you know better than I; because I understand from politics *"von Semri kein Wessle."*[43] We are not ready because the troops in the field still do not have all the necessities. There is the highest probability that the next campaign decides about victory or loss; non-confederation or confederation; about life or death. Before we can enter an important battle, the utmost attention is necessary; and the best possible preparations must be made for the attainment of favorable results for us. A spring campaign, therefore, is improbable.[44] We must fight in the hot summer. In consideration of these things one can only be led to belief that Halleck[45] neglects much—but also that Grant correctly understands his mission and has comprehended that he will attain the desired goal only through thoroughness.[46]

Our army corps, as I indicated in my last letter, was in motion. On the 6th of April we were finally released from the Army of the Ohio, and our Division, Wood's, arrived here on April 17th; where [Maj. Gen. David S.] Stanley's was already camped. Also, [Brig. Gen. John] Newton's division (previously Sheridan's) arrived here from Loudon and the whole 4th Corps lies here together and near Cleveland. [Major] General [Oliver O.] Howard has command of it and, although no one builds a gold mountain on him, one believes, in general, that he with one arm (the other was shot off him) is a more capable general than Granger with two.[47] The latter was given this proud command in the true American way; because he had found an acorn in the battle of Chickamauga. Providence used him there to our advantage.[48] Our division was in a fatal state; which is easily understood, if one considers that for 5 months, since the Missionary Ridge battle, it was almost constantly on the march and had to endure the hardest and most wearing privations. (Many soldiers went for a long time without shirts and without shoes.)[49] Here all missing items will be replaced and all customary repairs be made. The troops should be clothed and provided with all types of camp utensils; the means of transportation should be supplied and improved; the books, reports, bills (accounts) brought into order; and altogether the whole command put into a capable condition to serve in the field. All relevant authorities have performed the most valiant work to reach this goal quickly and completely. As soon as that happens we will be pushed to Ringgold, without doubt; where the whole Army of the Cumberland will be united again and will be ready to make its mark through so many victories.[50]

Our number has been very much reduced through this winter campaign. The 6th Kentucky regiment has only 106 "valiant men" present. Two of its companies are attached as Provost Guards—Co. B, Captain [Richard C.] Dawkins,[51] at the division headquarters—Co. H, Captain [Isaac N.] Johnston,[52] at brigade headquarters. The remaining 8 companies number some 13 men per company present and capable of bearing arms. Captain [William] Frank, "The Fat,"[53] commanded the regiment about a month, during the absence of Lieutenant Colonel [Major] Whitaker.[54] He commanded capably. He has become, however, somewhat thinner from it. What is established is that it must be no easy thing to be a regimental commander. Captain H. Schmitt [Schmid] came back to the regiment on April 15th. We regret that he will have to arrange to resign because of his severe wound, because he is one of the best officers of our brigade.[55]

Also the 5th Kentucky Regiment (Louisville Legion) has merely about 225 men capable of bearing arms at present. The word "Legion" is no longer suitable for this regiment, because one remembers the Roman Legion's each had 12,000 men.[56]

G. Rentschler

LETTER 11 (Continued)

Published May 5, 1864
The Daily Work of the Soldier—Misery of the Residents of East
Tennessee.—A Tragi-Comical Finale

Although lying in camp, one should not imagine the soldiers are lying still. Following I give to you an excerpt from the daily orders of our general. It is quite obvious that we have enough to do.

1.	Reveille	Daybreak
2.	Camp Cleaning	5:30 A.M.
3.	Breakfast	6:00 A.M.
4.	Sick call	6:30 A.M.
5.	Company Exercises	7:00–8:00 A.M.
6.	Guard Mounting	8:15 A.M.
7.	Regimental Exercises	9:00–10:00 A.M.
8.	Noon meal	12:00
9.	Brigade Exercises	4:00–5:00 P.M.
10.	Camp Cleaning	6:00 P.M.
11.	Dress Parade	Sundown
12.	Tattoo (Last Post)	8:30 P.M.
13.	Taps (Lights Out)	8:45 P.M.

The newly-arrived recruits also have an Extra Exercise Hour from 10–11 in the morning.

From that you may see that we do not become bored. They will often enough "stir" and move. Incidentally, I have heard the best doctors say that it is indispensably necessary for the fitness of the troops to keep active, and the doctors' reports show that sickness in regiments and brigades that are allowed to completely suspend activity for a long time is far more frequent than in those which will maintain a constant moderate amount of activity. The former is certainly not the case in our brigade, because our General is a professional soldier (a West Pointer); and the torrent of the drum sounds all too sweet to his ears not to have activity at least a dozen times daily.[57]

At the sight of the country in East Tennessee, one's heart is overcome with a deep pain; and perhaps in no other season more than in the springtime. The fields lie fallow because the farmers who remain find it useless to cultivate them, because there are no fences anywhere.[58] The areas that are distant from the military roads may certainly offer favorable prospects. These areas cannot be large, however, because our troops have marched through part of the country and part has been marched through by the Rebel troops.

The homeless and destitute residents of this country who are wandering around still present but a sorrowful sight. It is heart rendering to see here the weakened, emaciated, pale figure of a mother, who has 5 or 6 or more ragged children following, creeping up or sitting huddled up together in the corner of a house. The war has made her a widow and unspeakably miserable—it is deplorable to see there a man reduced to a beggar, with his large family for which he has no more bread, move with a searching look to view up and down the road, in order to seek a home for himself and his charges—because his home was burned down or torn down by a boisterous band of soldiers. His fields lay fallow. He has no draft animals for his plowshare. He has no seeds for planting. He has no hands to work in the fields—his grown sons are in the army or already have been shot and are lying under the grass.[59] The misery of these people would be bottomless if the Americans themselves felt bound to the soil with heart and soul in the same degree as the Germans. Fortunately, the American has a lighter spirit and his home is where he finds the most plentiful bread. If that is true about him, so is the word of the poet: "Wherever man/woman is born, the heavens cast a unique magic over him/her."

The number of these unfortunate people in East Tennessee is not small. We have not marched a day that we have not encountered them. It is a sacred duty of the residents of the Northern, Western and Eastern states to make these emigrants, at their arrival, forget their exceptional misfortune through a warm reception and helpful assistance. Those to whom the war has brought pecuniary advantage should especially make it their responsibility to give these poor people a hand, with counsel and deed.

In Washington, there is dispute; some want peace. However, the peace advocates are getting the worst of it;[60] which reminds me of a little tragic-comic family story. For the peace advocates it has gone almost as with the pastor of Feverbach, and how it went with him I will only explain in passing. The story is a bit old because it came from the year 1850. The pastor was the cousin of the schoolmaster whose wife was a "hellcat," and had more hair on her tongue than many Newfoundlanders had on their pelts. She usually began to thunder lightly in the morning, she flashed lightning at noon and continued in the evening. There were, however, no "cold bolts". They were hot. Fisticuffs. On one unfortunate day there was a bad storm in the morning before coffee and Mr. Schoolmaster received his coffee roll on his cheek. That was just too much for the patient man, and "what is too terrible, is too terrible," and he went to his cousin, the pastor, and complained to him of his bitter plight. The pastor took off his sleeping gown and put on a large black "Gottfried."[61] He buttoned the white collar, so that he would make a right venerable impression on the wife; and went with the schoolmaster "in order to bring about peace," as he said. He went into the schoolhouse and heard his cousin's wife so terribly busy in the kitchen that his heart begins to pound; and he timidly opened the kitchen door, stuck in there his otherwise wine-red face, that by now had become totally white like the Schoolmaster's, and began with a moving voice: "Frau — — —."; Frau cousin's wife, he wanted to say. Hardly had the cousin's wife heard the word "wife," when she flew to the kitchen door like lightning, and mistaking the venerable cousin for her husband, angrily hit him around his face with the dripping wet kitchen rag, one time right, one time left, then again right, and again left, with shocking quickness, so that to the venerable pastor everything was green and brown before his eyes, and he barely could see the remorseful look of the repentant wife of his cousin when she realized her tragic error. The pastor has told this story to me many times and assured me from that since that time he has only acted as the peacemaker in the pulpit.

The gentlemen in Washington should take a lesson from this story and either let those who are in rage rage on until they have expended it, or, if they want to "establish peace," take a secure, as high as possible stand; if they do not accept my advice, then it is their own fault if the abolitionists one day throw a plantation full of niggers in their face.[62]

I fear that I already have taken more space in your treasured pages than is proper to claim, and bid you until later a friendly farewell.

G. Rentschler

The Beginning of
Their Last Campaign

John Daeuble *continued with his diary entries at the camp at McDonald's Station on May 2, 1864.*

MAY 2

Our Brigade held Inspection the 2nd May. Our extra Baggage, Co[mpany] Desks and etc. were sent off.

MAY 3

The 3rd we received marching orders and marched off around noon from Camp near McDonald's Station. On the Ringgold road in the evening after 7–8 miles march we pitched night camp.

■ ■ ■

P*rivate Rentschler's brief letter dated May 3, 1864, begins with a humorous description of generals and ends with a tribute to the soldiers in the ranks.*

LETTER 12

Published May 10, 1864
Written Five Miles from Cleveland, Tennessee, May 3, 1864

Dear Editor:

On the 29th of April, Major General [Oliver O.] Howard, our new corps commanding officer, held a review of his whole corps.[1] A large number of General Officers assembled in our headquarters. If one thinks of himself as a commanding officer, then he likes to think that with every step the ground crashes under him or when on horseback that his eyes dispatch lightning and, in general, his appearance is sort of majestic. Not many generals of this country make this imposing appearance; many of them have lawyers' faces and, in Germany, several of the thin ones of this class would be mistaken for a meditating schoolmaster, or a tailor plagued with galloping consumption. Several of the fat ones would be mistaken for well-fed village or city mayors. However, as all that shines is not gold; in comparison, some gold does not shine and some of these high officers have proven through shining deeds that looks can be deceiving.

The review itself was a magnificent affair. The troops made an imposing impression and General Howard expressed his greatest satisfaction with the results of his inspection in an Order. Right after the review other orders were also released; among which the most important was to make ready to move, in order to be able to be on the march after 30 minutes notice. Today, at 12 noon, we will break camp departing for ————. If we only knew where we are going![2] But since Grant[3] commands the ship of war, the immediate future is also a closed book for us. Good, come, then what may come; we are ready and willing to meet the most dreadful. The weak regiment is allowed one wagon, the stronger two.[4] Every man has to carry his little bit of belongings on his body, along with three-days cooked rations and, as the order says, they possibly must last for 5 days.[5] The officers have sent their overflow baggage to Bridgeport for storage.[6]

> Oh, how soon, oh how soon
> Fades beauty and figure.
> You are resplendent with your dancing,
> Which stands out like milk and crimson;
> Oh, the roses soon wilt!
> . . . .
> Today still stands proud roses,
> Tomorrow shot through the breast[7]
> . . . .

It is true, when he hears the drum begin the signal to move toward the enemy, a melancholy shadow enters his soul—he thinks about his loved ones at home! The thunder of war soon drives away the soft heartedness, and each grasps his rifle with a firm grip, to bring the highest honor to his profession by fighting the detested enemy with lion-like courage.

In my next writing I will undoubtedly be able to report interesting news. Until then—good-bye.

G. Rentschler

■   ■   ■

In early May 1864 Maj. Gen William T. Sherman launched most of his grand army of 110,000 men, consisting of the Army of the Cumberland, Army of the Tennessee, and Army of the Ohio, toward Dalton, Georgia, where General Joseph E. Johnston's 54,000-man Confederate Army of Tennessee was assembled. First Sergeant Daeuble detailed the southward movement of his unit beginning on May 4, 1864, and the subsequent fighting on Rocky Face Ridge, during which: "We found protection near the rocks and spent the whole day through [under fire] with anxious hearts."

MAY 4

The 4th we marched off again at daybreak. Our Regt and Battalion were in Front of the brigade, toward 10 o'clock we reached the East Chickamauga Creek and crossed over it. Around noon we arrived by a resort *Catoosa Springs* and [?] County and turned off the street into the woods where we crossed over the Chickamauga Creek again and formed a Line on the hills. We were some 2½–3 miles distant from Ringgold, 12 miles from Dalton, and 6 miles from Tunnel Hill, and had covered about 9 miles, when we pitched camp,

MAY 5

The 5th [of] May the 14th Army Corps or rather part of it camped below in the valley. According to a statement the enemy is supposed to have their outposts only ½ mile or 1 mile [away]. At noon the 6th our Regt came on outpost. Pioneer Co. A, remained back in camp because Pioneers [engineers] perform service on the march. We ran around in

FIG. 7. *Maj. Gen. Oliver O. Howard, commander of the 4th Corps. U.S. Army Military History Institute.*

the bush about 2 miles before we could find the post of our Brigade. The enemy outpost which was cavalry was located one half mile distant from us. We saw them clearly on the open field at the edge of the forest. The 23rd Ky Veteran Regt also arrived by the hill.

MAY 7

At daybreak the 7th our army moved forward. Some shots were exchanged whereupon the enemy posts moved back. We proceeded immediately to the Brigade. We had a miserable march because on the way back we had to run a mile through the woods, and because the Batteries and Troops of the 1st–3rd Brigades had to pass before we reached our Brigade. Blankets and knapsacks, etc., lay on the road from all quarters, after 4 miles march we reached Tunnel Hill [, Georgia]. Some cannon shots were exchanged, we were deployed in Close Columns by Battalion, after a half hour we moved forward in Close Columns through the woods. The enemy had moved back, and we marched in flank march through the little city of Tunnel Hill, [Georgia, where] some of the houses had been drilled through by cannon balls. We made a halt on top the hill. Tunnel is 1480 feet long. The enemy was located in front of us on the Rocky Face Mountain [Ridge] Bosseht Root [Buzzard Roost] Gap.[8]

MAY 8

The 8th May we received marching orders. We lay around here for an hour packed, and marched out of here in a Line of Battle through the woods and down into the valley and pushed from one side to the other. Skirmish fire was maintained the whole day [and] toward evening we saw the enemy march along the top in the flank march. *Appeared [to be a] maneuver.* We camped the night over in the valley.

MAY 9

The 9th May our Regt. [and] the 23rd Ky were ordered up as Advance and Skirmishers on big hill Rocky face [Ridge]. We climbed it under skirmish fire until 300 Yards. Our Brigade followed in Close Columns. The whole day a heavy Skirmish fire was maintained. When we neared the top in the morning the enemy fired a Battalion fire on us, whereupon we found protection near the rocks and spent the whole day through with anxious hearts. There were about 30 men wounded and shot dead from the 23rd Ky and 6th Ky.[9] From our company Corp[ora]l [Engelbert] Emig[10] was wounded[,] at nightfall we were ordered back into the valley. There was a heavy fire maintained on the right wing.

MAY 10

The 10th it was gloomy weather and rained off and on. We had to fall in several times. There was continuing skirmish fire together with cannon fire maintained the whole day. The enemy fired with cannon from the R.[ocky] F.[Face] Mountain [Ridge] into the valley below on the troops who had pitched their tents at the edge of the forest. An Order appeared in the morning that Gen[era]l Grant hit the enemy in Virg.[inia] and

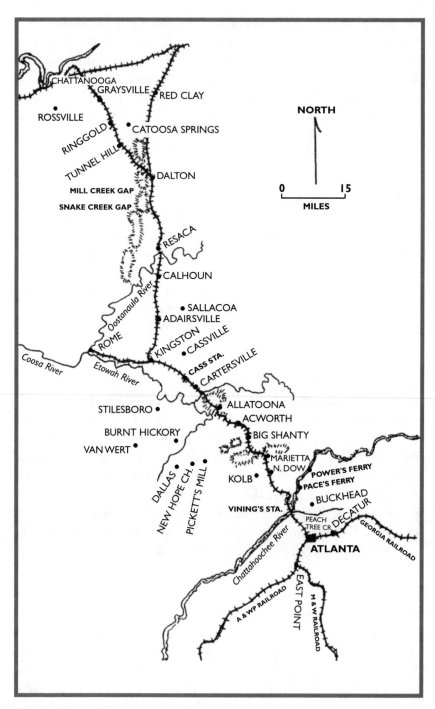

MAP 4. *Theater of operations—May 1864 to August 1864.*

pursued him for 10 miles and appeared to be in pursuit. Loss was heavy on both sides.[11] Toward nightfall a Regt. from [Brig. Gen. Walter C.] Whitaker's Brigade came marching over the open field. The enemy directed his fire from the hill down on it whereupon they ran toward the forest in the double-quick. During the night there was a terrific storm, it rained terribly, so that we were dripping wet in our Dog huts [shelter tents]. It rained the whole night through, the outposts fired continuously toward one another, when the enemy found out their bullets reached our camp, they fired continuously into our camp.

MAY 11

On the morning of the 11th 1 man was shot dead and one from the L.[ouisville] Legion wounded, shot through the body,[12] the previous day a large number in the camp were wounded. Early on the morning of the 11th we moved our camp out of the range of the enemy bullets on a hillock in the valley.

■ ■ ■

Gottfried Rentschler's thirteenth letter also covers the advance to Rocky Face Ridge in northern Georgia and the fighting there, but includes many interesting details not found in Daeuble's diary.

LETTER 13

Published May 17, 1864
Written Tunnell [Tunnel] Hill [Mill Creek] Gap, Georgia,[13]
May 11, 1864
Operations And Fights Of The Army Of The Cumberland Up To
May 11—The Louisville Legion

Dear Editor,

I give to you only briefly and quickly a short excerpt from my diary from May 3rd until today. I write under a furious roar; and you will, therefore, excuse me that I write with a pencil and not in excellent style.[14]

None of us thought that we would have a battle so quickly and probably you and your readers too. I can write to you only the details of our own brigade; of the other troops of our army, it is possible that others can share the details with you.

Before our departure from Catoosa Springs, the 8 regiments in our brigade were formed into battalions; not only because the regiments are small, but also because the brigade can be better handled by the general through this consolidation. 124th and 93rd Ohio, Col. O. H. Payne, 124th Ohio, commanding; 5th Ky. and 6th Indiana, Col. W. W. Berry, 5th Ky., commanding; 23rd Ky. and 6th Ky., Lt. Col. J. C. Foy, 23rd Ky., commanding; 41st and 1st Ohio, Lt. Col. R. L. Kimberley, 41st Ohio, commanding.[15]

The 3rd of May. The 6th Ohio, which up to now was part of our brigade, has been ordered to Cleveland, Tenn. to function there as Provost Guard, and to prepare at the same time for their muster out and completion of paperwork. Their service is to end on June 18th.[16] At 12 o'clock noon we left our camp (5 miles from Cleveland) in order to go to the front. We marched 8 miles through rather heavily wooded country

The 4th of May. Marched 9 miles and made a halt 2 miles from Ringgold and one mile from Catoosa Springs. These springs are a true natural wonder. On one flat area of about one-half of an acre there are 52 springs, and the water in each one is different from the rest. Earlier, by each spring was a plaque with its name. Now only 16 plaques remain. The following springs are described: 1. White Sulfur (has a disgusting death-like taste); 2. Healing; 3. Buffalo; 4. Black Sulfur; 5. Magnesia; 6. Chillie Betha; 7. Red Sulfur; 8. Congress; 9. Emelia; 10. Choumosdusca; 11. Red Sweet (famous mineral water); 12. Bedford; 13. Coffee; 14. Essam; 15. Alkali; and 16. Free Stone (a splendid, cold, drinking water; has, however, an acidy taste).

This bathing establishment must have been, before the war, the most magnificent in the South. Now, of course, everything is rather ruined and destroyed. The buildings were used by the Rebels as hospitals.[17] The earth in this whole area is stony, hard and broken.

The 5th of May. Lying quietly. General Hazen gave the brigade orders to mainly fire in "volleys" when in battle.[18] It is said that we have 6 army corps here with a supposed manpower of 90,600, without the cavalry and artillery.[19]

The 6th of May. The 23rd Ky. Regt., that had re-enlisted, came back this morning. It numbers 25 officers and 232 men. Our effective strength today amounts to 8 regiments, 136 officers and 2,356 men.[20]

Late in the evening received orders to send all wagons and baggage back to Ringgold. Only one wagon is allowed for brigade headquarters and a second for the fodder for the horses of the field officers of the entire brigade.[21]

The 7th of May. Left camp at 6 o'clock in the morning in order to move toward the enemy. We marched about a mile when a lively picket-fire was opened on the advanced posts of the enemy. This was about a mile in front of us, and was maintained about 30 minutes by [Maj. Gen. David S.] Stanley's division.[22] The way was strewn with blankets, coats

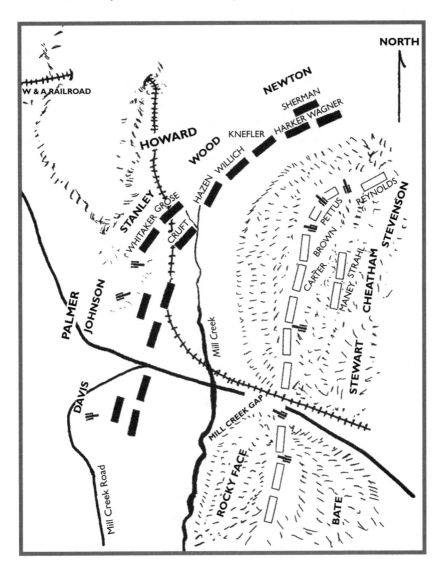

MAP 5. *Howard's and Palmer's Corps at Rocky Face Ridge.*

and pieces of clothing that our soldiers had thrown away in order to march lighter, because the day began quite unusually hot. On the entire way I saw only two Rebel blankets (or actually rags), and some tattered and torn pants and jackets. They probably have little surplus baggage.[23] Came through Tunnel Hill, some six miles from Catoosa Springs. Tunnel Hill is located in a romantic basin-shaped valley; and is a little town of 30 to 40 houses, of which only 2 or 3 are still occupied.[24] Camped on an eminence. On the mountain line across from us the Rebels had a signal station and a very strong force. This mountain line is perhaps 6 miles long and runs from north to south. Between the south end of it and moving across the mountain range in a southwestern direction is situated Tunnel Hill [Mill Spring] Gap; through which [Maj. Gen. John M.] Palmer, in February, if I am not mistaken, wanted to force a way through with the 14th Army Corps, but was unsuccessful.[25] Our corps was mainly asked to storm the 6-mile long mountain line, which I will henceforth call signal hill [Rocky Face Ridge] for the sake of brevity, and force a passage through its gap.[26]

The 8th of May. Around 9 A.M. advanced to the signal hill. Newton's division on the extreme left. Ours, Wood's division, to the right of Newton's, and our brigade to the extreme right of our division. A strong and unceasing picket fire the whole day on our left side;[27] only a little fight on our right. Late in the evening Stanley's division advanced (to our right) toward the gap, and drove the Rebels back in a wild chase. Stanley conquered half of the Gap this evening.[28] Our brigade fired only a few shots the whole day. We did not lose a single man in the brigade. When our brigade moved up the signal hill a good piece, the Rebels called down to us: "Come up here and get your whiskey"; to which we called: "Come down here and get your coffee,"; they called: "Come and get your cotton"; which we answered: "Come down and get your soap to wash your pig skin." Also the Rebels yelled, "If your Lincoln is elected, we will fight with you four more years."[29]

This evening received the official news that Grant has fought Lee in a 2-day battle, and is making preparations to renew the battle. The cheers from our troops were deafening; never have I heard such jubilation. Sherman told several of his generals today that he wanted to give Johnston, "a final hearing."[30]

The 9th of May. In the morning, 7 o'clock, the dance was opened with a very strong skirmish-fire that soon resulted in a regular battle.—

Horrible butchery of the Rebels as well as our troops. Our brigade received orders not to try to storm the ridge on the signal hill, if it should cost too many people. The main purpose of our attack was to keep the enemy busy, in order to draw his attention away from other points; because the 23rd Corps was expected on the eastern [northern] side, while McPherson's two corps were expected on the southern side of the signal hill.[31] The ridge could not be taken without large losses on our side; because the ridge itself is bordered with an almost uninterrupted natural rock wall and, besides, the Rebels have erected strong breastworks made of stones. Our brigade moved up until just below the rock wall; there, however, we could go neither forward nor backward. We lay there stretched out on the ground for several hours, because everyone that stood received a bullet from the Rebel sharpshooters who held the ridge of the mountain in an enormously long and strongly-occupied line. A soldier of the 23rd Ky. Regt., for fun, hung his handkerchief on a small branch of a tree; as fast as the Rebels saw it, three shots were fired; two bullets went through the handkerchief. This may serve as evidence of the skillfulness of the Rebel sharpshooters; who, for the most part, have large rifles on stands. Our soldiers named these rifles "young cannons," because they almost have as great a bang as a howitzer.[32]

The signal hill is densely wooded, stony and steep. In our front there is only a little place, some 50 to 60 feet wide, through which it would be possible to reach the ridge on the mountain. Sherman said today, in the circle of his generals, that by tomorrow around 2 P.M. the battle would be won for us and Johnston under arrest, i.e., be taken prisoner.[33]

From 6 o'clock until in the night, a horrendous cannon fire was maintained by our side. Never have I seen our army so happy and desirous of being drawn into a fight as today. The music bands of the army also make their contributions to keep the soldiers happy.

The Rebels shoot down from the ridges, a distance of more than a mile, and wound many of our people, many mortally. Before we came, they placed targets below in the valley and practiced shooting at this distance.

Four from the 6th Ky. Regt. were wounded today, including two Germans, namely: Engelbert Emig, from Louisville, shot through the left hand; and Karl Fischbach, also from Louisville, shot through the stomach. The latter was taken to the hospital, where he died after a half an hour. Rest in peace! He was a brave young man. In the brigade, in total, we lost about 60 men, dead and wounded.[34] Since the 3rd of May very hot weather.

The 10th of May. This day was opened with a very unmilitary operation by the 96th Ill. Regiment, which was situated ½ mile from the signal hill. [Thomas E.] Champion, the Col. of the regiment, sent them over here to the mountain into our picket line to fire their rifles; which happened in such confusion, that we generally believed that the enemy had made a bayonet attack down the mountain; our whole corps was set up in a line of battle, posthaste.—Scarcely had we learned the cause of the shooting before we were immediately sent out again, when a second regiment of the same brigade came over here and began the same stupid thing. A foolish screaming was maintained the whole morning in that brigade.[35]

This morning we heard a rumor that Schofield is under arrest because last Sunday he was still lying with his whole corp., the 23rd, while he had strict orders to advance as quickly as possible.[36]

The day was relatively quiet. A weak infantry and artillery fire was maintained the whole day. Several from our brigade who were stationed at the bottom of the signal hill were wounded, because the bullets from the Rebel sharpshooters whistled around their ears. Toward evening a regiment of Stanley's division was led across the valley in order to go on picket duty.—The picket line is half way between the foot and the ridge of the mountain. The Rebels opened a lively fire on them. The back half of the regiment ran and sought shelter in a nearby woods; the front-half of the regiment moved forward in the double-quick. I do not believe that anyone was wounded. The whole corps laughed heartily.[37]

The weather was gloomy and rainy. During the night a terrible storm came and the rain ran in rivers. Many of us had to abandon our "beds" in order not to be swept away.

The 11th of May. This morning two men from the Louisville Legion were shot; one dead and the other mortally wounded.[38] They were laying at the foot of the mountain with the rest of the regiment; the bullets came from the ridge. Several others from our brigade were wounded, and it was not advisable to remain there for long. We fell back about 600 yards, 200 yards further to the left. Here we were safe from the Rebel sharpshooters. It is certain that we cannot take the signal hill without enormous casualties, and it is not worth it to suffer such casualties for this position of the Rebels. Sherman, through maneuvers on the flank with different parts of his army, will make this mountain worthless to the Rebels; and I do not doubt that they will leave the mountain in a short time, in order to avoid capture.[39]

Up to this hour, 11 A.M., our brigade has 100 to 125 killed and wounded. We have not received official reports in the Brigade Headquarters yet. I will share the further operations of our brigade as soon as possible.[40]

G. Rentschler

CHAPTER EIGHT

The Battle of Resaca

The Southern army abandoned Rocky Face Ridge and Dalton during the night of May 12–13 and Sherman's army pursued it to Resaca (located on the north bank of the Oostanaula River) where the Rebels made a determined stand on May 14 and 15. However, another flanking movement by Sherman forced the Southern army to retreat again. John Daeuble survived the fierce fighting near Resaca that claimed the lives of eight of his comrades in the 6th Kentucky and bloodied six other members of the regiment.

MAY 12

On the 12th we were kept under Skirmish fire together with cannonading. The 1st and 3rd Brigade[s] were ordered to a different position during the previous night. On the 12th toward noon we received orders to get ready. During the night was still vigorous fire.

MAY 13 TO 14

Towards morning the 13th it was quiet, one heard no more shots. The enemy had withdrawn however we were not certain of it until 9 o'clock. I and [Pvt. August] Lamprecht,[1] proceeded up the Rocky face Mountain which is near 1000 feet high and has remarkable rock projections. When we reached the top we had a wonderful view, the enemy had fortifications all along the hill from 4–5 feet high made out of stone. Down in the valley all was fortified just as a mass of well built abandoned Rebel camps were located there. We saw also the highest point where our Signal Corps was [located]. One could distinguish everything exactly through a spyglass toward Tunnel Hill. The enemy blocked the river [creek] in order to make a swampy barrier against artillery. Around noon I visited the hill again and the Gap Buzzard Roost together with Rebel camps. Our Brig[ade] marched off before we came back again. On our march there was nothing to see for six miles but abandoned Rebel camps in 5 miles. Dalton was all ruined and abandoned. One saw there some women residents. We marched about 10 miles and made a halt in the woods. Our

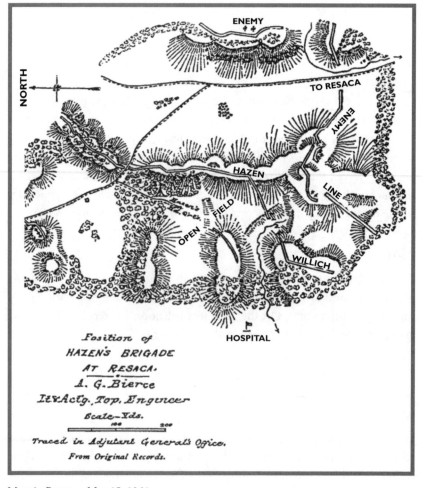

MAP 6. *Resaca—May 15, 1864.*

Regt. came on outpost [and] we were there scarcely 2 hours, when strike tents blew. We marched off again. At the beginning it went very slow and stopped every 5–10 steps. The road was horribly muddy many places, which caused us so many stops. We marched some 3–4 miles, then we ran into our Division which was camped on the road. We made a halt on the road. It was 12 o'clock [and] our Regt. was again ordered on picket. After some coming and going we marched up the road [and] were finally halted. We were ordered to proceed into a swampy thicket in order to set up the post, [but] we could not find it in the dark night. After [a] long wait and stumbling around here and there we made a fire and set up the post. Shortly after that our Major [Whitaker] came and ordered us out farther and spread out wider. Some slept because we were already very tired, now we were again disturbed, some continued to sleep or hid themselves, the others blundered in confusion and were mixed up etc. In the woods around the area [it] was very damp, with a great deal of insects of all sorts. It was toward 2 o'clock in the morning before we were properly posted. The 14th the battle was opened.[2]

MAY 15

The 15th [Pvt.] Joh.[n] Deisinger and [Pvt. Franz] Zanger from our Comp[any] were shot to death and [Sgt.] Franz Maas wounded.[3] During the night around 11 o'clock the Rebels made a charge on us which lasted ¼ hour, we spent the night with changing and improving our fortifications. Our Regt received this day 9 wounded and 4 dead. In the afternoon our Brigade was requested to make a charge toward the enemy fortifications but we were driven back again. We had day and night neither quiet nor rest and lay or crouched behind the fortifications. We could not cook or eat.[4]

MAY 16

At daybreak the 16th [illegible] [we found that] the enemy had withdrawn during the night.[5] Our whole army moved forward. [Maj. Gen. Joseph] Hooker's Army Corp[s]. passed us. We marched through Resaca which is a RR [railroad] Station. We saw fortifications located on every hill [and] the R.[ail] Road Bridge going over the river there was close to half burned down. We crossed over the [Oostanaula] river on a wooden bridge and marched upon the R.[ail] Road nearly 5 miles farther, where we Camped at nightfall.

■   ■   ■

A*fter providing daily accounts of the events preceding the Confederate withdrawal from their fortifications around Resaca, Private Rentschler expressed
his woefully mistaken beliefs that: "They will probably not make a stand
until in Atlanta. . . . This place is very strongly fortified and the fact they left
it proves . . . that they have completely lost confidence in themselves."*

LETTER 14

Published May 28, 1864
Written near Coosa [Oostanaula] River, May 16, 1864
From the Army of the Cumberland—From the Diary of Our
Correspondent. From the11th to the 16th of May—Wounding of
General Willich—List of the Killed and Seriously Wounded Germans

Dear Editor:

On the 11th of May, around 11 A.M., I ended my last letter. I forgot
to insert in it that as soon as the Rebels on the Signal Hill [Rocky Face
Ridge] noticed our withdrawal, they opened a heavy fire on our with-
drawing columns from the back of the mountain; however, without
much damage to us. Only 2 or 3 men from our brigade were lightly
wounded. We marched to the edge of the forest, which covered us. The
rest of the day was quiet. Only the pickets on each side maintained an
unbroken fire. The day was rainy and gloomy.[6]

The 12th of May. Last night, persistent picket-fire. In the afternoon,
at 5 P.M., received the "grapevine" from Stanley's headquarters that Grant
had taken Richmond.[7] The whole day and late into the night there was
heavy picket-fire. Only our corps, the 4th, still lies here. All the other
troops moved southwest.

The 13th of May. Last night the Rebels left the signal hill. [Maj. Gen.
David S.] Stanley's division chased them after daybreak and drove them
through Dalton. We left the camp at 1 P.M., marched through Buzzard's
Roost Gap (not Tunnel Hill Gap as I wrongly put in my last letter), and
were amazed that the Rebels gave up this place without stronger resistance. The gap is a natural fortress and could almost be made impregnable with little support from the pioneers. The gap is almost 2- miles
long. We saw several commemorative plaques that were placed to honor
those of [Maj. Gen. John M.] Palmer's command who fell here in

February. Came through Dalton, a little, but pretty country town, in a wild region. All around here are valleys, mountains and wilderness. Almost all residents fled last night. I saw several females; ⅔ of them were covered in black cloaks and black veils, and had weeping eyes. They are mourning Mrs. Sesech, who is close to drawing her last breath.[8] One loyal old woman told me that the weeping and crying of the women and children was truly awful, because Yankees and devils have the same meanings in the dictionary of the Sesech women. Who here does not remember the word "Turks," that in Germany frightens the children and makes them stop their crying?![9]

The destruction in Dalton was terrible. The stores were open, their contents stolen by the Rebels and strewn around. The streets of the city were strewn with "peanuts." One hundred fifty-thousand bushels were supposed to be in the storehouses, from which the soldiers and residents made coffee.[10] The houses themselves had not been damaged. A half mile from Dalton we headed down a wrong road and only a quick turn "by file right" saved us from captivity.—Camped four miles from Dalton on the farm of a Rhine-Prussian.[11] Received about 2 hours later, at 8 P.M., orders to go farther. Marched 3 miles farther and camped in the woods.

The 14th of May. Left the camp at 6 A.M. in the morning. Marched 5 miles toward the Coosa [Oostanaula] River. Our cavalry was attacked on a large open place and they retreated; many without their hats, a few wounded, a few horses killed, some wounded. The cavalry appeared to be disorganized because they could not stay in rank and file.[12] Hot battle on our right.[13] At 2 P.M. our division was led into the battle, but was not strongly engaged. Today our brigade had 15–20 dead and wounded.[14] Late in the evening Hooker came over here from the right with his 20th Corps, in order to help our corps tomorrow.[15] A brigade from the 23rd Corps got quite lost today. Nobody knew what had become of it. Staff officers were sent out in order to find the lost sheep. They were successful in finding 2 regiments in our rear. They were without a commander. [Major General] Howard assigned one of these regiments to Willich.[16] The 124th and 93rd Ohio of our brigade made a bayonet charge on a hill on which a Rebel battery was set up. They drove the cannoneers back. The two cannons had to stay in no man's land because our 2 regiments received a strong fire from the Rebels who fell back without the cannons. They stood on the hill without an owner late into the evening. Neither we nor the Rebels could ascend the hill without exposure to devastating

fire. There was no gain today. Certainly, we had the outermost breastworks of the enemy, which to us, however, was hardly an advantage.[17]
Tomorrow morning is Sunday and we probably will not have much to
do, because Sunday is held "holy" in this land.[18]

[Brigadier] General [Mahlon D.] Manson from our side was
wounded.[19] Our brigade took a Rebel colonel prisoner.[20]

Sunday the 15th of May. Berthold Auerbach in his book
"Lauterbacher" says: "Way back when, eons ago, when people still were
pious and were a good friend of the Almighty, they could afford to have
some fun with Him. Nowadays, however, since the world has become so
knowledgeable, there no longer is any room for a teeny little joke."[21]

Usually, Hooker will also think this way—but on this holy Sunday he
would like to earn a few "credits"; as he firmly believes that his name will
be underlined in the "Book of Life," if he plays some trick on the devil and
if he beats the rebels convincingly. And that he did accomplish. He took the
Rebels' battery and about 800 prisoners, and hit them in his whole front. I
do not know all the details about it, and I do not want to send "grapevine"
dispatches[22]—our brigade made a bayonet charge on the Rebel breastworks directly in our front. The attack, however, was not crowned with
success. The Rebels opened a devastating cannon and small-arms fire on
our ranks and forced us back into our works. Our casualties were considerable. We lost over 100 dead and wounded. The 5th and 6th Kentucky lost
many brave men. As soon as I have the official report I will provide the
names of the Germans of the 6th Kentucky who fell today.[23]

General Willich was severely wounded, one fears mortally wounded.[24] The whole division is sad over this misfortune—and [Brigadier]
General [William T.] Ward was wounded.[25] While I am writing this letter (9 P.M.), all our artillery that we could not use at this place until now
is being sent to the front.

We expect a bloody battle in the morning.

The 16th of May, in the morning, 6 o'clock. The Rebels left the battlefield this morning and have retreated over the Coosa [Oostanaula]
River. Our army is hard-on-their-heels. They burned the bridge over the
river. We captured a large number of prisoners yesterday. They will probably not make a stand until in Atlanta; you will probably receive my next
one from there.[26]

Greetings,
G. Rentschler

POSTSCRIPT

RESACA 9 A.M. the 16th May 1864

Following is the list of dead and wounded in the 6th Kentucky Regiment:[27]

Co. E

John Deisinger, shot through the breast—dead

Franz Zanger, shot through the head—dead

Franz Maas, shot through the mouth—severely wounded[28]

Co. C

Conrad Wittig, shot through the body—dead

Heinrich Pope, wounded in the right leg[29]

Co. I

Michael Reuther, shot through the body—dead

William Hetzel, slightly wounded[30]

Co.G

August Noll, shot through the breast—dead[31]

The losses in dead and wounded for the Rebels is supposed to be dreadful. The prisoners say that our fire directed into their ranks was devastating; like their fire into our ranks at Chickamauga.[32]

The conduct of the 6th Kentucky Regiment has been excellent, and up to now it has constantly been in the front ranks when it was intended to attack the enemy. The forest lays full of dead Rebels, who present a hideous sight in their coarse, torn up, nauseating clothes.[33] They left a large number of their wounded behind. Paths and forests are full of dead horses.

In the 51st Ohio Regiment the last of six brothers was shot yesterday.[34]

The bridge over the river was burned. We are enthusiastically busy rebuilding it so we can follow the Rebels.[35] This place is very strongly fortified, and because the Rebels have left it proves: first, that we have completely beat them up to now; and second, that they have completely lost confidence in themselves.[36]

G. Rentschler

CHAPTER NINE

Death at Pickett's Mill

Between May 17 and May 19 the Confederate army retreated to Cassville—located just north of the Etowah River—with Sherman's army in close pursuit. The advanced units constantly skirmished with Johnston's rearguard and significant bloodshed was anticipated at any time. Two weeks filled with fighting, marching and almost continuous fire from sharpshooters was wearing down the men physically and, in many cases, psychologically. John Daeuble was among those becoming despondent and confided in his diary on the nineteenth: "Each day brought us sad hours and weariness with life."

MAY 17

On the morning of the 17th 1½ [1:30] o'clock we were awakened and drew rations. At daybreak we again went forward. Our Regt and Brigade were in Front of the Division [and] our Regt and the 23rd Ky had to march sidewards of [down] the RR [railroad] in Line of Battle and Columns. We always drove the enemy before us here. We made some 6–7 miles and met the enemy in strength in our Front, who had intended to flank around us and advance. We fortified immediately. Our Battery opened fire on them and held them back. [Pvt.] Henry Webert was wounded, our troops lost nearly 250 dead in a charge.[1]

MAY 18

The 18th we marched off again, the enemy had moved back during the night. The enemy's Rear Guard consisted of a whole Corps [of] Cavallry [cavalry]. By the little city of Cassville [Adairsville] our Corps came together again along with other troops. We marched in 8 files on the wagon road and along the railroad, We did not meet the enemy the whole day and marched some 8–9 miles.[2]

MAY 19

The 19th we marched off again at daybreak [and] we reached the little city of Kingston. The enemy was located in the front, where we were deployed in Line of Battle and fortified. The enemy withdrew slowly. We followed immediately after [and] at nightfall our Battalion came in the Front Line whereupon we fortified. Night 1 o'clock we drew rations, it was cool and very foggy. Each day brought to us sad hours and weariness with life.[3]

MAY 20 TO 21

The 20th and 21st we remained still. It was terribly hot.

■ ■ ■

Private Rentschler also wrote of the movement to Cassville, but gave no indication of sinking morale among the campaign-weary men. Rather, he punctuated his letter with some humorous little stories.

LETTER 15

Published May 29, 1864
Written from Headquarters, 2nd Brig., 3rd. Div., 4th A.C., Four Miles
South of Kingston, Georgia, May 21, 1864
How It Stinks in Dixie.—Fight by Calhoun.—The Starving Out Theory
Nonsense—Fight by Kingston

In Resaca, through which we marched on May 16, the Rebels left behind a large quantity of cornmeal, corn, beans, etc.; which they did not haul off quick enough. It again appears that the Rebels have practically nothing to eat except cornmeal; which is sent through the digestive chan-

nels without being digested, and is expelled as fast as it is eaten. The
Rebel army is like an octopus, and would be better suited than a million
sheep for one of the sheep corrals in Germany. Their camps are so horribly soiled, all Dixie stinks.—In three hours our troops put three bridges
over the river. We marched still 5 miles the same day.[4]

The 17th of May we came through Calhoun, a truly southern country town in a superb valley. Each house is enveloped in a little grove of
decorative ornamental trees. The owners have almost all fled—a gentleman who remained threw peanuts into the street for our thankful soldiers. The somersaults that the soldiers turned over each other while
gathering up the nuts cannot be described. The shells, however, were for
the largest part "empty"; the gentleman was a knave.

Hardly had we left Calhoun when our general received the news that
the enemy stands in our front. We had to fight our way through until
4 miles past Calhoun, where to our left, a heavy fight, that one may call
a little battle, between [Brig. Gen. John] Newton, commander of the
2nd Division of the 4th corps, and a considerable Rebel force, eased.[5]
Our skirmishers maintained an uninterrupted fire toward the retreating
enemy. Our brigade made a halt in a large open field of about one square
mile by the little river [Oothkaloga Creek].[6] We wanted to help Newton
urgently and attack the enemy on his left flank; however, the enemy acted
quickly and he threw a strong force in front of us on our right wing, and
tried to cut us off from the rest of the troops. He almost succeeded, but
through the quickness of our generals his troops were foiled.[7] This is
the second time we have been threatened with capture.[8] Today
150,000–200,000 shots fell toward our brigade.[9] In spite of this, only
5 men were wounded and 2 killed. Among the slightly wounded was
Henry Webert, Co. E, 6th Kentucky, who was shot through the left arm.[10]
The main causes of these unsuccessful shots by the Rebels, as well as our
troops, are: first, the soldiers fire at such a great distance, that it would
require the skill of that marksman in the fable, who wanted to shoot the
left eye out of a goat sitting on a church tower three-miles away; and second, many officers engage in a deafening yelling that they believe will
inspire the soldiers. In this act, however, it excites them so unnaturally
that their entire bodies start to vibrate; thus the balls travel through the
air, instead of into the body of the enemy. The Rebels made a determined
resistance here—because they wanted to gain time so they could move a
large quantity of quartermaster and commissary supplies to the south,

out of Adairsville, which was situated 2 miles from the battlefield.—They had 5 large railroad trains in this little town.[11]

The farther we moved through Georgia, the more it proved the star-vation theory as [only] a theory. The fields are all well fenced-in and well-built. With its abundance of vegetables, the assumption that the South can be starved out makes as much sense as what the Rebels express; that they generally believe the North cannot raise 300,000 troops from the call of the President and no veterans will reenlist.

During the night of the 17th to 18th the Rebels ran away. Early in the morning we began to pursue them further. Came through Adairsville, a poor little town in a pretty region. Our whole army assembled at this place and advanced toward Kingston in a tremendous stream. Marched 8 miles and camped four miles from Kingston. Trampled young crops, and burning and burned houses, marked our path.[12]

On the 19th we came through Kingston. We marched on the railroad from Calhoun to this place. Kingston is an impoverished little town without a single brick house, just little wooden huts. Not a single resident has stayed behind. It is deserted, except for a fat, dirty, woman. She knew quite well that the filth on her would be her security.[13] The small town lay in a charming little valley. We marched 3 miles, then we saw the enemy set up in a line of battle on a large plantation covering two square miles. A spirited battle eased because the Rebels could not bear our artillery long and moved back into the woods, where we subjected them to strong small-arms fire until late evening.[14] The Rebels made a stand here because they could not move their wagon train away fast enough. We are always so hard-on-their-heels that they either must fight or let their trains and goods fall into our hands. Our losses today in killed and wounded were very small. Our brigade has had up to today, 200 to 300 dead, wounded and missing; which loss must appear very moderate, if one considers that we have now been under fire for 16 days. Only 2 or 3 officers have been wounded.[15]

As we awakened on the morning of the 20th of May we learned that the Rebels had again run away. They had saved their trains. Thomas gave us a rest-day today, which we very much needed. We had been on the march since the 3rd of May, and unceasing vigilance has been required of each one of us.[16]

The weather is very hot. The troops suffer much from headaches. The sunny South causes us to sweat thick beads, and we are beginning to change color. Which color we turn I will express through a Swabian short story. A man from Württemberg who was not one of the "smart Swabians," but instead belonged to the group of "dumb but good-natured Swabians," came to New Orleans where he heard a very dark Negro speaking German in the Swabian dialect. This Swabian was highly pleased to find a fellow countryman here and politely shook the Negro's hand, asking: "How long have you been in this country?" "Three years," answered the Negro. "Dear God how will I look when I am in America six years?" asked the dumb but good-natured Swabian. Similarly, I exclaim: "How will we appear next fall if we are to spend the summer in Georgia?" Our women will be greatly surprised if their returning sons of Mars are blackish-brown, as in the above-stated fashion. I will give them some good advice, and I believe no doctor knows it better: "Close your eyes when you embrace us, like you do when swallowing a bitter medicine."

This morning about 6 o'clock we again resumed our march in order to pursue the Rebels. I do not believe we will have to fight a large decisive battle before we reach Atlanta.[17] We will decide there, whether we will drown the Rebel rabble in the Atlantic Ocean or in the Gulf of Mexico.

Yours,
G. Rentschler

■   ■   ■

John Daeuble continued to update his diary as Sherman's juggernaut made its stormy voyage through the wilds of Northern Georgia. However, John's anxiety pressed more heavily on him each day and, on May 24, he confided in the small leather-bound notebook containing his diary entries: "If a bullet is meant for me, it will hit me wherever I am, dead or wounded. God have mercy on me, protect and comfort my parents . . . , God, let the time of liberation be fast coming. John Daeuble. Oh dear God, this sinner pleads to you in his own misery, release me from my evil and have mercy on me, the poor sinner. My heart is bleeding in my own misery when I think of my poor parents." Sergeant Daeuble's premonition of his own death became a reality late on the afternoon of May 27 when was mortally wounded by a gunshot to his breast during ferocious fighting—while his brigade and division valiantly but unsuccessfully tried to turn the Confederates' right flank near Pickett's Mill. John died in a field hospital on May 28, 1864.

MAY 22

The 9th and 10th Ohio marched away from here [on] the 22nd.[18] Their terms of enlistment had expired. The 22nd we had an Inspection. Our Brig. was in Front of the Corps.

MAY 23

The 23rd we marched off around noon. It was extraordinarily hot and terribly dusty. When we arrived at the river we marched a detour of about 3 miles, where we had to go back again and cross over the river on a covered bridge. Blankets etc. were discarded by the soldiers, a number [of men] fell out and stayed back. We marched about 15 miles and only made a halt about 10 o'clock at night. It was all mixed up [and] nearly half the men were back there. The 23rd Capt [Isaac N.] Johnson took command of our Regt.[19]

MAY 24

The 24th we marched about 12–14 miles and camped at nightfall. We went mostly through the woods however it was dusty and hot. Our Regt came on outpost, we ran and stood around for about an hour before we were posted. During the night it rained very hard.

If a bullet is meant for me, it will hit me wherever I am, dead or wounded. God have mercy on me, protect and comfort my parents. . . . God, let the time of liberation be fast coming. John Daeuble. O dear God, this sinner pleads to you in his own misery, release me from my evil and have mercy on me, the poor sinner. My heart is bleeding in my own misery when I think of my own parents.[20]

MAY 25

The 25th we took up our march again, it went through the woods and from hill to hill. We only seldom came on the road. Toward evening Hooker had a fight with the enemy [near New Hope Church], where he lost about 1600 men.[21] We marched in the night farther to the Front, it rained tremendously, I fell out and made myself comfortable by the fire until the next morning.

MAY 26

The 26th our Corps advanced, as usual our regiment came in Front of the Brigade. The wounded from Hooker's Corps lay everywhere in the woods. We threw up fortifications, when they were finished we moved forward, we went over a Creek and at first were all alone for ½ hour. Skirmish fire was maintained the whole day together with cannonading, several were wounded from the 23rd Ky. Towards evening we saw a large wagon train of the enemy start back. With pensive heart the day disappeared, oh Dear God, I do not know how I should thank you. During the night we had to throw up fortifications.

MAY 27

On the morning of the 27th we were relieved by the 93rd Ohio.[22]

[First Sgt. John Daeuble was mortally wounded on May 27 and died on May 28.]

■ ■ ■

Gottfried Rentschler's sixteenth letter reported the marching and fighting for the last nine days of May, including the significant bloodlettings at New Hope Church on May 25, Pickett's Mill on May 27, and Dallas on May 28. Gottfried paid special tribute to Sergeant Daeuble who fell at Pickett's Mill, writing: "He was the favorite." He closed out the letter with speculation about troop strength and casualties.

LETTER 16

Published June 10, 1864
Written from Sherman's Army, near Dallas, Georgia, June 1, 1864

Dear Editor:

The order to resume the pursuit of the Rebels around 6 A.M. was cancelled, and we remained three miles east of Kingston near the little town of Cassville the whole day, and the day after, Sunday, in order to provide our army with 20 days rations, forage, and so forth. The wagons sent back to Ringgold on 5 May followed, in order to transport these supplies with the army. Three rations of sugar, coffee, meat and crackers had to last for 5 days, and 4 pounds of corn or oats per horse or mule for one day.[23] The further essentials must be pressed from the countryside in the same way as during our march to Knoxville in November and December of last year. The same, ugly, outrageous scenes, which I tried to draw a picture of in my letter of 1 January have repeated.[24] To the honor of the Germans, it is said: no single German soldier of the 6th Kentucky Regiment thus far has participated in these acts of plundering and robbery.

This preparation indicates a long and arduous march, with the prospect that our lines of communications behind us could be cut off; which fortunately up to now has not been the case, because the railroad comes down to Kingston about 25 miles in our rear. On May 23, 12 o'clock noon, we left our camp, in very hot weather and through clouds of dust, to continue the pursuit. [Brigadier] General [Thomas J.] Wood misled us, and we finally camped late at night in the woods. This leading astray of a group of veterans, through the stupidity of one individual, disheartened and fatigued the troops more than anything else.[25]

On the 24th we marched toward Dallas, where on the 25th a battle to our left began. Hooker was attacked. One of his divisions is supposed to have lost 1,200 men.[26] Our brigade, which did not meet the enemy this day, lost one man on picket on the 26th.

Here, in and around Dallas [Georgia], the whole Rebel army has fortified itself in a wild, hilly and stony area; and will give long and stubborn resistance at this place for as long as possible, because this is supposed to be the last place toward Atlanta that they are capable of defending.[27]

On the 27th, late in the evening, our division was ordered to storm the Rebel breastworks directly in our front. We advanced toward the Rebels' breastworks with fixed-bayonets. The Rebels themselves encouraged our people to come up there; they said that they would not shoot anymore, but, rather, wanted to surrender. Our men had come near the breastworks when the Rebels rushed up and opened a terrible cannon and small-arms fire in our front and on both flanks. There remained for us no other choice than to fall-back quickly. The Rebel bullets sowed death in our retiring lines.[28] In approximately 30 minutes [several hours] our division had lost nearly 1,700 [1500] men. Our brigade had 585 [467] killed, wounded and missing.[29] Of the missing, most were dead or severely wounded and fell into the enemy's hands. It was a massacre; as

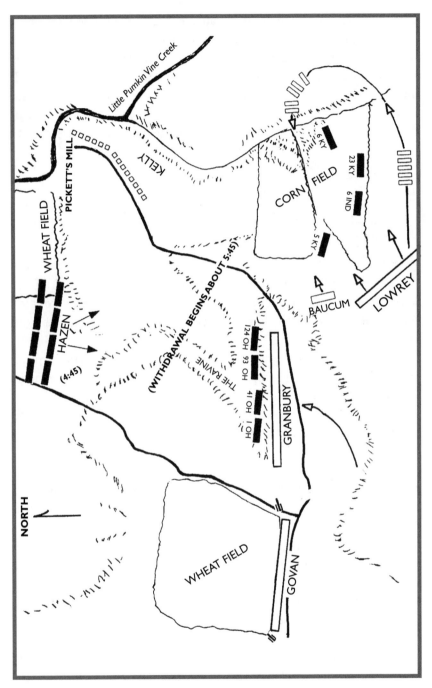

MAP 7. *Pickett's Mill—4:45 P.M. to 5:45 P.M., May 27, 1864.*

Brigadier General Hazen, himself, called it. Our brigade had completely dissolved, and could not be brought together again until that night and toward morning.[30] Willich's [former] brigade suffered just as terribly as us. The 32nd Indiana Regiment had 11 officers wounded and 2 killed; among the dead is found Max Hupfauf.[31] Among all the participating regiments in the affair, the 6th Kentucky was the luckiest; it lost 2 killed, 8 wounded and 10 missing.[32] Among them are the following Germans.

Killed
John Daeuble, Ord.[erly] Serg. from Co. E[33]

Wounded
Conrad Seibel, Co. I, shot 5 times, (later died)[34]
Philipp Necker [Nocker], Co. I, wounded in the elbow[35]
Lorenz Ultsch, Co. E, wounded in the foot[36]

I could not learn the names of the missing today; however, I do not know if the list is finished or not, because I have not been in the front for 6 days due to illness. I had to go back about 5 miles, where I found more comfort.

The whole regiment grieves about John Daeuble. He was the favorite. He was just as true and competent in the service as he was charming in private life. I spoke the truth in my letter of 1 May, that the falling blooms this year will be strewn over the graves of many fresh, healthy and brave soldiers. John Daeuble is a snapped-off spray of flowers, and with him withers the most beautiful hopes of his family.[37]

Who carries the guilt for what happened to our division I will not dare to assume at this time. The future will bring the guilty to light.[38] Allow me to set forth here just a point of my practical knowledge. As is well known, Napoleon was always victorious against the Austrians because he concentrated an overwhelming power with lightning speed on one point, and either hit the center or the right or left wing of the enemy army; while the antiquated Austrian generals inefficiently clung to the old ways and spread out their army in tremendously long lines. Our generals sometimes are guilty of making the same errors as the Austrians, while the Rebels some of the time have made use of Napoleon's tactic as their own.[39]

On the 28th our brigade was eagerly engaged in perfecting our breastworks and making new ones. Late in the evening, [Maj. Gen. James B.] McPherson paid the Rebels back with interest what we owed them from yesterday. The Rebels attacked the breastworks of McPherson with fixed-bayonets. The latter allowed no firing until the enemy had reached close to the works. Then McPherson's men jumped up and opened a dreadful, devastating cannon and small-arms fire on the Rebels. Many say that 2,000 Rebels covered the battlefield. This, however, appears to be an exaggeration. One of McPherson's officers who had participated in the affair told me that they had buried about 500 Rebels, which consequently suggests their total casualties from 2–3000. A rather large number of prisoners were sent to our rear today.[40]

On the morning of the 29th, at 2 A.M., heavy rifle-fire, mixed with heavy short-term cannon fire. A part of our line was attacked by the Rebels, especially [Brig. Gen. John] Newton's division. The Rebels were sent back with bloody faces.[41] Today, the 17th Army Corps came to reinforce us; which we needed very much, because we are not strong enough to make a week-long battle with the enemy; whom we are scarcely able to reach behind his fortifications.[42] Our ranks become weakened with each significant attack, while the Rebels defend themselves behind their works without suffering considerable casualties. Competent military men say that we need 2 to 3 against one Rebel to force them out of their present position. Until now we have hardly had more than man against man, and my assumption that the Rebels are stronger in number than one usually reads in the newspaper has been verified as absolutely true.[43] The enemy army opposite us has numbered, until now, about 80,000 men. Today they supposedly received 25,000 men, probably State-Militia, as reinforcements; which would make a total number of 105,000.[44] We supposedly have at the present time barely a larger number. We must become strengthened if our army is supposed to realize that which is hoped for; and the President will order a new conscription in the near future, in spite of the sour faces which the businessmen and other heroes will make who now are so complacent while laughing all the way to the bank.[45]

In Chattanooga, the people believe we are already below Atlanta. In Louisville, they undoubtedly believe we are a stretch farther. Some in the middle of Florida? However, if one considers: We are in the heart of the enemy's country; we must fight every step of the way, and have a train of 8,000 wagons and ambulances with us, which we must push through wild areas; then one will not easily lose patience when I express here the misgiving that we will not seize Atlanta, the sought after pleasure, during the next two weeks; yes, perhaps not during this whole month.[46] Until now our army has done all that could be expected of it, and [Major] General [William T.] Sherman has placed on him the hope not to disgrace it. Naturally we cannot wait until we receive sufficient reinforcements, in order to give us 2 to 3 against the one Rebel; we must drive the Rebels out of their present favorable position through direct attack,—how? We must leave it to the genius and talent of our commanding generals.[47]

The total losses of ourselves, as well as the Rebels, through our present campaign is not possible to give; and all public statistics up to now are raw estimates. It is known, however, that we have more killed and wounded than the Rebels; while we have taken more of them prisoner, than they of us.[48] Only when the campaign is ended, and the official lists consolidated, can accurate numbers be given.

> Friendly greetings,
> G. Rentschler.

CHAPTER TEN

To the
Chattahoochee River

*M*ounting casualties, the battle at Pickett's Mill, shortages of food and other hardships, the army's changed attitude toward property of civilians, and the movement of the army back to the Western and Atlantic Railroad dominated Private Rentschler's June 10 letter, in which he cleverly uses examples from the Bible to illustrate several points.

LETTER 17

Published Friday, June 24, 1864
Written from Sherman's Army, Two Miles from Ackworth [Acworth], Georgia, June 10, 1864

Dear Editor:

I give you the following list of the dead, wounded and missing of the 2nd Brig., 3rd Div., 4th Army Corps from the 6th to the 31st of May:[1]

Regiment	Killed Officers	Killed Enlisted Men	Wounded Officers	Wounded Enlisted Men	Missing Officers	Missing Enlisted Men	Total
1st Ohio	2	16	7	65			90
41st Ohio		28		92		7	127
93rd Ohio		12		53		8	73
124th Ohio	2	21	5	89		10	127
5th Kentucky	1	22	2	52			77
6th Kentucky	1	10	2	21		3	37
23rd Kentucky	2	5	4	61		12	84
6th Indiana	4	16	7	77		7	111
Total	12	130	27	510		47	726

Many slightly wounded, who have not been rendered incapable of service, are excluded from this list.

On June 2nd, bad weather arrived; lightning hit in the middle of the 1st Ohio Regiment and killed 2 soldiers and injured about 12 others who had to be taken to the hospital.[2]

On the evening of the 2nd of June, General Wood released the following order, which throws a little light on the unfortunate affair of May 27th:

Headquarters 3rd Div., 4th Army Corps,
In the field, [near Dallas,] Ga., June 2, 1864

General-Order No. 38

The general commanding desires to express to the division his high appreciation of their good conduct in the battles of the 27th ultimo, and to thank the officers and soldiers for their heroism displayed on that occasion. Ordered to assault a strongly intrenched position, the troops advanced to the attack with a vigorous, decided earnestness and heroic determination which covered all engaged with the highest honor, and would have insured success if their flanks could have been properly supported.

Advanced to within fifteen paces of the enemy's intrenchments, the troops were compelled to desist from the attack by the flank fire of artillery and musketry, not by the direct ones.

For the heroism displayed, the commanding general expresses the warmest thanks.

By command of Brigadier-General Wood:

On the order of Brigadier-General Wood.
M. P. Bestow
Capt and A.A.G.[3]

[Brigadier] General [Richard W.] Johnson's division was posted to our left, and a brigade of the 23rd Army Corps to our right. Neither Johnson's division, nor the brigade [McLeans's] of the 23rd Corps raised a musket in our attack; for which they will receive much criticism, if they received timely orders to cover our flanks. It was evident on this occasion, as on many occasions, that there was a failure of the different divisions and army corps to work harmoniously together.[4] Where the source lies is clearly evident to the private soldier, who, himself, has suffered the detrimental effects of this problem. He knows "where the difficulty lies." When one gives little people a big assignment, it is usually—Stupidity. "That's what's the Matter!"[5]

Our train animals are having a hard time again; because four pounds of corn without oats is not enough, and the foraging in the countryside yields insufficient results. So far while coming down here in Georgia we have usually found empty barns. Many of the farmers have previously had all their property stolen.[6] Atlanta is supposed to be crammed full of refugees.[7] We are not allowed to go far away from the main body of our army to collect provisions and forage, because the country is full of small bands of Rebels, that pick up everyone on our side, whom they come across, and who are capable of being overcome. They captured General Thomas' headquarters' mail a short time ago.[8] The battery of our brigade lost a wagon, along with its horses, and the men accompanying the wagon. The cook of our brigadier general [Hazen] was sent out in the countryside to buy provisions; he has been absent 8 days and there is no doubt anymore, that he was picked up by a party of Rebels; and thus we lose something every day, that eventually adds up to a large amount.

On the 3rd, 4th and 5th nothing new. During the night of the 5th to 6th the Rebels left their fortifications in reaction to the danger to them caused by the threatening flanking movements of the different corps of our army. They moved to our left toward the railroad. On the 6th we left our fortifications in order to pursue the Rebels. We, meaning the 4th and 14th Army Corps, marched some 8 miles to our left and camped 2 miles from Ackworth [Acworth] until today.[9] This region is extraordinarily productive and the crops are piled up. Naturally the plantation owners need not trouble themselves with harvesting their crops. We spare them the trouble and cut the crops before they are ripe.

One of the Egyptian plagues was swarms of locusts that devoured everything. If you consider that we are, likewise, large swarms of incomparably larger caliber and especially with much larger mouths than the Egyptian locusts; then it is possible for you to form an image of our "devouring." If we had been put on the Pharaoh, like the 12 plagues, the Pharaoh would have not only allowed the House of Jacob to leave, but the Pharaoh himself would have left the land.[10]

Nowadays the Rebels are treated with an iron hand, not with a silken glove as formerly; and thousands are scratching their heads, who in the past, with profound contempt, talked about the "Yankee Power," and acted accordingly. However, it is possible that because of this rougher treatment of the Rebels and of their earthly possessions—their heavenly possessions already were sold to the devil—some of our troops are going too far and become demoralized; but these damages are totally balanced by the impression which is made on the Rebels themselves, because of all the destruction in the Rebel country; because they can see now that their cause is irretrievably lost, because of our overwhelming strength.[11]

Because I write the word "demoralization" here, let me say to you that the soldiers life as such is not always demoralizing; just the opposite, it makes many strong believers in the bible. Earlier I could neither believe as true, e.g., that Esau was so utterly stupid as to sell his birthright for lentil soup, nor could I really believe that Jacob is supposed to have had his most favorite dream on his flight to Mesopotamia while using a stone as a pillow. A dream of angels![12] Now I believe both, because it is well-known that Experience is the Mother of Wisdom and the Lady Cousin of Beliefs. We out here would not only totally give up our birthright for a bowl of soup; but also would give our bow, arrow and sword to "boot."—and we lay in the evenings on the hard earth with a smile on our lips anticipating the delights of the ensuing sweet dreams about our loved-ones at home; that here in Georgia all too often will certainly be interrupted by the long, black snake, of which there are a large number in the local forests; and which not infrequently crawl over our faces while we are asleep. Snakes are the symbol of slyness. They want to remind us through their presence that the soldier should sleep with his eyes held open?!

The number of effective soldiers in our brigade has dwindled considerably. We only have about 1,500 officers and soldiers in our brigade who could be put to use in battle. It is often incomprehensible to me how the soldiers are able to endure for several months the severe burden caused by reduced rations, shortages of clothing, and without blankets and being without tents; but, truly man has a rough life, and the animal strength in him appears to be inexhaustible. The summer of the South is hot and we can expect and await lots of trouble and miseries from our military service. Also, it must be expected that it will last for some time. Meanwhile, the war will break the vigor of many and the number of brave men will be reduced considerably before we may venture to hope that we may be released from service and return to our homes.[13]

The 6th Kentucky Regiment, from all appearances, will not be mustered out on September 24th. The 2 companies, A and C, which were mustered in with the Louisville Legion, will, however, come home with the [Louisville] Legion on September 9th; as result of which, the 6th Kentucky's number will be so small that it would hardly form a full-strength company. The regiment will probably be sent to serve as Provost Guard in some small city.[14]

We just received this morning, about 8 A.M., the order to march. I am not allowed to reveal anything about the position of the Rebels or our own, or to tell of our movement tomorrow; it may be sufficient to note, that we will advance today on the route to Marietta.

We receive the mail here pretty regularly. Since the day before yesterday the railroad train has come to Ackworth [Acworth] Station. I always receive the *[Louisville] Anzeiger* on a regular basis. It is a very welcome companion to me on our long journeys. I always share it with my closest German acquaintances, and they read it with great interest. They would really like to order it for themselves, if $13 monthly was not so small a reward and they would not have to distribute it already for so many expenses.[15] As usual, I comfort you and myself with the hope of better days after our service time expires; and in the hope, that hope has not become shameful. With friendly greetings to you.

Your humble servant,
G. Rentschler

Almost *four weeks passed before Rentschler wrote his next letter to the* Louisville Anzeiger. *Perhaps he was kept busy by the combination of the army's movements to Kennesaw Mountain, Marietta, and the Chattahoochee River (eight miles north of Atlanta), and the continuous contact with entrenched Rebels. Gottfried stated that: "From the 6th of May up to the present day, the firing has not ceased for over five minutes." Heavy losses incurred by two companies of his regiment near Kennesaw Mountain, the suffering caused by the intense Georgia summer heat, and friendly meetings between pickets of both sides are some of the news items he shared in his lengthy letter.*

LETTER 18

Published July 15, 1864
Written from Sherman's Army, on the Bank of the Chattahoochee River, Eight Miles from Atlanta, July 6, 1864

Dear Editor:

As I wrote to you in my letter of June 10th, we advanced that same day toward Marietta. We pushed the Rebels back to Lost and Ken[n]esaw Mountains, where they prepared fortifications and set up a battle line. Our army was deployed in the following order from left to right: 23rd, 20th, 4th, 14th, 15th, 16th, 17th Army Corps. Skirmish fire was opened on both sides and maintained both day and night. The results of this fire were hardly different than a useless waste of ammunition. The weather was cold and damp from the 10th until the 18th and, for the soldiers, uncomfortable in the highest degree. On the 19th we maintained a heavy cannonade toward the Rebels' works, which I heard. The earth trembled for 10 miles around. On this day Sherman wanted to move his headquarters to Marietta, and he had packed up and sent his wagon forward. The Rebel Johnston, however, was not yet quite ready to "move out"; and, therefore, the new landlord had to be patient for a while, and had to order his effects back to the old quarters.[16] Angry about that, the next day, the 20th [27th] Sherman had the 14th and 4th Army Corps advance towards the Rebels' line in order to attack. Our two corps, however, were repulsed with approximately 3,000 casualties.[17] Around this time Sherman had all the sutlers' shops at Big Shanty Station closed because they had charged outrageously high prices and because he had been informed that the sutlers' goods had been illegally transported. The sutlers, Sherman was informed, had pressed money into the hands of the R.R. Conductors and Transportation Managers in order to get their goods delivered instead of government goods; perhaps under a false address. The results of this investigation is not known to me.[18]

On the 24th [23rd], a part of our picket line was ordered to advance attacking. Included in this party were 2 companies of the 6th Ky Regiment, one of which, Co. H, was almost completely wiped out. Out of 17 men, only 5 came back unscathed; 2 were killed and 11 wounded, some mortally. In this affair Captain Nierhoff of Co. I was killed. He held his rank only about a month. He was an excellent soldier and a competent officer.[19]

During the night of the 29th to the 30th of June, the Rebels attacked the line on the right of our division. Hundreds of thousands of shots were fired; however, only 4 men on our side were lost.[20] A night fight is something terrifying and puts troops in a really feverish state of excitement. The stillness of the night lays heavily on the hearts and emotions of the men. The effect of a night fight, however, is scarcely different from an attack of the blues for a very short time.

Orders had been given that conversations with the Rebels were strictly forbidden, and that our pickets should fire on the Rebels. When the commanding officers were lenient, a friendly relationship was sometimes formed between the Rebel pickets and ours. Pickets on both sides traded tobacco, newspapers, whisky, coffee, sugar, etc., and agreed to lay down their weapons and to meet each other half way; where they often had long, friendly conversations. One day, a company of one of our regiments received an order to open fire on the Rebels after they had not fired on them the whole day. After the company was given this order, they called to the Rebels to lay behind their rifle pits because they had been ordered to shoot at them. The parting words of the friendly enemy were in the rule: "If I see you in the battle, I will spare you."[21]

On the 2nd and 3rd of July, general troop movement. Our line was adjusted and all preparations made for battle on the 4th; however, the Rebels sensed this danger and scrammed on the 4th. General Howard learned from his spy around 7 P.M. on the evening of the 3rd that the Rebels were pulling back. On the morning of July 4th all camps were broken in order to pursue the Rebels.[22]

As a result of the adjustment of our front on the 3rd, our brigade was thrown one mile further to the left, and so close to the Rebel breastworks that it was not possible to put out pickets. On the morning of the 4th, as soon as it became light, we discovered the source of the pestilential smell in our new position. A large number of dead, half-decomposed Rebels layed strewn outside of the former Rebel works. Among the half-decomposed bodies was Major O'Neal [O'Neill] of the 16th South Carolina Regiment. Papers in his pockets gave us his rank, name and several other things.[23] Several of our dead troops also lay there. The heart aches with the thought that so many brave men decay here in the wilderness, being eaten by vermin, without burial. Poor widows, grieving orphans.

When we left our camp on the 4th and advanced over the Rebels' works, we were all amazed by the excellent and almost impregnable entrenchments and fortifications that they had erected and built. The Rebels' works were much stronger than ours. Earlier ours were much stronger by far than those of the Rebels. They have exceeded us during this campaign in this highly important skill. We learned from prisoners that Johnston had a large number of Negroes, some say 6,000, who provided the construction labor. These Negroes, probably under the control of excellent engineers, had already completed the works, so the army only needed to fall back to them in order to show a menacing front.[24]

All the trees between the Rebels' line and ours at Lost and Ken[n]esaw mountains were fully spiked by cannon and rifle balls from their roots to their tops.

In pursuit of the Rebels we passed very close to Marietta, which is situated in a truly paradise-like area. The forests which surround the city are the most beautiful that I have ever seen. A large college building is surrounded by nice residences for professors and pupils, and graces the heights southeast of Marietta; and the whole area breathes fortune and well-being. It is tragic that such a beautiful countryside has been covered by such black clouds as produced by the war.[25]

The Rebels had constructed a line of breastworks three miles from the river to cover their crossing over it. Their resistance was not stubborn. We had easy work to throw them back. Our brigade lost a few dead and wounded in the operation. The 6th Ky. Regiment did not suffer any casualties.[26] Yesterday, the 5th, there was light skirmish-fire against the rearguard of the enemy; who retreated over the river on pontoon bridges in the biggest hurry. And now we lay very close to the bank of the river. A mutual picket fire has been maintained over the river and I doubt not in the least that in a short time our army will cross the river and be in and around Atlanta.[27]

During the whole campaign, from the 6th of May up to the present day, the firing has not ceased for over five minutes. We are as used to the crack of the rifles, as a miller is used to the clatter of his mill, as we wake up in the middle of the night if the firing ceases for a moment; like the miller, whose mill, or the Black Forest farmer whose wall clock, suddenly stops.[28]

The weather has been unbearably hot since the 19th. If our whole army marched down through a narrow valley, the sweat that ran off us would form a river as large as the Mississippi, in which river the lice and wood ticks replace the fish and alligators; and all would drown miserably. Fortunately the land is hilly and the army marches steadily on a dozen different paths. That this heat has a very detrimental influence on the troops is easily understandable. Our paymaster clerk wandered happily through the streets of Marietta when a sunburned soldier stuck out his hand to greet him and called him by his first name. "Who the hell are you?" asked the clerk. "I am your brother, John," answered the soldier. "Not by a d—d sight," replied the clerk arrogantly. When he proved to John that he really was his brother, and no other, the paymaster had a fatted-calf butchered; and they were happy, without however being troubled by jealousy as the father in the gospel, who found his son who had been lost and previously relegated to feeding the pigs.[29]

The effect of the heat on the outside of the troops is not the worst part. The heat kills the appetite and produces a burning thirst. Up to now we have certainly found rather good water in Georgia, but the different nature of the water has also been detrimental to the organs; and drinking it has been very frequently followed by sickness.

The wounded suffer the most from the heat, and very many died who could have easily recovered in milder weather. Wounds through the hand and lighter flesh wounds have up to now often been fatal; while such wounds with milder weather would hardly be noticed. Therefore, many slightly wounded in our division die. The conclusion from this should be that our division has had a year of harder service than some of the others in the army, and the constitutions of the men are extraordinarily weakened and for many totally ruined. The result is that our effective force is small and will fast become smaller.

By the way, the Rebels also appear to have lost a lot of people because I know from a trustworthy source that they do not have more than 41,000 infantry to oppose us. I do not know about their cavalry force. Their artillery consists of 106 cannons with a probable crew of 2,000.[30]

We took many prisoners yesterday. I spoke with a large number of them; however, their statements are not worth publishing. The Rebel soldiers are ignorant for the most part and their various statements only prove that they know very little about the size of their army, and don't understand the administration of the army. Many of them appear to have the same level of education as their Negroes.[31]

Many things appear to be wrong in the Quartermaster Department, because never before have the means of transportation been administered so badly; and never before have the various wagon trains been in such disorder, as in this campaign. One does not know who is "cook or waiter." The trains of the different brigades, divisions and corps have so often been mixed up that it requires a day to find a certain regiment's wagon.[32]

A very small part of our brigade's music band had an amusing adventure yesterday. Three of them were filling their canteens in a stream 1mile from the river when they heard a whisper close by, and heard the word "surrender." They went about 20 paces through the bushes, towards the whisper, and they found 4 six foot (that means six feet tall) Rebels stretched out on the ground. The Rebels jumped up when they saw our heroic musicians, and one called, "We surrender." The musicians turned pale. They heard the word "we," and believed the Rebels wanted to take them as prisoners. One of the musicians said, almost whining, "We have no arms." The Rebels saw the anxiety in these poor souls and explained that they, the musicians, were not supposed to surrender; but rather they, the Rebels wanted to surrender to the musicians. "Hm, hm," said one of the musicians—a heavy stone lifted from his heart—and so the 3 musicians brought the 4 towering Rebels here to General Hazen, who laughed uncontrollably when he heard the circumstances under which these Rebels had been captured. The musicians let the 4 rifles belonging to the Rebels lay. They probably thought like the Jew who believed a rifle could fire even if its not loaded.[33]

In the course of the month of June our brigade lost 121 officers and soldiers; 14 killed and 107 wounded. We had none missing.[34] Our troops fought well and all are certain of a favorable outcome. Of course, no one knows how long this campaign will last. However, two things are certain: first, that this campaign is not over by any means, and second, that this campaign will not end the war.

We are making at this moment all preparations to throw bridges over the river and to cross over as soon as possible. We do not believe that there will be a battle in Atlanta itself. The Rebels will retreat behind Atlanta. It is true this city is heavily defended, as we can see with field glasses from a mountain 1 mile from the river—but the Rebels will not want the darling of Georgia exposed to bombardment. They will, as always before, attempt to seek safety by retreating; in order to weaken our army through strain, delay and small battles.[35] Johnston has demonstrated just as great a skill in retreating as Sherman has in flanking.[36]

The greatest misfortune that could befall us would be having our line of communications cut off. If they attack us on an open battlefield, it is certain that they will meet complete disaster.

Perhaps I can announce to you in a few days the capture of Atlanta.

Friendly greetings,
G. Rentschler

CHAPTER ELEVEN

Two Miles from Atlanta

Sherman's legions began crossing the Chattahoochee River north of Joseph E. Johnston's river defenses on July 8, 1864; however, it would take more than two weeks and two bloody battles to force the Confederate army back to its fortifications ringing Atlanta. Gottfried Rentschler's first letter, written "Two Miles from Atlanta," related both major and minor events during this critical period in the campaign, and correctly predicted: "We will lay here a considerable time. . . ."

LETTER 19

Published August 3, 1864
Written Two Miles from Atlanta, July 25, 1864

Dear Editor:

Near the bank of the Chattahoochee River 16 Rebel soldiers hung from trees at various distances from one another. One suspects that they were deserters. The bodies were horrible to look at; they were almost totally decomposed, and some already half shriveled-up.[1]

During the night of the 7th of July our division made a night demonstration which has been so frequently used during this campaign. Twenty of our cannons fired over the river as quickly as they could be loaded. All our wagons were brought down to the bank of the river and dashed along there and were driven around with as much noise as possible. Men were

141

stationed at different posts to issue commands with loud voices, as if our whole army was in motion on the bank of the river. Everywhere, all were in motion in order to allow the Rebels to believe that the devil is loose in all corners and that we would cross the river. These demonstrations were made to cover up Schofield's crossing 5 miles up above [the next day]. The Rebels were led astray in the desired way. They believed we wanted to cross, and they cut the pontoon bridge that lay over on their side of the river in order to let it float downward. The bridge, however, floated over to our side of the river, where we lashed it up the following night. Schofield crossed that same night with the largest part of his corps and seized four Rebel cannons.[2]

On the night of the 9th, one of our men on picket sang the "Star Spangled Banner." When the Rebel pickets fired at him, he called to them across the river not to make such noise; because his song is not yet at its end, and he bravely finished his stanza. You see our soldiers take it "cool."

On the 10th we marched 5 miles upriver to the same place where [Maj. Gen. John M.] Schofield had crossed; and on the 12th we crossed it ourselves, 2 miles below, on a cotton pontoon bridge that bent like a piece of canvas under the weight of the heavy cannon and wagons. These pontoons followed us on wagons, and the widest river can be bridged over in an unbelievably short time. They are made of water-proof cotton stretched over wood, and a wagon can transport 5 to 6 of these pontoons. We camped 2 miles south of the Chattahoochee, where we threw up breastworks. On this day I saw the first, and until now, the first and only, cotton field in Georgia. It was only 100 square meters in size.

On the 16th, [Maj. Gen. William T.] Sherman, [Maj. Gen. Oliver O.] Howard, [Maj. Gen. David S.] Stanley and [Brig. Gen. Thomas J.] Wood and a number of other generals came to our headquarters, in order to gain a view of what lay before us in the Rebel-occupied countryside. Our brigade headquarters was located on a mountain ridge and, on this ridge, a tremendously high pine tree stood in front of General Hazen's tent. Hazen had a ladder made, and from the top of this pine tree one could see the country in a wide circle and could see Atlanta. Sherman appears very ill, and anyone who saw him last fall would not recognize him. Three months of restlessness has made him age a year. However, he has remained the same friendly, laconic, diligent and slow-speaking man.[3] Sherman appeared to have obtained the information he wanted from this lookout, because the next day, the 17th, an unbelievably beautiful Sunday, our division was sent down 2 miles toward the river, in order to protect the crossing of the 14th Army Corps, the last one still on the north side of the river. The Rebel pickets were driven back easily. Our flankers fired only a few shots. The 14th Corps crossed with luck and took 200 prisoners.[4] Toward evening our division returned safe and sound.

By now our whole army had crossed over the Chattahoochee—and the enemy's rear guard, consisting fully of cavalry, had fallen back. So "Sherman's Company," as a Sesesh Lady naively called our army, pressed toward the first-desired main objective, Atlanta; always moving nearer and nearer.[5] We marched through many farms with rich and well-cultivated soil. The houses stood empty. The men are in the army, and the women and children hurried through the country with bewildered, confused looks; not knowing which way to go in order to hide. The people act very foolishly when they leave their houses. If they would stay at home they could get off with the fright. The empty houses and the furniture and house wares left behind will be, more or less, totally demolished.

Intelligence, even in the simplest form, does not seem to have found its way into this part of the country yet, because the mile posts are not marked with numbers, but the number of miles is given in notches. That is the Southern Chivalry.

Our division was in the rear and pushed on no enemy. [Brig. Gen.] John Newton's division marched in our front and had light skirmishes with the enemy's rear guard. One soldier of the division pursued several retiring Rebels, including a captain. The soldier called out to those fleeing, "halt." However, he could not see the "halt" until after he had sent a bullet to confirm it, which severely wounded the captain. The wounded man appeared to be an honorable man because he immediately acted friendly toward the soldiers, gave them his pocketbook which contained several hundred dollars, his pocket watch, and mainly everything of value he had. The promise of an exchange of letters, if the captain should survive, was mutually given. The captain belonged to the "1st Regt. Georgia Line," as he called it.[6]

On the 19th our Division crossed Peachtree Creek against fruitless resistance by the enemy. While crossing this creek [Brigadier] General [William B.] Hazen's Provost Marshal was severely wounded by a musket ball, perhaps mortally. This wound had our staff doctor much perplexed because the Provost Marshal had a wound in his body, but his clothing showed no sign of the entrance of the bullet. I do not know whether there was a bullet in his body or not, because he was taken to the hospital immediately. Four men had to carry him on the stretcher to the hospital. He did not want to be transported in an ambulance because, as he said, he did not want to catch lice. An officer on his deathbed and worried about not catching lice!! Is it necessary to assure you that the soldiers did not cry into their handkerchiefs when they heard of their Provost Marshal being wounded?[7]

Four weeks ago the Top.[ographical] Engineer in Hazen's staff was severely wounded in his temple. He is said to have shot a wounded soldier who went to the rear. Many presume that the Top.[ographical] Engineer was wounded by one of his own soldiers for revenge. It is not very clever of an officer to mistreat a soldier who made him an officer.[8]

On the 20th our brigade went back again on the north side of Peachtree Creek, in order to take a place in the line a mile to the east. The brigade had hardly marched over the creek when several were wounded by stray Rebel bullets.[9] [Maj. Gen. Joseph] Hooker's corps and Newton's division were attacked by the enemy and driven back a short distance, where they made a stand and efficiently burned the Rebels. Rebel prisoners said they lost over 2,000 in the attack.[10]

Howard asked Sherman about the direction of our line. Sherman made a point in the sand and said, "Here's Atlanta"; and then drew a circle around this point with his finger and said, "Here we are." In the action Atlanta was almost completely surrounded on the same day.[11]

Our brigade was not needed in the front line there, so we went back a half-mile and camped in the area of a match and a chair factory. We threw away our old headquarters chairs and sat in new ones. The match factory caught fire, probably through carelessness of a soldier, and went up in smoke.

On the 21st our brigade was again given a position in the front, where the 6th Kentucky Regt. lost 4 men while they were building breastworks.[12]

On this same day I received the *"Anzeiger"* of the 16th, which brought news that our army had taken possession of Atlanta a long-time ago. Such things touch us in a funny way when we fight at this very time with lead and iron, and thunder and lead, for prizes which the telegraphers 1,000 and 2,000 miles away have already reported as won long ago.

A heavy cannonade and unceasing small-arms fire were maintained this whole day by both sides. Luckily, our demonstrations were successful;

because on the morning of the 22nd the enemy had left our direct front and moved back to their works 1½ miles outside Atlanta. We followed them hard-on-their-heels and took many prisoners. A hot fight ignited on the outside left of our line. The Rebels fell on [Maj. Gen. James B.] McPherson's rear, but were totally beaten. Each part of our army had a hard fight. McPherson was killed, and also [Brigadier] General [Manning F.] Force who commanded a division [brigade] in the 16th [17th] Army Corps. McPherson had earned a glorious name through the campaign of the summer.[13]

Nowadays, Rebel prisoners that are brought in say to us that [General John B.] Hood, who had taken [General Joseph E.] Johnston's position, would defend Atlanta to the last; and that he has said from now on he will fight us on even ground and no longer attack entrenchments. "Bully for Hood"—Cedar Bluffs is a lone mountain where he has remained, and Cedar Bluffs is 9 miles south of Atlanta; ergo, Hood wants us to fight on even ground, because he wants to defend it to the end.[14] Hood it is said, and all Rebel prisoners say, is not popular in the Rebel army and his troops do not have any trust in him. Johnston raised their spirits to the heavens and they are pained that they lost him as their commander. As all Rebel prisoners here agree, as does everyone agree, the Rebels will not stop fighting as long as they still can assemble a company.

On the 23rd [Maj. Gen. Lovell H.] Rousseau came up here from Alabama with 2,100 men. He left Nashville with 2,400 men, of which 300 became so very sick on the way that they had to be sent back. Rousseau rode along our line in order to see old acquaintances and was received by the solders with general jubilation. He and his soldiers will take a place on our extreme left.[15]

We just learned that the Rebels' General Hardee was seriously wounded yesterday. In the fight yesterday [called the battle of Atlanta] the Rebels lost 6,000 men—1,000 dead, 1,500 prisoners and the rest wounded. We (McPherson's command) lost 2,000 men, and 10 cannons; however 6 were recovered.[16]

An uninterrupted small-arms fire of the pickets, with cannon often mixed, was maintained day and night. We threw shells into the city. Atlanta is surrounded by countless forts. However, the forts are empty. The whole Rebel army is set up in a line opposite us.

Last night we advanced our line considerably. There is a large open field between the 4th Corps (ours) and the Rebel line.[17] To attack the

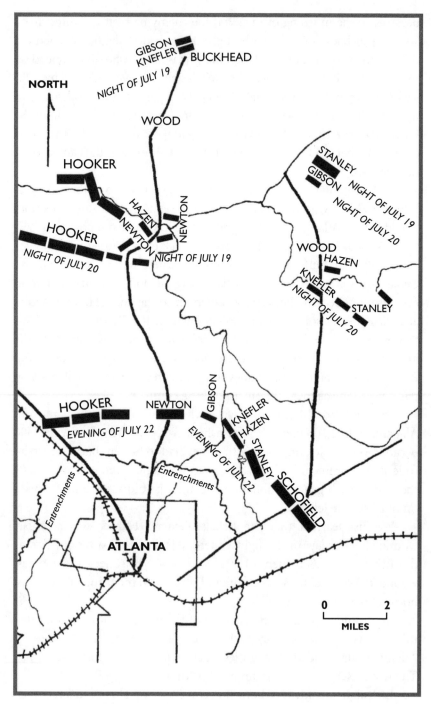

MAP 8. *Approach to Atlanta.*

enemy over this field would be ruin; therefore we must make our main operations on the flanks. Through these flanking operations, the Rebels will have to give up their position before long; and at the same time, give up Atlanta.

I do not believe our army will advance on Atlanta. I believe the opposite, that we will lay here a considerable time in order to reorganize the whole army.

The last two nights were bitter cold and very uncomfortable for us. We threw our blankets away long ago and have nothing to keep ourselves warm.

Since my last letter only 2 Germans have been wounded: Henry Flottman of Co. I in the leg, and Charles Stoesser of Co. I also in the leg.[18]

In my last letter I gave the number of enemy cannons at 106. This is wrong, the source from which I draw said 166.

Wheeler has 6,000 cavalrymen and the State Militia is stated at from 10[,000]–40,000. The round number of Hood's Veterans is 50,000.[19] Almost too many nuts to crack. However the President has called for 500,000 more nutcrackers—so we may not grow any gray hair.[20]

With friendly greetings,
G. Rentschler

■   ■   ■

A *short communication forwarded to the* Louisville Anzeiger *on July 27 included a circular issued by Maj. Gen. George H. Thomas about the battles on July 20 (Peachtree Creek) and July 22 (Atlanta).*

LETTER 20

Published August 9, 1864
Written Two Miles from Atlanta, July 27, 1864

Mr. Editor,

In a great rush I send to you an extract of a circular from the Headquarters of the Department of the Cumberland, as correction of my letter of the 25th of this month. My numbers given in that letter were from Staff Officers of various headquarters; since then exact reports have been received in the Department Headquarters.

The Louisville Legion and the 1st Ohio left our brigade early yesterday morning. The Louisville Legion was transferred to the 4th Division of the 20th Corps through the efforts of Major-General Rousseau,[21] in order to go to Nashville, and give the regiment time and opportunity to prepare the papers necessary for the mustering out on September 9th. The 1st Ohio has been ordered to Chattanooga for the same purpose. That the delight of these two regiments was great needs no assurance.

We still lay in our old position. This morning I heard a general officer say that Atlanta will be in our hands in 3 or 4 days. (?) Sherman flanks and Hood retires. Sherman is supposed to have said yesterday that this campaign will reach its end with the capture of Atlanta. God grant it, because our troops need recuperation and reorganization. Nothing noteworthy happened yesterday or today. A very lively picket fire was maintained day and night.

As soon as I have made a walk through Atlanta, I will send you a line.

Greetings,
G. Rentschler

[Circular]
HDQRS. DEPARTMENT OF THE CUMBERLAND
Near Atlanta, GA., July 25, 1864.

The major-general commanding congratulates the troops upon the brilliant success which has attended the Union arms in the late battles, and which has been officially reported, as follows:

In the battle of the 20th instant, in which the Twentieth Corps, one division of the Fourth Corps, and part of the Fourteenth Corps, was engaged, total Union loss in killed, wounded, and missing, 1,733. In front of the Twentieth Corps there were put out of the fight 6,000 rebels. Five hundred and sixty-three of the enemy were buried by our own troops, and the rebels were permitted to bury 250 additional themselves. The Second Division, of the Fourth Corps, repulsed seven assaults of the enemy with slight loss to themselves, which must swell the rebel loss much beyond 6,000. Prisoners captured, 300, and 7 stand of colors. No report has yet been received of the part taken in this battle by the Fourteenth Army Corps.

In the battle of the 22d the total Union loss is killed, wounded, and missing, 3,500, and 10 pieces of artillery. Rebel loss, prisoners captured, 3,200. Known dead of the enemy in front of the Fifteenth and Sixteenth

Corps and one division of the Seventeenth Corps, 2,142. The other division of the Seventeenth Corps repulsed six assaults of the enemy before it fell back, which will swell the rebel loss in killed to at least 3,000. There were captured from the enemy in this battle 18 stand of colors and 5,000 stand of arms.

Brigadier-General [Kenner] Garrard, commanding Second Cavalry Division, has just returned from a raid upon the Georgia railroad, having lost 2 men and brought in 200 prisoners and a fair lot of fresh horses and Negroes. He destroyed the railroad bridges across the branches of the Ocmulgee and the depots at Conyers, Covington, and Social Circle.

By command of Major-General Thomas:
WM. D. WHIPPLE,
Assistant Adjutant-General[22]

■ ■ ■

Irresponsible newspaper correspondents and Maj. Gen. Joseph Hooker's self-ish resignation from command drew Private Rentschler's ire in his next letter, while others received his praise. Heavy skirmish fire continued unabated as the Federals strengthened their fortifications and General Sherman formulated his plan to capture Atlanta.

LETTER 21

Published August 10, 1864
Written Two Miles from Atlanta, August 1, 1864
Dear Editor:

The poultry with miserable noses, called correspondents, wrote more than 10 days ago: "Atlanta, the etc." I alone, a normal human being with blue pants, must also write today still far "in front of Atlanta." I can only think of one reason why the correspondents perpetrate this deception on the public. It is that they live in the strong hope that Atlanta will fall into our hands by the time their letters reach their destinations, and the people "know" that they were the first in Atlanta. However, Atlanta is still not ours. No Union soldiers have entered Atlanta except as prisoners. It appears at the present time that we must still be patient for a while with regard to capture of Atlanta, because the most magnificent preparations have been made to put us in this position and to be able to repulse a rebel attack.

Howard took over command of the Army of the Tennessee in McPherson's place. General Stanley took over command of the 4th Army Corps in Howard's place.[23] Howard's character reveals itself so well in his written letter of departure from his corps, that I cannot paraphrase it.

HEADQUARTERS FOURTH ARMY CORPS,
Near Atlanta, GA., July 26, 1864.
To the Fourth Army Corps:

Having been assigned to another command, the duty, by no means a pleasant one, devolves upon me to take leave of a corps that I have learned to love and trust. The time of our service together has been short, but crowded with remarkable events. The words "Dalton," "Resaca," "Adairsville," "Kingston," "Cassville," "Dallas," "Ken[n]esaw," "Smyrna Camp-Ground," and "Peach Tree Creek," suggest to us fields of conflict, more or less severe, where we have buried many an endeared comrade, where you have won honor for your country and yourselves, and where the enemy has learned anew to fear and respect the power of the Government for which we fight. It is with pain that I realize my inability to reward your cheerful devotion to duty, your arduous and prolonged labor, and your uncomplaining sacrifices. I heartily appreciate the constant co-operation of the division commanders, and the cheerful manner in which they have sustained me, and in which they have been sustained by their own officers. To them, and, through them to their commands, I tender my warmest thanks and unqualified commendation. No officer could have received more ready and untiring assistance from his staff than I have from mine. To them also I am more than grateful. Believing from my heart that our cause is right and just before God, as I take leave of you I commend you to His blessing, and trust He will assist our armies to complete the work which He has enabled them so gloriously to bring to the present stage of success.

O. O. Howard,
Major-General.[24]

The 4th Army Corps generally regrets having lost Howard as its commander. In his successor, General Stanley, we have again received an excellent corps commander who is just as popular. Hooker, jealous over Howard's promotion, tendered his resignation; which was "approved" by Sherman and sent to Washington. Hooker was ordered to report to

Washington. Let him go! Through his resignation request he has only proven that, to him, his own interest is closer to his heart than that of his country. He has always merely considered the soldiers as numbers. Incidentally, he has proven through a whole host of examples that he is a capable general and his corps (the 20th) is the best disciplined of our army. The jealousy of the higher and lower officers has already caused much damage in our army.[25]

On the 28th of July our brigade took the rifle pits of the Rebels and captured the Rebels in them who were not able to flee quick enough.[26]— On this day Howard's 3 corps (the Army of the Tennessee) were attacked by the Rebels in the same way as it was on the 22nd [of July] while under McPherson. Howard, however, drove them back. He is supposed to have lost 500–600 as opposed to the Rebels who are supposed to have lost 5,000 men in this affair.[27] On this occasion the Rebels used their 64-pounders for the first time.[28] These large cannons had been sent from Atlanta to Macon. Johnston, however, who was replaced by Hood as commander of the Rebel Army, had them brought back to Atlanta again. On the 28th they fired a bomb out of one of their cannons into our brigade's camp. It did not explode and I measured it. Following are the results: 6½ inches in diameter on the thick end; 1 inch, and 5 lines on the pointed end; 10 inches, and 3 lines in length; 20 inches in circumference around the body; 7 inches and 6 lines deep cavity; 6 inches long; the same thick; and then the shell comes quickly to a point. The bomb is surrounded by 2 iron hoops and weighs 44 pounds. A solid ball weighs 64 pounds. When one of these cannons is fired a person believes, "A white frost has burst out of Hell". Consequently, those of us here can imagine, in part, the Last Judgment.

During the night of the 28th, on the 29th of July, a terrible cannon and small arms-fire was maintained. Our cannon were positioned so that they raked the Rebels' works right next to Atlanta, and it is beyond doubt that the Rebels suffered considerable casualties that night.[29] On the 29th our brigade had to be prepared to march off at a moment's notice because an attack by the Rebels was expected. It did not occur. On the 30th, the line of the 20th Corps advanced a short piece under a very lively, but relatively harmless cannonade by the enemy. On the 31st all was quiet. Because it was the "Lord's day," only occasional picket fire interrupted the quiet of the day.

No one knows at this time when we will capture Atlanta. The Rebels will fight here fanatically. However, before long, the lack of provisions and other supplies will cause them to leave this place; which they will not do without attempting to attack us again and again, in order to give us a bloody defeat. Our works are strong and become more secure each hour. The variety of them is too extensive to describe and for the nonmilitary too boring to read.[30]

The army will provide everything that is needed. Full rations will be provided, and the small amount of clothing that is necessary for the summer will be promptly delivered.

Sherman lets one of his chief concerns be facilitating the delivery of the day's most essential needs in order to relieve the uninterrupted arduousness to which his soldiers have been subjected for three months. Officers and soldiers of a regiment draw their rations together, and the Commissary Sergeant allots them in the regiment's camp. I am sorry to have to say that some officers, especially those in the headquarters, sometimes take a lion's share for themselves; and therefore, shorten the rations of the soldiers! However, wherever there are so many of them, i.e., officers, one always can find some small and other souls. Perhaps you are interested in a price list of the different articles of foodstuffs that the army provides, and what must be paid by the officers. I therefore submit, herewith, the list which was given out for the month of July.

Those with a * denote articles which are usually provided to the troops in the field. Those with a † are sometimes delivered to the officers.[31]

Pork*	per barrel	$30 —
Bacon*	per pound	— 15
Ham†	" "	— 20½
Flour†	" "	— 04
Hard bread*	per pound	— 5¼
Beans*	" "	— 5
Peas	" "	— 3½
Rice	" "	— 12
Hominy	" "	— 3
Coffee, roasted and ground*	per pound	— 51½
Tea†	" "	1 38
Brown sugar	per pound	— 20
White sugar	" "	— 25
Vinegar (very seldom received)	per gallon	— 25½
Adamentine candles†	per pound	— 22¾
Soap (very seldom received)	per pound	— 8

Salt*	per pound	—	1
Molasses	per gallon	—	79
Desicated potatoes*	per pound	—	12
Mixed vegetables*	per lb.	—	20¾
Pepper†	per lb.	—	35½
Whisky†	per gallon	1	52

The Quartermasters in Chattanooga and Nashville sometimes are guilty of hilarious errors; and they sometimes send a box of shoes to us, size 14, 15 and 16, which were made for the Nigger soldiers. Of course, we cannot use them. The only use we could make of them would be to build a pontoon bridge over a river with them; only we have enough cotton pontoons, which have the advantage, that they are lighter than the Nigger shoes; therefore, the Brigade's and the Division's Headquarters must return the shoes again and again.[32]

The loss to our Brigade in manpower was not significant during the past month. The brigade had the luck not to be involved in the bloody affairs of that month. There were 3 officers wounded, 6 privates killed, 38 wounded and missing.[33]

The 5th Kentucky and 1st Ohio regiments have left our brigade, as I informed you in my last letter. Sherman is supposed to have been very annoyed when he learned of their departure, at a time when every single man is so essential here; only Thomas had issued the order to relieve the 2 regiments, they were gone, and nothing more changed.[34]

The railroad bridge over the Chattahoochee is still not finished.[35] Sherman is not in a hurry with it. Our corps train is still on the north side of the river, 10 miles in our rear; and our daily needs are being transported here by wagon trains every 2nd or 3rd day, as we consume the supplies. It is not advisable to amass larger supplies south of the river, because the area is very insecure and the possibility of a successful Rebel attack on our lines is always present [illegible] this side of the river, must fall into enemy hands.

Yesterday evening we had a substantial amount of rain; today we have a cloudy, misty day.

The pickets have opened fire on each other this morning, and the accustomed baff, baff, baffbaffpaff fills the sunburned ears of the sons of Mars.[36]

Friendly greetings,
G. Rentschler

CHAPTER TWELVE

From Atlanta to Louisville

Maj. *Gen. William T. Sherman realized that a direct attack on Atlanta had little chance of success and would be overly costly in his soldiers' lives. Lacking sufficient troops to surround the heavily fortified city, the Federal chieftain decided to cut the railroad west of the city. Private Rentschler's letter dated August 10 reported that cavalry raids launched late in July by Maj. Gen. George Stoneman and Brig. Gen. Edward M. McCook had failed, and Maj. Gen. John M. Schofield's attempt to move south over Utoy Creek was soundly repulsed. However, Rentschler believed "the Rebels cannot hold Atlanta much longer because of lack of supplies." He ended his letter because "my Sambo just calls me to coffee."*[1]

LETTER 22

Published August 16, 1864
Written Two Miles from Atlanta, August 10, 1864

Dear Editor:

Do not become annoyed when I always, and this time too, write to you "2 miles from Atlanta." The air of the city of Atlanta is still not healthy for us, and to date we hold up "for health reasons." Back in February or March a friend wrote to me from Louisville that I should send a correspondence from Atlanta very soon. I would have made the friend bored if other events had not occupied his time. The good friend has become a veteran since that time because he was drafted, and only released after he presented proof that he was over forty-five years old. We also had a veteran who had not tasted Sow-Belly [salted pork] one time; nor sharpened his teeth on hard-tack [hard bread];[2] nor still much-less, smelled powder [saw action]. Smelled powder—that is a meaningless expression for us here. We not only smell powder, we are stuck in a thick cloud of saltpeter and smell, taste, hear, feel and swallow powder; reek of powder; stick our heads out through the cloud of saltpeter, and appear to the outside world as the Grass Devil;[3] with which the old Fritz [Frederick the Great][4] compared his veterans, because we also bite like him. In order to prove all this in black and white, and to provide you with an approximately correct idea of the powder expended in larger and smaller fights and battles; and how the powder gets on us; and how it effects our appearance; I will present below the intensity of our picket fire.

One regiment from each brigade is normally on picket. The regiment stays on picket 24 hours and fires an average of 5,000 cartridges during the 24 hours. Take as an average, 3 brigades for a division and 3 divisions for an army corps. Therefore, each day 63 regiments come on picket because Sherman's army consists of 7 corps: the 4th, 14th, 15th, 16th, 17th, 20th and 23rd. These 63 regiments fire, according to the above-given average number,—5,000 per regiment—315,000 cartridges per day. Estimated in terms of money, this makes a daily expenditure of $4,725 because the cartridges cost $15 per thousand. Add to this the artillery fire, and one can estimate the usual daily expenditure for munitions when the army is quietly lying in camp as at least $6,000. Now I flee the vapor of powder and go to my diary.[5]

On the 1st and 2nd of August nothing worthy of note occurred. On the 3rd, about 5 P.M., our picket regiment, the 6th Md. [Ind.],[6] was pushed forward. The 23rd Kentucky was advanced as a reserve. Our pickets took the Rebels' rifle pits. The Rebel pickets scattered in all directions and were quite amusing to watch. When these rifle pits were evacuated by their Secesh inhabitants, it was like we frightened a number of hares out of their nest. However, we could not hold the pits longer than an hour, and the part of our line to our right fell back. The Rebels flanked us and it was necessary for the 6th Md. [Ind.] to fall back to its own pits. The Rebels opened a raging artillery fire and we replied sharply. Our brigade took 3 Rebels as prisoners. The brigade to our left ([Brig. Gen. William] Grose's) took 21 prisoners, and the rest of the brigades engaged, [captured prisoners] in the same ratio. A man from the 23rd Kentucky was shot. He was collecting "roasting ears" in the cornfields that were occupied by both ours and the Rebel pickets. His officer advised him several times to lay down. He paid for his carelessness with his life.[7]

It was not our objective to hold the rifle pits of the Rebels. The whole thing was a demonstration through which we wanted to find out the present position of the enemy and especially his artillery, which was fully achieved.

The prisoners taken here and elsewhere say that the Rebel armies all have been called upon to hold fast until after the presidential election is held, because the Arch-Rebel, i.e., the leader of the Rebellion,[8] is aware that if Lincoln is not elected again peace had to follow; if Lincoln is elected again, then the South will fight to the last man (about which so much has been written); ergo, with Lincoln: War; without Lincoln: Peace.

On the 4th only the usual picket fire interrupted the quiet of the day. A fight is supposed to have taken place on our extreme right but I have not been able to learn the details. On the afternoon of the 5th a large demonstration was made. Schofield, on the right of our line, was hard-pressed, and in order to give him fresh air and thus let him breath easier, we were supposed to knock a hole through the wall; and to plug up the hole already punched, through which stale air streamed.[9]

The open field between the 4th corps and the Rebel breastworks had a round shape. The surface is very undulating, and about in the middle of the field is a hollow that is not deep and not wide. The field is about a mile in diameter. Our regiments left their works and marched out, so that they came into full view of the Rebels. Only half of a regiment was advanced at the same time; and, in fact, at the slowest step and with billowing flags leading the way. After one-half [of our men] lay in the immediate area of our pickets, and under protection of the elevation; the flags were brought back into the middle of the second half of the regiment in order for the Rebels to see. Through that, it appeared to the enemy that our number had doubled. Spontaneously came to my mind the Russian Katharine [the Great] and her bed-friend Potemkin, as he led the Empress through Russia and had canvas cities appear in the distance; which just as quickly were transported as Katharine traveled, in order to be set up repeatedly in other places. Whether the Rebels were deceived by our "trick," just as successfully as Katharine was deceived by Potemkin's

"Trick," in that she took home with her a far too high idea of the number of Russian cities; I don't know.[10]

We did not attack the Rebel pickets and, in the evening, when it
became dark, our regiments returned to our works. Next day I learned
from a source that Schofield had lost 1,000 out of 1,600 men. I still do
not know at this time whether these 1,600 men were the only ones who
fought with the Rebels.[11]

On the 6th we heard that [Maj. Gen. George] Stoneman and two of
his [cavalry] regiments had been taken prisoner. His campaign was a failure because the objective of the campaign was to lay the groundwork—
to free the prisoners at Andersonville [Georgia][12] and that was not
achieved. The Rebels received wind of the undertaking and transported
our prisoners from Andersonville to Charleston, S.C. Also, Stoneman
could not reach Macon [Georgia]. There was a brigade of Rebel infantry
and a brigade of Rebel cavalry there. [Gen. Joseph E.] Johnston was in
Macon at this time visiting his wife and personally took over command
of the two brigades. Incidentally, Stoneman is supposed to have done
much damage to the Rebels at other places.[13] Colonel [James P.]
Brownlow from the 2nd [1st] Tennessee Cavalry Regiment is supposed
to have swum over the river naked. He came to Marietta wearing only
pants and a jacket, which he borrowed from one of his people. Luckily,
he brought back his regiment which formed a part of Stoneman's force.[14]
The demonstration program was the same today as yesterday. Many of
our troops were thrown on our left wing. We expected an attack by the
Rebels, but it did not come. The Rebels understood our demonstration
and did not worry themselves further with our exhibition and our noise.
They remained ready for battle, in case it became necessary, and that is
all. Fights occur each day; indeed, almost each hour, at some part of our
long, half-circle line. Where we would like to attack, the Rebels are vigi-
lant and in strong numbers. This and Stoneman's and [Brig. Gen.
Edward M.] McCook's experiences prove that the Rebels are stronger in
numbers than many newspapers say. A violent small-arms fire was maintained on our right wing for a considerable time. Parts of the 14th and
23rd Army Corps were at loggerheads with the Rebels and lost approximately 500 men. In retaliation they took 500 Rebel prisoners and made
mincemeat out of [Maj. Gen William B.] Bate's Division of Rebels
(Napoleonically speaking).[15] On the 7th many believed that the Rebels
had moved out of Atlanta, but, "Millers blow barley," as the Bavarian

farmers say. The Rebels did not move and fierce shooting to the right informed us that the Rebels have not yet given up hope. I did not hear any artillery fire on this date.[16]

On the morning of the 8th, General Thomas assured our brigade's General Hazen that our prospects were excellent; and that Sherman could wish for no better success in the action for this operation than he has achieved up to now. There is no doubt, however, that Sherman could take Atlanta if he wanted to expose his army to the danger of very large losses in human life. That he could do this in two hours and do quite easy, as several newspapers in the world have written, is a very erroneous assumption and the composers of this sort of flowery language prove through this, only a total ignorance in military matters and the conditions of our present situation. If Sherman wants to take Atlanta by storm, it must happen by carrying out a skillful flanking movement and the high bars of the piece must be played on the southern side of the city. The operation, however, would demand time and require such a large loss of life on our side that the humanitarians would advise against it. It is the view of the best informed, that the Rebels cannot hold Atlanta much longer because of the lack of supplies; which they cannot supply in sufficient quantities because their lines of communication have already partly been cut off and before long will be completely blocked.[17] Meanwhile, one generally knows that Sherman does not press with the capture of Atlanta as long as the situation in Virginia is not decided favorably for us. This is because after the evacuation of Atlanta, Johnston [Hood], without doubt, would send the larger and better part of his army to strengthen Lee, or would supply in person anything positive to prevent trouble.[18]

To my knowledge nothing new and worthy of note took place today [August 8]. In the afternoon we had thunder, lightning and rain, as has been normal during the afternoons of the last eight days. The pickets banged the whole day as usual, and the artillery mixed temporary cannon shots in between. Thunder up in the sky, thunder below on earth, thunder right, thunder left, thunder behind, thunder in front, which adds up to, as a Louisville friend who is from the Black Forest [in southwestern Germany] has so often said, a "Million-Thunderstorms."

Yesterday, the 9th, rain the whole day. Of today, the 10th, I still do not know anything to say, because it is still early in the day and my Sambo just calls me to coffee, that is too costly a surrogate for the soldier's stomach;

and I must lay down my pen and respond in the double-quick to the African's call.

Friendly greetings,
G. Rentschler

■   ■   ■

Gottfried Rentschler's last letter from the front contained the welcome news that the 6th Kentucky was being sent back to Tennessee. Two of its companies' enlistments would be expiring on September 9 and a third on November 1. The small number of men fit for duty comprising its remaining seven companies would not be sufficient to justify keeping it on the front line.

LETTER 23

Published August 20, 1864
Written Two Miles from Atlanta, August 11, 1864

Dear Editor:

The 6th Kentucky regiment has just received orders to go to the rear. The place to which we are going is Decherd, on the railroad from Chattanooga to Nashville, about 4 miles on this side of Murfreesboro and 14 miles from Tullahoma. It is a place where our Captain Frank says "the sparrows die during the harvest [i.e., it is a desolate place]."[19] The regiment departs from here as soon as the 71st Ohio regiment, which is supposed to take the place of the 6th Kentucky, arrives here. General Hazen thinks that this regiment will come in 3 or 4 days and the 6th Kentucky will leave.

This so-welcome order was effected for the regiment through Capt. Johnston who has commanded the regiment for 3 months and has made, in that position, every contribution within his power for the welfare of the regiment.[20]

The regiment has only 184 officers and soldiers present, of which 8 officers and 143 soldiers are capable of service; 3 officers and 16 soldiers are on "Extra Duty," 12 soldiers are sick and 2 under arrest. Absent are 12 officers and 226 soldiers. The regiment therefore has in total 422 men, namely 23 officers and 399 soldiers.

The 6th Kentucky Regiment has been at the Front constantly since it left Camp Sigel and has performed so well in all the skirmishes and battles in which it has participated that it has received the highest praise in the official reports of the brigade's general, of which I will publish extracts some day, for which I have already received permission from the general himself.[21]

General Hazen invited me to stay with him a while longer and I accepted with pleasure, because I would very much like to stroll through Atlanta.

Greetings,

G. Rentschler

■　■　■

Gottfried Rentschler was promoted from private to captain of Company E on August 15, 1864, but was unable to walk through Atlanta with General Hazen because Hazen was appointed commander of the 2nd Division of the 15th Corps on August 17 and left the brigade. The new captain's last letter was published in the Louisville Anzeiger on September 3, 1864, and it described the trip to his company's post on the railroad and the easy duty there. It is unknown whether the native German wrote any more letters to the Anzeiger; if he did, they were not published.

LETTER 24

Published September 3, 1864
Written from the 6th Kentucky Regiment, Block House No. 32, N&C [Nashville and Chattanooga] Railroad, August 30, 1864

Dear Editor:

On the evening of the 20th we finally received Marching Orders. Although the orders were given by Headquarters on the 9th, General Wood held up the written orders and they were not sent to us until the 20th. The regiment was on picket that day and not relieved until the morning of the 21st. We packed up that same morning and left the front "two miles from Atlanta," and moved with priceless humor to the rear. We marched up to Vining Station—10 miles—from where we headed to Chattanooga by railroad. We spent an unpleasant night in railroad cars that were so packed we barely were able to sit upright. We could not even think about sleeping because the cars contained an enormous amount of lice, and there was insufficient space between the large number of men in the overcrowded cars.—If one stood up, it cracked under his feet because each step cost half-a-thousand lice their lives. These railroad cars appeared to have never been cleaned; today, they contain a load of cattle; tomorrow, a load of people; the day after tomorrow, a load of cattle hooves or other fancy articles; without removing the droppings of the first, nor the other race or thing.

It was 5 o'clock in the evening on the 22nd when we arrived at Chattanooga; gnawed, scratched, crushed, corroded—generally half-dead. Here, however, we recovered quickly; because after being without for so long, we again had the opportunity to have wine and beer. On the 23rd, at 4 o'clock in the afternoon, we went to Decherd, where we arrived on the morning of the 24th. From then on the regiment's commander had to report by letter to General Rousseau.[22] On the 25th we stayed in Decherd, and on the 26th Rousseau sent orders that we should guard the railroad between Anderson [Tennessee] and Stevenson [Alabama].[23] Company F is situated 3 miles, Company D 1½ miles north of Anderson. Companies A, B and C, which will muster out in September, are situated in Anderson; where the regiment's headquarters are located. Company I is situated 2 miles; K, 4 miles; H, 6 miles; E, 6 miles; and G, 8 miles south of Anderson, and the last company 2 miles from Stevenson.

Each company has a blockhouse that is strong enough that artillery fire will not seriously damage it. A well has been dug in each of these blockhouses, and 20 days rations and firewood stored, in order to be able to endure a siege for a short time. At night each blockhouse sends out patrols that go up to the next blockhouse and must observe whether everything is in order; similar to the mounted-policemen in Germany. Rousseau has given much attention to guarding this railroad, and there have been so many precautions taken that it takes more intelligence then the Rebels possess to damage the railroad.

We are situated very comfortably; in fact, we only have to work several hours each day in order to keep the area surrounding the blockhouse clean and well-maintained. We do not work any harder than is necessary to work up a good appetite for meals. Therefore, the relatives of the soldiers of the Sixth Kentucky do not have to worry about our fate. Our lot is pleasant. Here we have the time to fill out our thin cheeks and to provide our wives with a well-fed filled-out husband as a Christmas present on December 24—the day of our muster out.[24]

Letters to the 6th Kentucky should from now on be addressed to

2nd Brig. 4th Div. 20th A.C.
Anderson, Tenn.

Those who would like to send their loved ones in the regiment something edible, drinkable, wearable, smokable or snuffable, use the news that Adam's Express Company has an office in Anderson.

Friendly greetings,
G. Rentschler

EPILOGUE

General John Bell Hood abandoned Atlanta on the night of September 1–2, 1864, and escaped with his army. Gottfried Rentschler and the rest of his regiment missed the bloody Tennessee battles at Franklin (November 30) and Nashville (December 15–16) that virtually destroyed Hood's Army of Tennessee. The 6th Kentucky's last seven companies and its regimental headquarters mustered out at Nashville between December 31, 1864, and January 2, 1865, and headed back to Kentucky, leaving a record of service that, according to Capt. Thomas Speed (10th Kentucky Volunteer Infantry), author of *The Union Regiments of Kentucky*, was second to none of the other regiments its state furnished to the Union.[1]

During its three years of existence, almost one-half of the 937 men who served in the 6th Kentucky suffered wounds, and 94 were killed in action or died from wounds. Four men were missing and presumed dead. Its combat losses placed the hard-fighting regiment in William F. Fox's list of "300 fighting regiments" of the Union army. Another 82 of its men died of diseases or illnesses, including three in Confederate prison camps.[2]

■ ■ ■

First Sergeant John Daeuble was initially buried near the field hospital in which he died. After the war ended his remains were moved to the National Cemetery at Marietta, Georgia, and re-interred on a grassy hillside (possibly in 1866). After John's death, his mother was able to obtain an army pension of six dollars a month until her death in 1875; his father applied for a pension after Anna Maria's demise and received eight dollars a month until his death in 1878. He died penniless. John's and his parents' hopes for a better life in America had been destroyed by a tragic civil war.[3]

Although the last company of the 6th Kentucky mustered out of service on January 2, 1865, Captain Rentschler remained in the service to temporarily command a group of around fifty-five men from his regiment who had reenlisted or had additional time to serve. On March 15, 1865, after his charges had been absorbed by the 4th Kentucky Volunteer Mounted Infantry, he mustered out and returned to Louisville.

Gottfried's return to civilian life was marred by a drinking problem he may have developed in the army. The talented Württemberg native worked as a reporter for the *Louisville Anzeiger* for a short time, then taught music, and later worked in a music store; however, he often went on long drinking binges and was soon deep in debt. Gottfried's wife Paulina put up with his destructive behavior for about a year and a half before obtaining a divorce. During the last half of 1866, the former soldier-correspondent moved to Lawrence, Kansas, and worked at a German-language newspaper (*Lawrence Freie Presse*, later the *Kansas Freie Presse*) for which he eventually served as editor. Gottfried married Anna Thoman Englemann, widow of William Englemann, on March 8, 1873, in Topeka, Kansas, and they moved to St. Louis, Missouri, where he secured the position of teacher at the Independent Protestant Church of North St. Louis. A year later he accepted the call as preacher at a church in Fayetteville, Illinois, and in 1879 moved to Highland, Illinois, to become the pastor of the German Evangelical Church located there. Gottfried Rentschler resigned as pastor in 1887 due to failing health; he died from a stroke or heart failure in November 1897 at age seventy and was cremated. He had no children.[4] It is not surprising that this man whose Civil War letters were punctuated with references to God, biblical passages, the devil, sin, and guilt became a minister.

■   ■   ■

A postwar study by Benjamin A. Gould published in 1869 revealed that more Germans served in the Union army than any other foreign-born nationality.[5] The large majority of Germans served in mixed regiments; however, an estimated thirty-six thousand or about one in five served in all or mostly German regiments.[6] German units achieved the purpose of raising the visibility of the German element in the war but also made them easy targets for critics and led to allegations of widespread cowardice by Germans at the battle of Chancellorsville in Virginia in May 1863. American newspapers quickly reported rumors that the German regiments of the 11th Corps posted on the army's right wing fled without offering significant resistance, causing its army's defeat. The Germans were called "Dutch cowards" and "flying Dutchmen." This unearned reputation for cowardice lasted well beyond the end of the war. Historians now agree that the defeat was caused by errors of American senior commanders who let the Germans take the blame for them. Further, the American regiments in the 11th Corps gave less resistance than the Germans, and even if all the troops there had been Americans they could not have withstood the overwhelming Confederate force that burst unexpectedly out of the woods.[7] The reputation of Germans in the Civil War has improved with time and study, but more research and study is needed.

Despite the disrespect and prejudicial actions manifested against Germans in the army, the process of their assimilation into American culture and society accelerated after the war. Forty-eighters tamed their radicalism, gave up the idea of returning to a democratic Germany, and joined with their fellow German immigrants in the process of Americanization.[8] An early sign of the change in Louisville was the election of Peace Democrat Philip Tomppert as mayor in 1865. Louisville historian George H. Yater noted: "Perhaps the most remarkable thing about Tomppert's election, however, was . . . the fact that only a decade after the horror of [the] Bloody Monday [election rioting], Louisville had chosen a German for its highest office." Yater attributed the German's election "not only to war weariness, but the rapid decline of nativism, the growing strength of immigrants in the city, and their strong allegiance to the Democratic party. Tomppert's election demonstrated the integration of the immigrant into the mainstream of society, one of the significant changes the war brought in Louisville."[9] The German population of Louisville increased by approximately 1,000 persons or 7 percent from 1860 to 1870, but by 1880 fell back to the 1860 level of 13,300. Kentucky's German residents increased about 10 percent from 1860 to 1870 and remained at about 30,000 persons through 1880.[10] Post–Civil War German immigrants benefited from the groundwork laid by those before them. Unfortunately, World Wars I and II led to new outbreaks of anti-German feelings that often found their focus on German Americans. The *Louisville Anzeiger* was published daily until 1933 and its circulation climbed from an estimated 3,000 copies in 1870 to 8,056 copies in 1900. Thereafter, declining circulation and advertising revenues led to its ultimate demise in 1933.[11]

■ ■ ■

Finally, a word about Kentucky after the war is in order. Most white Kentuckians who remained loyal to the Union wanted the Union restored as it was, i.e., with slavery. After all, early on, Lincoln had promised that the purpose of the war was to save the Union and not to abolish slavery. The Emancipation Proclamation (effective January 1, 1863) angered most white Kentuckians and they felt betrayed by President Abraham Lincoln. Slavery was abolished in 1865 by a constitutional amendment that Kentucky's General Assembly refused to ratify. In 1866, Congress granted citizenship to blacks and gave them access to federal courts, further rankling Bluegrass State whites who believed the federal government had usurped powers that belonging to the state. Kentucky was also still smarting from restrictions and abuses imposed by federal military authorities.

The state's Union soldiers, who were cheered in 1861 and 1862 when they marched off to war, subsequently became viewed as aiding the Lincoln administration and Radical Republicans who had and were abusing Kentucky—a loyal state. Many former Union soldiers experienced prejudice because of their army service. On the other hand, ex-Confederates quickly had their civil rights restored and with the help of most newspapers in the state gained control of the Democratic party and controlled the state's politics for decades. Union veterans had little chance of being elected in statewide elections or filling state government jobs.

Wartime enemies or their survivors often lived side by side in Kentucky after the war, and the animosities and bitterness created by the conflict frequently erupted into violence, instances of which even occurred after the turn of the century. Lawlessness and violence within the state also posed a serious problem in the postwar era. Assaults on blacks, crime and violence by roving bands of desperadoes against both blacks and whites (especially pro-Union people), and actions by vigilantes continued for decades after the war. In such an atmosphere, it is not surprising that Kentucky's Union soldiers and their fighting units have received short shrift in telling their side of the story.[12]

Appendix A

BOOKS CONTAINING CIVIL WAR DIARIES AND COLLECTIONS
OF LETTERS BY NATIVE GERMANS AND PUBLISHED IN ENGLISH

Ahsenmacher, Henry. *The Civil War Diary of a Minnesota Volunteer: Henry Ahsenmacher 1862–1865*. St. Paul: Minnesota Genealogical Society, 1990. 11 pages. 10th Minnesota.

Byrne, Frank L., and Jean Powers Soman, eds. *Your True Marcus: The Civil War Letters of a Jewish Colonel*. Kent, Ohio: Kent State Univ. Press, 1985. 353 pages. 67th and 120th Ohio.

Goyne, Minetta Altgelt, trans. and ed. *Lone Star and Double Eagle: Civil War Letters of a German-Texas Family*. Fort Worth: Texas Christian Univ. Press, 1982. 276 pages. 37th Regiment Texas Cavalry CSA.

Hedrick, David T., and Gordon Barry Davis Jr. *I am Surrounded by Methodists: Diary of John H. W. Stuckenburg, Chaplain of the 145th Pennsylvania*. Gettysburg, Pa.: Thomas Publications, 1995. 158 pages.

Horner, John B. *Captain John M. Sachs: His Long Road Back to Gettysburg*. Gettysburg, Pa.: Horner Enterprises, 1994. 42 pages. 5th Maryland.

Janeski, Paul, comp. *A Civil War Soldier's Last Letters.* New York: Vantage Press, 1975. 61 pages. 6th Pennsylvania.

Patrick, Charles, ed. *Giesecke's Civil War Diary: The Story of the Fourth Regiment of the First Texas Cavalry Brigade of the Army of the Confederate States of America (1861–1865).* Manor, Tex.: Patrick Historical Research, 1999. 70 pages.

Spurlin, Charles, ed. *The Civil War Diary of Charles A. Leuschner— Sixth Texas Infantry* (CSA). Austin, Tex.: Eakin Press, 1992. 120 pages.

Wickesberg, Alfred, ed. *Civil War Letters of Sergeant Charles Wickesberg.* Trans. Ingeborg Wolferstetter. Milwaukee: Alfred Wickesberg, 1961. 39 pages. 26th Wisconsin.

Winkler, William K., ed. *Letters of Frederic C. Winkler 1862–1865.* N. p.: William K. Winkler, 1963. 219 pages. 26th Wisconsin.

Appendix B

BRIEF HISTORY OF THE 6TH KENTUCKY VOLUNTEER INFANTRY REGIMENT, DECEMBER 24, 1861, TO JANUARY 2, 1865

The 6th Kentucky Infantry assembled at Camp Sigel (near Louisville) in mid-November 1861, and after about six weeks of training and the muster in of the regiment's final seven companies on December 24, 1861, moved to Camp Wickliffe in Larue County, Kentucky (about sixty miles south of Louisville), where it was assigned to the 19th Brigade commanded Col. William B. Hazen, a highly competent West Point graduate and veteran Indian fighter who forged his troops into one of the toughest brigades in the Union's western armies.[1] The 6th and the rest of its division (commanded by Brig. Gen. William Nelson) left Camp Wickliffe on February 14, 1862, and marched to West Point, Kentucky, where they boarded steamboats that took them down the Ohio River to the Cumberland River and then to Nashville, Tennessee, where Maj. Gen. Don Carlos Buell was concentrating a large part of his Army of the Ohio after Confederate troops abandoned the city.[2]

The 6th Kentucky and its division left Nashville in mid-March to reinforce Maj. Gen. Ulysses S. Grant's Army of West Tennessee, and arrived at Pittsburg Landing (on the Tennessee River) in time to fight on the second day of the two-day battle of Shiloh. In its bloody baptism of fire on April 7, 1862, the 6th suffered 103 casualties out of 484 men taken into the battle. The battle of Shiloh (also called the battle of Pittsburg Landing) was the largest battle of the war to date and resulted in a Confederate retreat to Corinth, Mississippi.[3]

During May, the 6th Kentucky participated in the siege of Corinth and by month's end the Confederates abandoned their fortifications there and retreated to Tupelo, Mississippi. The 6th Kentucky engaged in some skirmishing and was shelled during May but mostly pulled guard duty and worked on entrenchments.[4] After Corinth was secured the regiment moved to Iuka, Mississippi, and then Athens, Alabama, where they guarded bridges and the railroad.[5]

In August, the 6th Kentucky and its brigade moved to Murfreesboro, Tennessee, to garrison this important little city on the Nashville and Chattanooga Railroad, while the bulk of Buell's army operated southeast toward Chattanooga. They reunited with their division and most of Buell's army on September 6, 1862, when Buell was moving north to counter movements by Gen. Braxton Bragg's and Maj. Gen. Edmund Kirby Smith's Southern armies, which had marched north out of Chattanooga and Knoxville and soon headed for Kentucky.[6] The officers and men of the 6th Kentucky Regiment made the grueling 200-mile march to Louisville with its army, which began reaching this important Union city on September 26.[7] Part of Buell's army clashed with Bragg's army at Perryville, Kentucky, on October 8, 1862, in a hotly contested battle that resulted in thousands of casualties on both sides, and a Confederate withdrawal during the night. The 6th Kentucky spent the afternoon on the Federal right listening to the raging battle because its corps was not ordered into the fray.[8] However, the 6th and its brigade were in the forefront of the Union forces that pursued the Rebel army down the rugged Wilderness Road, across Wildcat Mountain, and as far as London, Kentucky. The 6th suffered several casualties before its brigade turned about and marched for Nashville, Tennessee, near where they encamped on November 26.[9]

The day after Christmas 1862, Maj. Gen. William S. Rosecrans (who had replaced Buell as army commander) launched his 44,000-man Army of the Cumberland toward Murfreesboro, and was attacked by Bragg's legions near the Stones River on December 31.[10] The 6th Kentucky and its brigade fought stubbornly on their army's left and played a key part in denying the Rebels a stunning victory by their determined fighting at the Round Forest, where they repulsed numerous fierce enemy attacks.

Lt. Col. George T. Cotton was killed in the morning's fighting.[11] Significant combat resumed on January 2, 1863, when Braxton Bragg ordered a division to drive a Federal brigade off a hill on the east side of the Stones River. The Confederate brigades were successful in their initial attack and they pursued the fleeing Federals to the Stones River. The 6th Kentucky and its brigade waded through the ice-cold, chest-high water of the Stones River to reinforce their besieged comrades, while the destructive fire from over fifty Federal cannon—mostly massed on high ground on the opposite side of the river—routed the Rebels, who ran for their lives pursued by thousands of Rosecrans's vengeful blue-clads. Darkness ended the fighting and the Confederate army withdrew before dawn on January 4, 1863. The 6th Kentucky lost several men in the fighting on the second, bringing its total casualties for the battle of Stones River to 113, including 20 killed or dead from wounds.[12] The 6th Kentucky and the rest of Hazen's brigade forged an imperishable record of valor at Stones River, and Colonel Hazen reported that the 6th "fought unflinchingly, and is deserving of all praise."[13]

After the battle of Stones River, the 6th Kentucky and its brigade encamped at Readyville (about twelve miles east of Murfreesboro) to guard the left flank of the army and remained there almost six months, performing guard duty and sometimes skirmishing with enemy cavalry who often lurked nearby. During this period the Bluegrass State unit suffered nine men wounded, including two men who subsequently died. Also, Colonel Hazen won promotion to brigadier general for his gallant leadership at the battle of Stones River.[14]

The 6th Kentucky and its brigade broke camp at Readyville on June 24, 1863, and reunited with the rest of the division and corps, which was tasked to get around the enemy's right flank. However, rain, mud, and swollen rivers prevented their corps from engaging any sizable enemy force before the Confederates retreated out of Middle Tennessee into northern Georgia under pressure from the other Federal corps.[15] The 6th Kentucky encamped at Manchester, Tennessee, on July 8, and remained there until August 16, when Rosecrans put his army in motion toward Chattanooga, Tennessee, and Braxton Bragg's army. Meanwhile, on July 14, the Kentuckians bid adieu to Colonel Whitaker who had been promoted to brigadier general and appointed commander of the 1st Brigade of the 1st Division of the Reserve Corps. Lt. Col. George T. Shackelford of Richmond, Kentucky, a deputy circuit court clerk in civilian life, was advanced to colonel and replaced Whitaker as leader of the regiment.[16]

The Army of the Cumberland and Bragg's Army of Tennessee next collided near Chickamauga Creek in northern Georgia on September 19 and 20, 1863, in another great American slaughter. The 6th Kentucky fought stubbornly in this bloody battle; however, a Federal error on the second day of the battle allowed the Confederates to break through the Union line, and the blue-clad army was forced to retreat back to Chattanooga and fortify the city.[17] The 6th fought in the Brock and Brotherton fields and near the Poe house on the first day of the battle, and at the Kelly field and on Snodgrass Hill on the second day, suffering a staggering 118 casualties out of 302 men engaged in this great western bloodletting. Colonel Shackelford and Lt. Col. Richard C. Rockingham were both seriously wounded in the first day's fighting, and Rockingham was killed the next day by a shell. Command of the regiment then passed to Maj. Richard T. Whitaker (Brigadier General Whitaker's younger brother). Federal casualties totaled sixteen thousand and Confederate casualties totaled over eighteen thousand in this major Southern victory.[18]

The Confederate army besieged Rosecrans's army at Chattanooga by occupying the west bank of the Tennessee River, Lookout Mountain, and Missionary Ridge, and the Federals suffered severely from lack of food and supplies. The War Department ordered reinforcements sent to Chattanooga from the Army of the Tennessee and the Army of the Potomac and, on October 23, Maj. Gen. Ulysses S. Grant arrived in Chattanooga to take charge. Rosecrans was replaced as Army of the Cumberland commander by Maj. Gen. George H. Thomas, a highly competent Union-loyal Virginian, who had been dubbed the "Rock of Chickamauga" for his courageous leadership in that battle.[19]

While at Chattanooga, the Army of the Cumberland was reorganized and General Hazen's brigade became the 2nd Brigade of the 3rd Division of the 4th Corps. Brig. Gen. Thomas J. Wood commanded the division and Maj. Gen. Gordon Granger headed the corps. After the reorganization, Hazen's brigade consisted of the 6th Kentucky and eight other battle-reduced regiments, and aggregated about 2,200 men.[20]

The 6th Kentucky and its brigade helped open a supply line from Bridgeport, Alabama, by conducting a daring amphibious raid on October 27, 1863, at Brown's Ferry, west of Chattanooga. The enemy was driven away from the area, and reinforcements previously transferred from the

Army of the Potomac moved from Bridgeport, Alabama, to Brown's Ferry, opening the critical line of supply. On November 23, 1863, the regiment helped seize fortifications near Orchard Knob, located east of Chattanooga and about halfway between Chattanooga and Missionary Ridge. Two days later, over 22,000 troops of the Army of the Cumberland stormed Missionary Ridge and drove the Confederates from their fortifications and won one of the most stunning Union victories of the war. The 6th Kentucky was among several units credited with being the first to reach the fortifications on the crest of the ridge. Twenty-four members of the 6th became casualties of combat during the battles around Chattanooga.[21]

The 6th Kentucky, along with the rest of their division, spent December 1863 through mid-April 1864 marching around in East Tennessee looking for General James Longstreet's Virginia corps, which was in the area, but they fought no significant battles. Mostly they suffered from cold and hunger, and were elated when spring arrived.[22]

On May 3, 1864, the regiment began its last campaign of the war— Maj. Gen. William T. Sherman's Atlanta campaign—sometimes called "the 100 days under fire" because of continuous contact with the enemy. Still serving in General Wood's division, the 6th Kentucky fought at Rocky Face Ridge near Tunnel Hill, Georgia, on May 9; Resaca on May 14–15; Pickett's Mill on May 27; and Kennesaw Mountain in late June. The 6th Kentucky also participated in the siege of Atlanta, which began on July 23, 1864. Because three of its companies' enlistments were close to expiring, the 6th Kentucky was sent back to Tennessee on August 22, twelve days before Atlanta was captured. The 6th suffered twenty-one killed and mortally wounded plus thirty-seven more wounded or missing during the Atlanta campaign.

During its three years of existence, almost half of the men in the 6th Kentucky suffered wounds, and ninety-four were killed in action or died from wounds. Four men were missing and presumed dead. Its battle-related losses placed the regiment in William F. Fox's list of "300 fighting regiments" of the Union army. Eighty-two men died of diseases or illnesses, including three in Confederate prisons.[23]

From September through December 1864, the regiment guarded a twenty-five–mile stretch of the Nashville and Chattanooga Railroad running between the tunnel at Cowan, Tennessee, and Stevenson, Alabama. The regimental headquarters and last company of the regiment mustered out in Nashville on January 2, 1865.[24]

Notes

Introduction

1. William K. Winkler, ed., *Letters of Frederic C. Winkler 1862–1865* (n.p.: William K. Winkler, 1963), 26th Wisconsin; Frank L. Byrne and Jean Powers Soman, eds., *Your True Marcus: The Civil War Letters of a Jewish Colonel* ([Kent, Ohio]: Kent State Univ. Press, 1985), 67th and 120th Ohio; Minetta Altgelt Goyne, trans. and ed., *Lone Star and Double Eagle: Civil War Letters of a German-Texas Family* ([Forth Worth]: Texas Christian Univ. Press, 1982), 37th Regiment Texas Cavalry CSA; Heros von Borcke, *Memoirs of the Confederate War for Independence* (Edinburg and London: W. Blackwood and Sons, 1867), Confederate cavalry officer; Carl Schurz, *The Reminiscences of Carl Schurz,* vol. 2 (1852–63), vol. 3 (1863–66), (New York: McClure, 1907–8), Union major general; Bernhard Domschcke, *Twenty Months in Captivity: Memoirs of a Union Officer in Confederate Prisons,* trans. and ed. Frederic Trautmann (Cranbury, N.J.: Associated Univ. Press, 1987); Carl Schurz, *Autobiography,* abridgement in one volume by Wayne Andrews, introd. by Alan Nevins (New York: Scribner's, 1961).
2. Wilhelm Kaufmann, *The Germans in the American Civil War,* trans. Steven Rowan and ed. Don Heinrich Tolzmann, with Werner D. Mueller and Robert E. Ward, (Carlisle, Pa.: John Kallmann, 1999), 74, 72.
3. William C. Burton, *Melting Pot Soldiers: The Union's Ethnic Regiments* (New York: Fordham Univ. Press, 1988); Ella Lonn, *Foreigners in the Union Army and Navy* (Baton Rouge: Louisiana State Univ. Press, 1951).
4. Burton, *Melting Pot Soldiers,* xiv–xv.
5. Lonn, *Foreigners in the Union Army and Navy,* 648–49.

6. Bell Irvin Wiley, *The Life of Billy Yank: The Common Soldier of the Union* (Baton Rouge: Louisiana State Univ. Press, 1978), 308.

7. Electronic mail from Earl J. Hess to the editor, Sept. 10, 2002. Hess is the editor of *A German in the Yankee Fatherland: The Civil War Letters of Henry A. Kircher* (Kent, Ohio: Kent State Univ. Press, 1983), containing letters of an Illinois-born son of German parents.

8. Ella Lonn, *Foreigners in the Confederacy* (Chapel Hill: Univ. of North Carolina Press, 1940).

9. Kaufmann, *Germans in the American Civil War.*

10. Joseph R. Reinhart, *A History of the 6th Kentucky Volunteer Infantry U.S.: The Boys Who Feared No Noise* (Louisville: Beargrass Press, 2000), 386, 387, 10, 17. Unless otherwise stated, personal and service information for individual soldiers belonging to the 6th Kentucky Volunteer Infantry Regiment is taken from Compiled Service Records of Volunteer Soldiers Who Served in Organizations from the State of Kentucky, microcopy 397, rolls 201–9 and 401, except for men whose surnames begin with Rag–Reu, for which the information was extracted from Compiled Military Service Records, Records Group 94, National Archives, Washington, D.C.

11. Kaufmann, *Germans in the American Civil War,* 74, 72.

12. John Daeuble wrote two journalized accounts of his experiences. One narrative covers December 30, 1861, to August 27, 1862, and the other encompasses December 30, 1861, to February 18, 1863. John wrote the first journalized account while on picket duty at Camp Brown near the Elk River Railroad Bridge in Tennessee during August 1862. He wrote the second and longer account in March 1863, while in Louisville recovering from a wound received at the battle of Stones River on December 31, 1862. Because the journalized accounts are so detailed—with miles marched, notations about rain and snow on specific days, and other independently verifiable items—the editor believes that Daeuble wrote the two journalized accounts from diary entries and that the diary or diaries covering December 30, 1861, to November 12, 1862, no longer exist or their whereabouts are unknown to the Daeuble family.

13. John Daeuble's paternal grandparents were Johann Ludwig Daeuble (1767–1820), a butcher and member of the village council, and Anna Katharina Gühl Daeuble (1768–1807). Mühlheim am Bach, Kingdom of Württemberg, Evangelical Church Registers: Vol. 1, Taufregister, 1653–1794; Totenregister, 1654–1809; Eheregister, 1654–1808; Vol. 2, Taufregister, 1794–1833; microfilm no. 1732307; Taufregister, 1809–1862; Totenregister, 1809–1862; Eheregister, 1809–1878; microfilm no. 17323078; Family History Center, Church of Jesus Christ of Latter Day Saints, Salt Lake City.

14. Ira A. Glazier and P. William Filby, eds., *Germans to America: Lists of Passengers Arriving at U.S. Ports 1850–1855* (Wilmington, Del.: Scholarly Resources, 1989), 6:262.

15. Glazier and Filby, *Germans to America*, 7:25. Many persons from southern Germany came to America via Havre, rather than by way of the north German ports of Bremen, Bremerhaven, and Hamburg.
16. George H. Yater, *Two Hundred Years at the Falls of the Ohio: A History of Louisville and Jefferson County* (Louisville: Filson Club, 1987), 65–71; Ludwig Stierlin, *Der Staat Kentucky und Die Stadt Louisville mit besonderer Berücksichtigung des Deutschen Elementes* (Louisville: Printed in the Offices of the *Louisville Anzeiger*, 1873), 172; *Statistics of the United States in 1860: Compiled from the Original Returns and Being the Final Exhibit of the Eighth Census under the Direction of the Secretary of the Interior* (Washington, D.C.: Government Printing Office, 1865), lviii.
17. John Daeuble Pension File No. 173731, Record and Pension Office, Record Group 15, National Archives, Washington, D.C.; conversation with Gustave A. Daeuble III in 1995.
18. John Daeuble Pension File No. 173731.
19. Louis Daeuble married Catharine Hausch on June 18, 1855; and Maria Magdalena Daeuble married Andreas Wegenast on August 14, 1856. Jefferson County, Ky., Marriage Index and Register 1853–1860 (microfilm), Filson Historical Society, Louisville, 120,194; Population Schedule, Eighth Census of the United States, 1860, Louisville, Kentucky, First Ward, 153; John Daeuble Pension File No. 173731.
20. John Daeuble diary, unnumbered page showing purchases while in the hospital at Nashville after the battle of Stones River.
21. Photograph of John Daeuble in possession of Mrs. Gustave A. Daeuble III.
22. *Louisville Anzeiger,* June 10, 1864.
23. Grömbach, Kingdom of Württemberg, Evangelical Church Registers: Taufregister, Totenregister, Eheregister, microfilm no. 1201985; Family History Center, Church of Jesus Christ of Latter Day Saints, Salt Lake City.
24. "Gottfried Rentschler," *Highland (Illinois) Journal,* Nov. 25, 1897. Information about Michael Rentschler and his family's places of residences provided to the editor on a family group sheet by Jerry Bruhn of Wheeling, West Virginia, in 2000. In the Ohio County, (West) Virginia Marriage Register, book 3, p. 25, July 24, 1854. Gottfried Rentschler is inadvertently listed as Gottfried Renesohler.
25. Gottfried Rentschler Pension File No. 605075, Record and Pension Office, Record Group 15, National Archives, Washington, D.C.
26. Reinhart, *A History of the 6th Kentucky,* 253.
27. Lowell H. Harrison, *The Civil War in Kentucky* (Lexington: Univ. Press of Kentucky, 1975), 8, 11–14. Harrison's excellent survey reviews the state's internal conflict between Unionists and secessionists, the course of the war within its borders, and postwar effects on the state and its people.
28. *Acts of the General Assembly of the Commonwealth of Kentucky, Passed at September Session, 1861,* 13–14. The General Assembly authorized the

governor to call for 40,000 volunteers for enlistments of one to three years, 1,000 sharpshooters and scouts, and 500 horsemen and scouts to repel the Confederate invasion of the state. *War of Rebellion: A Compilation of the Official Records of the Union and Confederate Armies*, 128 vols. (Washington: Government Printing Office, 1880–1901), series 1, vol. *OR* 4, p. 288 (cited hereafter as *OR*. Unless specified, all citations are to series 1).

29. *OR*, series 3, vol. 3, p. 314; Lowell H. Harrison and James C. Klotter, *A New History of Kentucky* (Lexington: Univ. Press of Kentucky, 1997), 195.

30. U.S. Census, Kentucky, 1860; Benjamin Apthorp Gould, *Investigations in the Military and Anthropological Statistics of American Soldiers* (1869; rpt. New York: Arno Press, 1979), 27.

31. Harrison and Klotter, *New History of Kentucky*, 195.

32. Reinhart, *A History of the 6th Kentucky*, 7, 11–12.

33. Ibid., 7–28.

34. Ibid., 8–9.

35. *Louisville Anzeiger*, Oct. 11 and 24, 1861.

36. Ibid., Oct. 11, 1861; Burton, *Melting Pot Soldiers*, 52.

37. A. H. Sampson to "Dear friends," Dec. 29, 1861, Terah Sampson Miscellaneous Papers, Filson Historical Society, Louisville.

38. Reinhart, *A History of the 6th Kentucky*, 8; *Louisville Daily Courier*, Aug. 11, 1857.

39. Reinhart, *A History of the 6th Kentucky*, 21, 30–31, 42–43, 76; Ezra J. Warner, *Generals in Blue: Lives of Union Commanders* (Baton Rouge: Louisiana State Univ. Press, 1964), 225–26; William F. Fox, *Regimental Losses of the American Civil War 1861–1865* (Albany, N.Y.: Albany Publishing, 1889), 11.

40. See Peter Cozzens, *This Terrible Sound: The Battle of Chickamauga* (Urbana: Univ. of Illinois Press, 1992), for an excellent description of this battle.

41. Thomas Van Horne, *History of the Army of the Cumberland: Its Organization, Campaigns and Battles* (1875; rpt., introd. by Peter Cozzens, Wilmington, N.C.: Broadfoot Publishing, 1992), 386–87, 392, 394–95. See Peter Cozzens, *The Shipwreck of Their Hopes: The Battles for Chattanooga* (Urbana: Univ. of Illinois Press, 1994), for an excellent description of the battles around Chattanooga.

42. *OR* 30, pt. 4, pp. 209–11; William B. Hazen, *A Narrative of Military Service* (1885; rpt. with an introd. by Richard A. Baumgartner, Huntington, W.Va.: Blue Acorn Press, 1993), 156.

43. John Daeuble Pension File No. 173731.

44. Robert Emmett McDowell, *City of Conflict: Louisville in the Civil War 1861–1865* (Louisville: Louisville Civil War Round Table, 1962), 8; Lincoln improved his showing in Louisville in the November 1864 presidential election by receiving 1,192 votes out of a total of 6,898 cast. It is not known how many Germans voted for Lincoln. *Louisville Journal*, Nov. 9, 1864.

45. *Louisville Anzeiger*, Feb. 17, 1863. The paper was owned by George Philip

Doern and edited by Ludwig Stierlin. Louisville also had a Republican German-language newspaper founded in mid-1862—the *Tägliches Louisville Volksblatt*. No publication statistics are available to compare the *Anzeiger*'s and *Volksblatt*'s circulation during 1862–1865, but the *Anzeiger* had a circulation of about three thousand in 1870 compared to the *Volksblatt*'s thirteen hundred for that year. Karl J. Arndt, *German-American Newspapers and Periodicals* (Heidelberg: Quelle and Meyer, 1961), 169–73.

46. La Vern J. Rippley, *The German-Americans* (Lanham, Md.: Univ. Press of America, 1984), 51–53; Bruce Levine, *The Spirit of 1848: German Immigrants, Labor Conflict, and the Coming of the Civil War* (Urbana: Univ. of Illinois Press, 1992), 16, table 1.
47. Albert Castel, *Decision in the West: The Atlanta Campaign of 1864* (Lawrence: Univ. Press of Kansas, 1992), 249.
48. John Daeuble participated in the fierce two-day battle of Chickamauga on Sept. 19–20, 1863; suffered through the siege and battles around Chattanooga (late September to the end of November 1863); spent four months (December 1863 to early April 1864) in East Tennessee with frequent marching, inadequate rations, and poor shelter in unusually inclement weather prior to start of the Atlanta campaign.
49. Burton, *Melting Pot Soldiers,* 205.
50. *Louisville Anzeiger,* Mar. 15, 1864. See letter 8 in chapter 5.
51. Ibid.
52. Ibid.
53. Burton, *Melting Pot Soldiers,* 101.
54. Henry Richards, *Letters of Captain Henry Richards of the Ninety-Third Ohio Infantry* (Cincinnati: Press of Wrighton, 1883), 31.
55. Burton, *Melting Pot Soldiers,* 202.
56. Joseph T. Glatthaar, *Forged in Battle: The Civil War Alliance of Black Soldiers and White Officers* (New York: Free Press, 1990), 12.
57. The Confederacy controlled East Tennessee until Maj. Gen. Ambrose Burnside's troops occupied Knoxville in September 1863. The best books on the conflict in East Tennessee are Digby B. Seymour, *Divided Loyalties: Fort Sanders and the Civil War in East Tennessee,* rev. ed. (Knoxville: n.p., 1982); Noel C. Fisher, *War at Every Door: Partisan Politics and Guerilla Violence* (Chapel Hill: Univ. of North Carolina Press, 1997); and W. Todd Groce, *Mountain Rebels: East Tennessee Confederates and the Civil War, 1860–1870* (Knoxville: Univ. of Tennessee Press, 1999).
58. Goyne, *Lone Star and Double Eagle,* 179.
59. *Louisville Anzeiger,* Jan. 20, 1864. See letter 4 in chapter 3.
60. Ibid., Feb. 6, 1864.
61. Burton, *Melting Pot Soldiers,* 205.
62. *Louisville Anzeiger,* Mar. 31, 1864. See letter 9 in chapter 5.
63. Ibid., Apr. 20, 1864. See letter 10 in chapter 6.

CHAPTER 1

1. See Cozzens, *Shipwreck of Their Hopes,* for details of the battles around Chattanooga.
2. Date headings do not appear in the diary and are provided for the convenience of the reader. The nine regiments John Daeuble listed comprised the 2nd Brigade of the 3rd Division of the 4th Corps of the Army of the Cumberland. The 2nd Brigade was commanded by Ohioan and West Point graduate Brig. Gen. William B. Hazen, one of the best officers in the Union army in the West. *OR* 31, pt. 1, p. 803.
3. Daeuble mentions Companies C, E, G, and I because they consisted principally of fellow German-born men from Louisville. A few natives of Germany were also scattered in the 6th Kentucky's other companies. Reinhart, *A History of the 6th Kentucky,* 17.
4. The soldiers who were on the list of the most capable men poked fun at the others by calling them the Invalid Corps. The Invalid Corps was established in April 1863 for soldiers who could not stand the hardships of a field campaign due to physical disabilities or ill health, but who could perform other necessary duties for the army, e.g., guards, clerks, cooks, and hospital attendants. In March 1864 the name of this organization was changed to the Veteran Reserve Corps. Mark M. Boatner III, *The Civil War Dictionary,* rev. ed. (New York: David McKay, 1988), 870.
5. Moccasin Point was a peninsula of land created by the course of the Tennessee River, which flowed west above Chattanooga, bent sharply south after it passed the city, curved in a westerly direction as it approached Lookout Mountain, turned northwest, and finally turned north before reaching Brown's Ferry. Although Brown's Ferry was only about a mile and a half west of Chattanooga by land, it was approximately nine miles distant by the route of the river. Reinhart, *A History of the 6th Kentucky,* 238.
6. Daeuble was a bit off in his estimate of the number of boats and their capacity. There were fifty pontoon boats that each carried twenty-five soldiers and some crewmen, and two flatboats each carrying about fifty officers and men and a small crew. Hazen's river-borne assault force contained approximately thirteen hundred men in total. *OR* 31, pt. 1, pp. 84, 79, 90, 92.
7. Daeuble referred to this eminence by the river as Sandy's Hill. He may have confused it with Sand Mountain, which was adjacent to Raccoon Mountain, but southwest of Brown's Ferry.
8. Daeuble refers here to Sgt. Nicholas Kelly of La Grange (Company B) who was captured at Brown's Ferry—not killed. Kelly was paroled and later returned to the regiment and served out his three-year enlistment.
9. The Confederate artillery Daeuble referred to was a section of Barret's (Missouri) Battery commanded by Lt. William G. Brown; however, the artillery support was not the 34th Alabama, but possibly the 4th Alabama.

Brig. Gen. Walter C. Whitaker commanded the 2nd Brigade of the 1st Division of the 4th Corps of the Army of the Cumberland. General Whitaker of Shelbyville, Kentucky, was the principal organizer of the 6th Kentucky Volunteer Infantry Regiment and its first colonel. He won promotion to brigadier general (ranking from June 25, 1863) and left the regiment in July 1863 to command the 1st Brigade of the 1st Division of the Reserve Corps of the Army of the Cumberland. He was brevetted a major general of volunteers for his service in the Atlanta Campaign and served in the army until discharged on August 24, 1865. *OR* 31, pt. 1, pp. 225, 802; *OR* 30, pt. 1, p. 46; Reinhart, *A History of the 6th Kentucky,* 7, 195, 355.

10. Just two days before the Federal attack at Brown's Ferry, Brig. Gen. Micah Jenkins (commanding Maj. Gen. John Bell Hood's division while Hood was recovering from a wound received at Chickamauga) recalled three regiments to the east side of Lookout Mountain. Cozzens, *Shipwreck of Their Hopes,* 58.

11. There were no 13½-pounder cannon, so Daeuble probably was referring to 12-pounders that fired a projectile of that weight.

12. Fort Whitaker stood north of the Tennessee River and opposite the point of Lookout Mountain. *OR* 30, pt. 1, p. 243.

13. Maine native Maj. Gen. Oliver O. Howard commanded the 11th Corps. General Howard had lost his right arm in the battle of Seven Pines in Virginia in 1862. Boatner, *Civil War Dictionary,* 413.

14. Maj. Gen. Joseph Hooker commanded the 11th and 12th Corps that had been sent from the East to aid the besieged Army of the Cumberland. Originally part of the Army of the Potomac, these two corps became part of the Army of the Cumberland on September 25, 1863. General Hooker lost command of the huge Army of the Potomac after its disastrous defeat in the battle of Chancellorsville in May 1863. *OR* 29, pt. 1, p. 151; Boatner, *Civil War Dictionary,* 193, 194.

15. Maj. Gen. Carl Schurz commanded the 3rd Division of the 11th Corps and Brig. Gen. Adolph von Steinwehr led the corps' 2nd Division. Both generals were natives of Germany. Maj. Gen. Daniel Butterfield was Major General Hooker's chief of staff, not a division commander. There was no 1st Division in the 11th Corps. Cozzens, *Shipwreck of Their Hopes,* 73, 401; *OR* 31, pt. 1, p. 804.

16. The small 2nd Division of the 12th Corps, led by Brig. Gen. John W. Geary, had encamped for the night at Wauhatchie (about three miles southwest of Brown's Ferry) and was attacked by a brigade of South Carolinians from Maj. Gen. John Bell Hood's division, now commanded by Micah Jenkins. Geary's division repulsed the Southerners, and General Howard's two 11th Corps divisions drove off the other two enemy brigades sent to prevent any reinforcements from reaching Geary. Geary and Howard each lost about two hundred men. The 1st Division of the 12th Corps commanded by Brig. Gen. Alpheus S. Williams was not engaged in the battle because it was

guarding the Nashville and Chattanooga Railroad between Wartrace Bridge, Tennessee, and Bridgeport, Alabama. For a detailed description of the battle at and around Wauhatchie see Cozzens, *Shipwreck of Their Hopes,* 78–100.

17. Maj. Richard T. Whitaker of Shelbyville, Kentucky, was the younger brother of Brig. Gen. Walter C. Whitaker. His promotion from second lieutenant to major on March 12, 1863, disgruntled most of the officers in the regiment, especially the large number senior to him in rank at that time. He assumed command of the 6th Kentucky on September 19, 1863, after Col. George T. Shackelford of Richmond and Lt. Col. Richard C. Rockingham of Covington were both wounded during the battle of Chickamauga. Shackelford never returned to the field because of his wound and resigned his commission because of disability on August 22, 1864. Rockingham, a native of England, was killed on the second day of the battle by a shell as he lay in a field hospital. Reinhart, *A History of the 6th Kentucky,* 182, 219–20.

18. Company B was composed almost entirely of men from Oldham County and led by Capt. Richard C. Dawkins of La Grange. Provost guards were equivalent to military police and also provided security for high-ranking officers. Brig. Gen. Thomas J. Wood was a regular army officer, a native of Hart County, Kentucky, and commander of the 3rd Division of the 4th Corps. Reinhart, *A History of the 6th Kentucky,* 9; Boatner, *Civil War Dictionary,* 946.

19. Fort Palmer lay about one-half mile southwest of Fort Wood and approximately a mile west of Orchard Knob. It was named after Maj. Gen. John. M. Palmer of Illinois who had led the 2nd Division of the Left Wing of the 14th Corps (Army of the Cumberland) from December 10, 1862, to January 9, 1862, and commanded its successor 2nd Division of the newly organized 21st Corps from January 9, 1863, to October 9, 1863 (except July 15 to August 17). Palmer then headed the 1st Division of the 4th Corps until October 28, 1863, when he was elevated to command the reorganized 14th Corps. General Hazen commanded the 2nd Brigade of Palmer's divisions in both the Left Wing of the 14th Corps and in the 21st Corps. The 6th Kentucky and 41st Ohio served in Hazen's brigade the entire time the brigade was in Palmer's 2nd Division. On October 9, 1863, the Army of the Cumberland was reorganized and the 20th and 21st Corps combined into the 4th Corps under Maj. Gen. Gordon Granger. General Hazen was given command of the 2nd Brigade of the 3rd Division (led by Brig. Gen. Thomas J. Wood) of the 4th Corps. The 6th Kentucky, 41st Ohio, and 124th Ohio remained with Hazen, and were joined by the 23rd Kentucky and 6th Ohio (both formerly of Col. William Grose's brigade of Maj. Gen. John M. Palmer's division of the 21st Corps), and the 6th Indiana, 5th Kentucky, 1st Ohio, and 93rd Ohio (formerly of Col. Philemon P. Baldwin's brigade of Brig. Gen. Richard W. Johnson's division of the 20th Corps). Wiley Sword, *Mountains Touched with Fire: Chattanooga Besieged, 1863* (New York: St. Martin's Press, 1995); Boatner, *Civil War Dictionary,* 617; Reinhart, *A History of the 6th Kentucky,* 234–35.

20. Soldiers had an annual clothing allowance. If they drew clothing costing in excess of the stipulated allowance the excess was deducted from their pay. If they drew less than the allowance, they would receive the savings at the end of their enlistments. August V. Kautz, *The 1865 Customs of Service for Non-Commissioned Officers and Soldiers* (1865; rpt. Mechanicsburg, Pa.: Stackpole Books, 2001), 15–16.

21. Daeuble has most likely misidentified the regiment of the third deserter. The 15th Missouri did not belong to Hazen's brigade. It belonged to Col. Francis T. Sherman's brigade of Maj. Gen. Philip H. Sheridan's division. *OR* 32, pt. 2, p. 284.

22. Fort Wood anchored the left flank of the Federal army and jutted out eastward toward Missionary Ridge. This large redoubt was manned by Brig. Gen. Thomas J. Wood's division and Fort Palmer stood next to it. Sword, *Mountains Touched with Fire*, map 9, following p. 260.

23. Peter Cozzens states that the 24th and 28th Alabama regiments suffered almost 175 casualties, including those captured. Most of the losses were in the latter unit. For details of the battle see Cozzens, *Shipwreck of Their Hopes*, 126–35.

24. Among the wounded of the 6th Kentucky were Capt. Robert H. Armstrong of Shelby County (Company F) who was shot in the foot, and Pvt. Conrad Seibel of Louisville (Company I). Captain Armstrong completed his three-year enlistment, but Private Seibel was mortally wounded on May 27, 1864, at the battle of Pickett's Mill in Georgia.

25. The 41st Ohio suffered sixty casualties (ten killed and fifty wounded) in the attack on November 23, 1863, not eighty as Daeuble stated. Daeuble was also in error when he remarked that the 41st Ohio had more killed in action on November 23 than the 6th Kentucky at Chickamauga. The 6th suffered twelve killed in action at Chickamauga and eleven more died later from wounds. The 93rd Ohio suffered twelve killed and forty-five wounded on November 23, 1863. *OR* 31, pt. 2, 298; *OR* 30, pt. 1, p. 176.

26. Three hundred prisoners seems excessive. See note 23 above.

27. Maj. Gen. Ulysses S. Grant, overall commander at Chattanooga, ordered Maj. Gen. George H. Thomas (commander of the Army of the Cumberland) to make a reconnaissance in force to determine the Confederate strength at Orchard Knob and the small rocky ridge to its right (located about halfway between Chattanooga and the base of Missionary Ridge). Brig. Gen. August Willich's brigade and Hazen's carried out the reconnaissance in their division's front, which surprised the enemy and developed into a successful full-scale attack. *OR* 31, pt. 2, pp. 94, 254–56.

28. General Braxton Bragg's army had occupied Chattanooga until early September 1863.

29. Maj. Gen. Philip H. Sheridan commanded the 2nd Division of the 4th Corps. *OR* 31, pt. 2, pp. 802–3.

30. On November 24, 1863, three Federal divisions fighting under the command of General Hooker forced the Confederates to withdraw from Lookout Mountain and move to Missionary Ridge. See Cozzens, *Shipwreck of Their Hopes,* 159–78, for a description of the battle.

31. A native of Germany, Second Lieutenant Valentine Melcher of Company E was from New Albany, Indiana. He was wounded and captured at the battle of Stones River, and paroled on January 16, 1863, but remained confined at Camp Chase near Columbus, Ohio, until exchanged on June 12, 1863. He served in the Veteran Reserve Corps before returning to the regiment. Melcher was sent to the hospital on November 28, 1863, because of illness, and never returned to the regiment. He resigned his commission on June 20, 1864, because of disability.

32. After Sherman's late morning and early afternoon assaults failed to force Maj. Gen. Patrick R. Cleburne's reinforced division off the north slope of Missionary Ridge at Tunnel Hill, Grant ordered the Army of the Cumberland to attack and seize the Confederate fortifications along the eastern base of the ridge and halt, hoping this would relieve pressure on Sherman's front. Upon reaching the base of the ridge the Cumberlanders were raked with a murderous fire from above and charged up the steep slope without orders. General Hazen believed: "To remain there would be destruction; to fall back would also not only be so, but would entail disgrace." After the battle, General Sheridan claimed that Hazen's men hauled off cannon that were actually captured by his troops. General Hazen went to great length in his published memoirs to document that not only was Sheridan's accusation regarding the cannon false, but also that his own (Hazen's) brigade was the first to reach the crest of the ridge. The battle of Missionary Ridge was one of the most surprising Federal victories of the war. Cozzens, *Shipwreck of Their Hopes,* 247–48, 265–81; *OR* 31, pt. 2, p. 282; Hazen, *Narrative of Military Service,* 179–235.

33. Burnside had requested that reinforcements be sent to him immediately because he was low on food and ammunition and Longstreet was expected to attack him. President Lincoln had been continually pressing Grant to secure control over Knoxville and East Tennessee because of the large number of Unionists who lived there and who were being persecuted by the Confederates. Burnside did not defeat Longstreet until the latter attacked Fort Sanders (located west of Knoxville) on November 29, so Daeuble was in error as to why the order to march to Knoxville was cancelled. Cozzens, *Shipwreck of Their Hopes,* 351–52.

34. The nine regiments comprising Brig. Gen. William B. Hazen's brigade are listed in John Daeuble's diary entry for October 27–28, 1863.

35. See John Daeuble's diary entry for November 25 and related footnotes for additional information.

36. Lt. Gen. James Longstreet and his corps departed for Knoxville, Tennessee, before the fighting erupted on Lookout Mountain and

Missionary Ridge. Rentschler assumed that Longstreet and Bragg would reunite, but they did not.

37. The *Louisville Anzeiger* was Louisville's principal German language newspaper. The 1860 U.S. Census revealed Louisville's German-born population aggregated approximately 13,000 persons.

38. See note 16 above.

39. Maj. Gen. Henry W. Slocum commanded the 12th Corps; however, Slocum was not present in Chattanooga during the battles. He established his headquarters at Tullahoma, Tennessee, and the 1st Division of the 12th Corps was employed guarding the railroad west of Chattanooga. Maj. Gen. Joseph Hooker commanded the Federal units engaged at Lookout Mountain on November 24, 1863. These units consisted of two brigades of the 1st Division of the 4th Army Corps, most of the 2nd Division of the 12th Army Corps, and the 1st Division of the 15th Army Corps (Army of the Tennessee). *OR* 31, pt. 1, pp. 43, 155; *OR* 31, pt. 2, p. 314.

40. Brig. Gen. John W. Geary, commander of the 2nd Division of the 12th Corps, reported that his division suffered 138 casualties and Brig. Gen. Walter C. Whitaker's brigade of the 1st Division of the 4th Corps incurred fifty-two casualties in the battle on Lookout Mountain. Geary estimated Confederate losses at slightly more than 2,400, including 1,980 captured; however, estimates of enemy losses were often overstated. *OR* 31, pt. 2, p. 409.

CHAPTER 2

1. Maj. Gen. Ulysses S. Grant placed Maj. Gen. William T. Sherman in command of the combined relief force, which consisted of Brig. Gen. Thomas J. Wood's and Maj. Gen. Philip H. Sheridan's divisions of the 4th Corps, Maj. Gen. Oliver O. Howard's two 11th Corps divisions, one division from the 14th Corps, and two divisions from the 15th Corps. Van Horne, *History of the Army of the Cumberland,* 2:1–2.

2. Because Hazen's nine regiments had been so reduced in size by cumulative battle casualties and other reasons, he combined eight of them into two-regiment units he called battalions. Companies were also consolidated to better approximate normal strength. The editor estimates that average battalion strength was about 450 officers and men. *OR* 31, pt. 2, p. 280.

3. The Tennessee and Georgia Railroad connected Chattanooga and Knoxville.

4. Although Tennessee had seceded from the Union and joined the Confederacy, a large majority of East Tennessee's residents were opposed to secession and loyal to the Union. The percentage of secessionists in a city or county varied, and in some places secessionists were in the majority. The Confederacy maintained military and political control of East Tennessee until Major General Burnside's army arrived in Knoxville in September 1863. For more information about East Tennessee in the Civil War see Fisher, *War at Every Door.*

5. Sherman's troops mentioned here would have been the non–4th Corps troops.

6. Brig. Gen. William B. Hazen wrote to Maj. Gen. George H. Thomas's chief of staff (Brig. Gen. William D. Whipple) on or about January 8, 1864, and pointed out that his men had been on greatly reduced rations for almost four months and, "during this time the command has not been able to procure clothing necessary for its health and comfort. There have been many men during all this time shirtless and shoeless." *OR* 32, pt. 2, pp. 45–46.

7. Forty-three-year-old Cpl. Engelbert Emig mustered in on December 24, 1861, and was promoted to corporal on November 10, 1862. He was wounded at Rocky Face Ridge on May 9, 1864, and mustered out on December 31, 1864.

8. Longstreet's troops attacked Fort Sanders, located just west of the city of Knoxville, on November 29, 1863, and were soundly repulsed by Burnside's Federals. Longstreet, knowing a large Union relief force was coming up in his rear, took his bloodied corps far northeast of Knoxville.

9. Maj. Gen. John G. Foster replaced Ambrose Burnside as commander of the Department of the Ohio on December 11, 1863. Burnside had requested that he be relieved of command. *OR* 31, pt. 2, p. 385.

10. Although enlisted men were not supposed to have alcohol in camp, they sometimes violated the rules. Sergeant Elisha Brown of Company D of the 6th Kentucky wrote in his diary on January 2, 1864: "Everything quiet as a lamb. Applejack has played out and regiment is sober." Elisha S. Brown diary, Jan. 2, 1864.

11. The fighting Daeuble mentioned occurred northeast of Blain's Cross Roads between troops of the 23rd Corps commanded by Maj. Gen. John. G. Parke and Confederate cavalry under Maj. Gen. William Martin.

12. Capt. Lyman Bridges' 2nd Illinois Light Battery, Capt. Cullen Bradley's 6th Ohio Light Battery, and Pennsylvania (Independent) Light Artillery, Battery B, comprised the 3rd Division's artillery The editor is uncertain as to which battery Daeuble referred. *OR* 31, pt. 3, p. 551.

13. Enlistments of soldiers who joined the army for three years in 1861 and early 1862 would be soon be expiring, and to encourage these men to reenlist for the duration of the war the army offered a cash bounty of $400 (payable in installments), a thirty-day furlough, free transportation home, and the privilege of calling themselves "veteran volunteers." Regiments in which at least 75 percent of the eligible men re-enlisted were able to remain with their original unit, and Veteran Volunteer was added to the regiment's designation. The 6th Kentucky did not veteranize. Forty-one of its men re-enlisted and transferred to the 4th Kentucky Mounted Infantry Regiment after the 6th Kentucky mustered out of service. Reinhart, *A History of the 6th Kentucky*, 269, 364.

14. See note 12 above.

15. Total bounty was $400, not $402.

16. The divisions referred to are the 2nd Division commanded by Maj. Gen. Philip H. Sheridan and the 3rd Division commanded by Brig. Gen. Thomas J. Wood. Maj. Gen. Ambrose Burnside's Army of the Ohio consisted of the 9th and 23rd Corps, and his headquarters were at Knoxville, Tennessee.

17. Rentschler incorrectly stated that the purpose of the mission was to reinforce (Maj. Gen. John G.) Foster. The purpose was to reinforce Maj. Gen. Ambrose E. Burnside. General Foster replaced Burnside as commander of the Department of the Ohio on December 11, 1863. Longstreet was Lt. Gen. James Longstreet, commander of a corps that belonged to the Army of Northern Virginia.

18. The top generals were Maj. Gen Ulysses S. Grant, commander of the Military Division of the Mississippi (comprising the Departments of the Ohio, the Tennessee, and the Cumberland), and Maj. Gen. George H. Thomas, commander of the Army of the Cumberland.

19. See note 8 above.

20. Albrecht von Wallenstein (1583–1634) served as a commanding general for Holy Roman Emperor Ferdinand II during the Thirty Years War (1618–48). During the Danish phase of the war he offered to raise an army of fifty thousand men for Ferdinand. The Emperor proposed Wallenstein raise half that number. Wallenstein replied that "twenty thousand men would die of hunger, whereas fifty thousand would enable him to levy requisitions as he wished." Captain B. H. Liddell Hart, *Great Captains Unveiled,* introd. by Russell F. Weigley (1927; rpt. New York: Da Capo Press, 1996), 170–74.

21. Rentschler did not exaggerate the lack of adequate clothing and shoes for the troops. Reinhart, *A History of the 6th Kentucky,* 270.

22. Blain's Cross Roads [not Blain's Bluff Cross Roads as Rentschler mistakenly calls it] lay northeast of Knoxville.

23. Jefferson Street was a principal east-west street in Louisville and was approximately six miles long at this time.

24. The identities of the "higher authorities" Rentschler refers to are not known, but probably included Maj. Gen. John G. Foster, department commander.

25. The temperature dropped well below zero on January 1, 1864, and stayed there for about two weeks. Even water in containers froze by a fire. Reinhart, *A History of the 6th Kentucky,* 270.

26. Louis H. Brauser of Louisville mustered in on December 24, 1861, and was promoted from corporal to first sergeant on July 1, 1864. He mustered out on December 31, 1864. Pvt. George Friedrich Dittrich of Cincinnati mustered in on December 31, 1861, and mustered out on December 31, 1864. Shorts (shortening) was used to make cornbread when eggs and butter were not available. E-mail to editor dated January 11, 2002, from historian Brandon Slone, Kentucky Department of Military Affairs.

27. First Lt. Lorenz Amon (Company E) of Louisville, mustered in on December 24, 1861, and was promoted as follows: February 1, 1862, from

sergeant to first sergeant; May 23, 1862, to second lieutenant; and November 8, 1862, to first lieutenant. He mustered out on December 31, 1864. Another German native, First Lt. John Sensbach (Company E) of Louisville mustered in on December 24, 1861, and resigned back on November 8, 1862, because his understanding of English proved inadequate to carry out his responsibilities as an officer.

28. The names of the first two men to re-enlist are not known. Also see note 13 above.

29. The identity of the several newspapers referred to is unknown. Perhaps the complaint resulted from a lack of any significant offensive action in Tennessee or Kentucky in December and to the date of the letter.

30. Reporters and some soldiers (like Rentschler) wrote letters to local and/or national newspapers telling of battles and other experiences. However, not every general or colonel or regiment had his or its own correspondent. Some officers used reporters for self-aggrandizement and some soldiers no doubt exaggerated in some of their letters.

31. Hannibal led Carthage's army during the Second Punic War (218–201 B.C.), conquered Spain and parts of Italy, and his army's crossing of the Alps on a march from Spain to Rome is still recognized as one of the greatest military feats in history. Scipio commanded the Roman army that drove Carthage's army from Spain and Italy (210–203 B.C.), and defeated Hannibal at the battle of Zema (202 B.C.) in North Africa, ending the war in 201 B.C. *Encyclopedia of World Biography,* 2nd ed., sr. ed. Paula K. Byers (Detroit: Gale, 1998), 7:128–29, 14:61–62.

32. Rentschler refers to the public's short memory and uses a fable to illustrate it. The editor does not know the name or author of the fable.

33. A Swabian is a person from the Kingdom of Württemberg, Rentschler's place of birth.

34. The origin of the story about Pfeffer is unknown, but he uses it to illustrate the virtue of frankness in reporting.

35. This story is used to point out that people are being deceived by newspaper reports.

36. Each regiment was authorized to have a chaplain who held the rank of captain. The 6th Kentucky's chaplain, Capt. James J. Johnston, a Methodist minister and brother of Capt. Isaac N. Johnston of Company H, mustered in on September 10, 1862, and resigned on September 23, 1863. Chaplain Johnston's resignation letter stated "from past experience . . . I can accomplish little or no good by remaining in the army in my present capacity." Reinhart, *A History of the 6th Kentucky,* 234.

37. See note 25 above.

38. Loudon lay on the west bank of the Tennessee River approximately twenty-nine miles southwest of Knoxville.

39. See note 20 in chapter 1.

40. Rentschler discloses how the soldiers were mistreated by certain persons in the army. Whether the "company savings" were ever distributed pursuant

to General Hazen's order is unknown. Maj. Gen. John G. Foster wrote to General Henry W. Halleck, general-in-chief, on January 11, 1864, and requested authority to order the chief commissary of the Department of the Ohio "to pay the troops the value in money of the rations to which they have been entitled, but which they have not received." The editor could not find General Hazen's order or a reply from General Halleck to General Foster. *OR* 32, pt. 2, p. 63.

41. Rentschler noted some improvements in the delivery of rations; however, inefficiency and corruption remained in the distribution system.

42. The 6th Kentucky and its division were still encamped at Blain's Cross Roads, about twenty miles northeast of Knoxville.

43. Rentschler's high opinion of the 41st Ohio was justified. West Point graduate Brig. Gen. William B. Hazen was the 41st Ohio's first colonel and he trained the regiment according to his high standards. He favored these Ohioans while they served in his brigade.

44. The 28th Kentucky Volunteer Infantry Regiment was organized at Louisville and New Haven, Kentucky, and its companies mustered in between October 10, 1861, and May 6, 1862. Although a member of the Army of the Cumberland, it was not attached to a brigade at this time and was posted at Clarksville, Tennessee. Rentschler probably mentioned it because it contained a number of German Americans from Louisville. Frederick H. Dyer, comp., *A Compendium of the War of the Rebellion* (Des Moines: Dyer Publishing, 1908), 3:1209.

CHAPTER 3

1. Capt. William Frank of Louisville was a native of Magdeburg in Prussia and served as an engineer officer in the Prussian army prior to his immigration to the United States in 1853. Frank mustered in on December 24, 1861, as a first lieutenant (Company I) and was wounded on December 31, 1862, at the battle of Stones River. He was promoted to captain of Company E on September 1, 1863, and served his full three-year enlistment. Reinhart, *A History of the 6th Kentucky*, 48.

2. Cpl. August Eversberg of Company E, a Louisville resident, mustered in on December 24, 1861. Eversberg reenlisted and was detached to General Hazen's headquarters on August 31, 1864. He was captured and exchanged; he died in the *Sultana* steamboat explosion on April 27, 1865, while on his way home.

3. Charles Grunewald of Company E mustered in on December 24, 1861, as a private. A resident of New Albany, Indiana, Grunewald was wounded on December 31, 1862, at Stones River, and promoted to principal musician on July 1, 1864. He reenlisted but mustered out on January 2, 1865.

4. Bridgeport and Stevenson in northeastern Alabama were located on the Nashville and Chattanooga Railroad and were the closest Federal supply bases to Chattanooga, Tennessee.

5. Although supplies and equipment began arriving in Chattanooga after the railroad was reopened, transportation difficulties deterred the delivery of those supplies to the troops operating in East Tennessee.
6. The spring campaign would not begin until May 1864.
7. At this time, the Tennessee River began northeast of Loudon, Tennessee, at the confluence of the Little Tennessee River, flowed southwest past Chattanooga, Tennessee, into northeastern Alabama, then turned northwest and re-entered Tennessee at the Mississippi-Alabama state line and finally flowed in a northerly direction until it emptied into the Ohio River. Many years after the war ended, the portion of the Holston River that ran from the French Broad River (located about four miles east of Knoxville) down to the confluence of the Little Tennessee River was designated as part of the Tennessee River.
8. Lack of support from home was a major concern for the soldiers in the field. The now well-known dangers and horrors of war, wartime employment opportunities, and—in Kentucky and some other places—changed war aims, deterred most military aged men from enlisting in the army. See chapter 2, note 13.
9. Maj. Gen. George H. Thomas commanded the Army of the Cumberland, the largest Federal army in the Military Division of the Mississippi.
10. Hazen, *Narrative of Military Service,* 240.
11. Pvt. John Lang of Company E mustered in on December 24, 1861. The Louisville resident reenlisted and transferred to the 4th Kentucky Mounted Infantry after the regiment mustered out.
12. Sheridan's and Wood's divisions of the 4th Corps and Col. Edward McCook's 2nd Division of its Cavalry Corps were being sent to Dandridge for the winter because it was thought that forage and subsistence was available there. *OR* 31, pt. 1, p. 22.
13. Federal and Confederate cavalry corps both contained artillery batteries. Cavalry units from Brig. Gen. Washington L. Elliott's Army of the Cumberland Cavalry Corps and Brig. Gen. Samuel Sturgis's Army of the Ohio Cavalry Corps became engaged with two divisions of Longstreet's infantry plus artillery on January 16. *OR* 32, pt. 1, pp. 79–80, 81–82, 93.
14. Part of Hood's infantry division and Maj. Gen. William T. Martin's cavalry (dismounted) made a strong attack along the advance Federal line and Maj. Gen. Granger ordered a retreat rather than bringing on a general engagement. It appears that the 6th Kentucky was not attacked. *OR* 32, pt. 1, pp. 79–80, 81–82, 93.
15. The Mudroad (mud road) was most likely the wagon road, as opposed to being posted on the railroad.
16. The editor did not learn why this move was made, but probably was made to a superior defensive or observation position.
17. Rentschler is wrong about General Braxton Bragg's location. The Confederate Army of Tennessee remained at Dalton, Georgia, about thirty

miles south of Chattanooga. President Jefferson Davis accepted General Bragg's resignation as commander of the Army of Tennessee on November 30, 1863, and Bragg was later appointed advisor to President Davis. Lt. Gen. William J. Hardee was appointed temporary commander of the army at Dalton. *OR* 31, pt. 2, p. 682.

18. Brig. Gen. August Willich's brigade of Brig. Gen. Thomas J. Wood's division moved to Maryville, Tennessee, not General Hazen's. Most of Hazen's command moved to Lenoir, about thirty miles southwest of Knoxville. Three of Hazen's regiments were each posted at towns on the East Tennessee and Georgia Railroad, approximately eight, fourteen and eighteen miles southwest of Knoxville. Lenoir was also on this railroad. Reinhart, *A History of the 6th Kentucky*, 272–73.

19. The 1,670-foot-long railroad bridge across the Tennessee River at Loudon had been destroyed by the Rebels on September 2, 1863. Gerald L. Augustus, *The Loudon County Area of East Tennessee in the War 1861–1865* (Paducah, Ky.: Turner Publishing, 2000), 3, 34.

20. *Floribus* is a Latin word meaning "blossom."

21. A sutler was a civilian appointed to sell food (butter, pies, cookies, etc.) and other items to the soldiers. He normally followed the regiment and set up shop near the unit's camp. Boatner, *Civil War Dictionary*, 822.

22. Only Companies A and C were mustered out in September 1864; their three-year enlistments would end on September 9, 1864.

23. Forty-one soldiers from the 6th Kentucky transferred to the 4th Kentucky Mounted Infantry Regiment as veteran volunteers in February and March 1865. Reinhart, *A History of the 6th Kentucky*, 364.

24. A $100 bounty was payable to soldiers in many units who were organized early in the war. It was payable at the end of the enlistment or death, but reenlistees received it earlier. The $400 reenlistment bounty was paid as follows: $60 at reenlistment; $50 at the first pay day after two months, six months, twelve months, eighteen months, twenty-four months, and thirty months; and forty dollars at the end of thirty-six months. If the war were to end before the enlistment was up the unpaid balance of the bounty was to be paid at muster out. In the event of the soldier's death, the balance due was to be paid to the soldier's heirs. The bounty was substantial, considering a private's pay was only thirteen dollars per month. Kautz, *Customs of Service*, 17–18.

25. Hazen's brigade was mostly at Lenoir and none of its regiments were at Maryville.

26. Rentschler is incorrect here. The 1st Division of the 4th Army Corps was not assigned to the Army of the Ohio, and it was commanded by Maj. Gen. David S. Stanley, not Brig. Gen. Richard W. Johnson. Johnson commanded the 1st Division of the 14th Corps. *OR* 32, pt. 2, pp. 283, 287.

27. The editor is uncertain as to the identity of "all."

28. First Lt. John L. Chilton (Company H) of Port Royal in Henry County mustered in on December 24, 1861. Lt. Chilton was detached to the

brigade commissary as assistant commissary of subsistence from March 10, 1863, to September 24, 1864. He mustered out on December 31, 1864.

29. Rentschler incorrectly identified East Chickamauga Creek as the Chickamauga River. The battle of Chickamauga (September 19 and 20, 1863) received its name from this creek.

30. Soldiers cut down trees and took fence rails for their fires.

31. Johann Wolfgang Goethe (1749–1832) is considered one of the greatest German men of letters, and his complex poetic drama *Faust: A Tragedy* is his most famous work. Faust is the story of a German necromancer and astrologer who sold his soul to the devil in exchange for knowledge and power. The fire pool is in Hell and Rentschler is most likely referring to lines from the scene "A Walpurgis Night," which translate as, "By thousands sputter out sparks of fire," and "A hundred fires are burning tier upon tier." Rentschler demonstrates his knowledge of literature as well as military history.

32. Capt. Snow may have been Capt. William Snow of Hamilton County, who organized Company C of Brazelton's 3rd Tennessee Cavalry Battalion CSA, and after his discharge formed Snow's Scouts. Zella Armstrong, *History of Hamilton County and Chattanooga, Tennessee* (1940; rpt. Johnson City, Tenn.: Overmountain Press, 1993), 2:295, 270.

33. The roster of the 3rd Tennessee Cavalry Regiment does not include a Major Baird, only a Pvt. Samuel Baird. Perhaps Rentschler has the rank, name, or regiment wrong.

34. Maj. Gen. Joseph Wheeler commanded all the cavalry in the Confederate Army of Tennessee.

35. Roberts is unidentified except by context.

36. The editor was unable to determine the veracity of Rentschler's account of a man named Roberts killing a Robert Carter. Some very prominent Unionist Carters were William B. Carter, Brig. Gen Samuel P. Carter, and Brig. Gen. James P. T. Carter, three brothers born in Carter County in East Tennessee. Oliver O. Temple, *East Tennessee and the Civil War* (1899; rpt. Johnson City, Tenn.: Overmountain Press, 1995), 447; Goodspeed Publishing Co., *History of Tennessee: Thirty East Tennessee Counties* (1887; rpt. Greenville, S.C.: Southern Historical Press, 1991), 1291–92.

37. The lieutenant is unidentified except by context. Revenge killings took place on both sides. Capt. George W. Lewis wrote in his history of the 124th Ohio regiment that he overheard one colonel of a veteranized Tennessee regiment tell his men leaving on furlough: "Take your arms with you; you will not be wanted here for thirty days. Go home and avenge the deaths of your fathers and brothers." George W. Lewis, *Campaigns of the 124th Regiment Ohio Volunteer Infantry* (Akron: Werner, 1887), 129.

38. Col. Eli Long commanded the 2nd Brigade of the 2nd Division (cavalry) of the Army of the Cumberland. He was a native of Kentucky. *OR* 31, pt. 1, p. 36; Boatner, *Civil War Dictionary,* 490.

39. A pontoon bridge was constructed from flat-bottomed boats.

40. Dipping is the act of taking snuff.

41. The water was supposedly made bitter by Federal troops fording nearby Sweetwater Creek on their way to Knoxville.

42. Rentschler is wrong in saying there was only one Unionist in Sweetwater. Maryanne Upton, circulation supervisor at the Sweetwater Public Library, advised the editor in a letter dated May 21, 2001, that there were three very prominent families there who were pro-Union, and the current county historian estimated that the population in Sweetwater was about evenly divided in sympathy for the Union and the Confederacy. Dr. Franklin Bogart and Dr. Richard Francis Scruggs both lived in Sweetwater during the war. Dr. Bogart had relatives who served in the Union army, but the editor was unable to determine with certainty either doctor's loyalty. William B. Lenoir, *The History of Sweetwater Valley, Tennessee* (Baltimore: Regional Pub. Co., 1976), 86, 260–63, 346–47; *Monroe County Tennessee Heritage 1819–1997* (Monroe County Heritage Book Committee, 1997), 63; Sarah G. Cox Sands, *History of Monroe County, Tennessee,* vol. 3, (Baltimore: Gateway Press, 1989), 456–57, 459.

43. Sexual morals decreased on both sides during the war, not just in the South. The principal reason for an increase in prostitution was that many of the women needed the money to survive. Some lacked skills to earn a living, while some pitifully low-paid factory women supplemented their income to support themselves, and in some cases their children. Mary Elizabeth Massey, *Women in the Civil War* (Lincoln: Univ. of Nebraska Press, 1966), 262–63; Wiley, *Life of Billy Yank,* 257–62.

44. See note 1 above regarding Captain Frank.

45. Col. William P. Sanders led about fifteen hundred men on a mounted raid into East Tennessee in June 1863 and upon reaching Lenoir burned the railroad depot and a large brick building containing weapons and military supplies. A local history indicates that the mill was saved from destruction because Dr. Benjamin Ballard Lenoir moved among the Union soldiers giving secret Masonic signs. There are many stories about lives being spared or aid given to enemy persons during the war because they identified themselves as Masons. An Arch-Secesh is a zealous secessionist. Dr. Benjamin B. Lenoir was one of twelve children of William B. Lenoir, who settled the area in the early 1800s. Augustus, *Loudon County Area,* 27–29.

46. The 1,670-foot-long Loudon railroad bridge was burned by members of the 5th Tennessee Cavalry CSA on September 2, 1863, to deny its use to Burnside's advancing army. A Confederate pontoon bridge was discovered a short distance upstream and used by the Federals until its removal on October 28, 1863, when Longstreet's corps was on the move to Knoxville. The Federals shipped the pontoon bridge to Knoxville by railroad where it was utilized. The Union army used boats to ferry troops and supplies across the Tennessee River at Loudon until the railroad bridge was completed on April 13, 1864. Augustus, *Loudon County Area,* 3, 34–35, 61, 108, 109.

47. Brig. Gen. Samuel Beatty was a Pennsylvania native who began his Civil War service with the 19th Ohio Infantry. Boatner, *Civil War Dictionary*, 54.

48. General Wood was on leave from January 8 to February 12, 1864. Boatner, *Civil War Dictionary*, 946.

49. Maj. Gen. John G. Foster was relieved as commander of the Army of the Ohio on February 9, 1864, due to an injury. Maj. Gen. George H. Thomas initiated the order that Foster issued before Foster was relieved. Maj. Gen. John M. Schofield, the former commander of the Department of the Missouri, succeeded Foster. *OR* 32, pt. 2, pp. 358, 271.

50. Soldiers sometimes referred to a battle as a dance or a ball.

51. Longstreet had sent cavalry to scout near Sevierville at this time but his whole army was not there. Longstreet's headquarters at this time were at Russellville, Tennessee. *OR* 32, pt. 2, p. 611.

CHAPTER 4

1. January 1, 1864, was the coldest day of the entire year.

2. The assistant inspector general for Grant's department reported that the appearance of General Wood's division was poor because of "bad clothing" and there were many "bad shoes and missing bayonets." Also, the records were generally far behind. *OR* 32, pt. 2, p. 484

3. Shooks Gap was located approximately ten miles southeast of Knoxville.

4. The principal festivity in Louisville on Washington's Birthday was the dedication of a base for a monument to the memory of the brave Union soldiers who died while serving their country. The base was sixteen feet by sixteen feet. The dedication ceremony took place at Cave Hill Cemetery after a long procession from downtown Louisville. The *Louisville Journal* reported on February 23, 1864: "The streets were thronged with people along the entire line and when they entered the Cemetery, the grounds were completely covered with anxious spectators hustling and crowding forward to secure a position near the spot where the great monument is to be erected." Prof. William Hailman, a former major of the 6th Kentucky, served as master of ceremonies, and one of the speeches was given in German. Some of Louisville's Germans initiated the movement to erect a monument to the fallen Union soldiers. The monument never advanced beyond the base, because some people felt any monies collected should instead be used for aid to soldiers' widows and orphans, and postwar prejudices against Union veterans that developed because of a disaffection with the government's interference in what most Kentuckians felt was their state's rights with regard to the institution of slavery and voting rights, and sympathy for the harsh treatment of the South during Reconstruction. *Louisville Journal*, Feb. 23, 1864; *Louisville Daily Democrat*, Feb. 23, 1864.

5. Rentschler compares the plight of the soldiers in East Tennessee to that of the Israelites whom Moses led out of Egypt into the desert, and who

suffered from severe hunger until God provided them with manna (bread that tasted like wafers made from honey) from Heaven. Exodus 16:1–4, 31.

6. Rentschler likens the hard bread (called "hard tack" or "crackers") provided by the army with "terrible Motzoth," an unleavened bread in the form of large crackers, typically square and corrugated, and eaten by Jews during Passover.

7. The regiment's chaplain resigned in September 1863 and Sunday prayer services were discontinued. Thus, the men lost track of time. Rentschler quips about not spoiling their Sunday best; they had only old and torn uniforms, and worn-out shoes at this time. Reinhart, *A History of the 6th Kentucky*, 275.

8. Rentschler explains how coats worn by several grades of officers differed, and why some officers wore uniform coats signifying lower rank than they actually held.

9. General (George H.) Thomas was a major general, one rank higher than brigadier general.

10. The brigade was sent to Shooks Gap [called Shuck's by Rentschler], approximately ten miles southeast of Knoxville. Rentschler incorrectly states the direction as northeast.

11. See John Daeuble diary entries for January 15–17, 1864.

12. The brigade did not move to Bristol, Virginia.

13. Rentschler was a clerk in General Hazen's headquarters, so he got to stay in Knoxville at this time.

14. Hazen's brigade did not return to Knoxville until April 7, 1864, and then it just passed through the city on its way back to the Chattanooga area to prepare for a spring offensive into Georgia. Until April 7 the brigade mostly marched around northeast of Knoxville looking for Longstreet's army, and went as far as Bean's Station and Morristown. The 4th Corps was not sent to reinforce the Army of the Potomac as Rentschler feared. Reinhart, *A History of the 6th Kentucky*, 275.

15. The *Knoxville Whig and Rebel Ventilator* was published by East Tennessean William G. Brownlow, a former Methodist clergyman often called "Parson" Brownlow. He was a highly vocal opponent of secession and had been persecuted by the Rebels for his outspoken views. Boatner, *Civil War Dictionary*, 93.

16. Rentschler paraphrases much of Brownlow's article and omits some parts. The full text can be found in Steven V. Ash, ed., *Secessionists and Other Scoundrels: Selections from Parson Brownlow's Book* (Baton Rouge: Louisiana State Univ. Press, 1999), 81–86.

17. A large majority of the people in East Tennessee was pro-Union and voted overwhelmingly against secession from the Union. The majority also wanted to separate from the rest of the state and remain in the Union, but Confederate forces in the area precluded this. Consequently, most of these Unionists suffered terribly at the hands of the Confederates in their state until General Burnside arrived with his army in September 1863. For more

information about East Tennessee in the Civil War see Fisher, *War at Every Door*; and Groce, *Mountain Rebels*.

18. Many East Tennessee men left the region and joined the Federal army, while others hid out in the mountains to avoid being forced to fight in the Confederate army. Women and children left behind were subjected to terrible privations. The estimate of 25,000 Union men who forced their way into loyal states is Rentschler's and does not appear in Brownlow's article. Peter Wallenstein, in his article, "Helping Save the Union: The Social Origins, Wartime Experiences, and Military Impact of White Union Troops from East Tennessee," estimates that it is likely that more than 30,000 white troops from East Tennessee served in the Federal army. *The Civil War in Appalachia: Collected Essays,* ed. Kenneth W. Noe and Shannon Wilson (Knoxville: Univ. of Tennessee Press, 1997), 17.

19. The words in this sentence following the semicolon are solely Rentschler's.

20. West Virginia split off from Virginia during the war and joined the Union as the thirty-fifth state on June 20, 1863. The East refers to present-day Virginia.

21. Rentschler often paraphrases Brownlow's article; Rentschler's added comments are indicated by < >.

22. The populations of some areas of mountainous Eastern Kentucky contained very strong Unionist sentiment, while others favored the Southern cause. Hambleton Tapp and James C. Klotter, *Kentucky: Decades of Discord 1865–1900* (Frankfort: Kentucky Historical Society, 1977), 7.

23. Brownlow used the word "State," not South, in his article.

24. Brownlow likens East Tennessee to Switzerland because of its physical features (as described in paragraph two of this letter).

25. The town of Knoxville was laid out in 1794 and its University of East Tennessee received its charter in 1807. Its 1860 population approximated six thousand. Ash, *Secessionists and Other Scoundrels,* 83.

26. Rentschler, no doubt, excludes East Tennessee's secessionists from the "warmest little group that exists in America."

CHAPTER 5

1. Confederate casualties in the November 29, 1863, attack on Fort Sanders by Knoxville were reported as 129 killed, 458 wounded, and 226 missing, for a total of 813. Some reported as wounded died later. After the battle the Federals buried their slain opponents in shallow mass graves. Some corpses only had a few inches of dirt spread over them. Ellen House wrote on December 1, 1863: "and the stench is horrible, particularly from the hospitals and there are one hundred and fifty of them. Many draft and other animals that died on the roads between Chattanooga and Knoxville lay unburied. Also, many animals died from starvation and strain during the Confederate siege of Chattanooga, and the Confederate killed in the battles

there were not buried with as much care as the Federals gave to their own dead." *OR* 31, pt. 1, p. 475; Daniel E. Sutherland, ed., *A Very Violent Rebel* (Knoxville: Univ. of Tennessee Press, 1996), 57.

2. Official records do not indicate any "stone in the way [enemy force]" that caused the 3rd Division move back to New Market from Morristown.

3. Subsequent to the date of Rentschler's letter no major battles were fought in East Tennessee. The fighting there would consist of actions between Federal soldiers and Rebel guerillas, and Unionist civilians and Rebel civilians. See Fisher, *War at Every Door,* for more information about this subject.

4. The 1st Division of the 4th Corps did not march to the relief of Burnside at Knoxville and on February 21, 1864, was attached to Maj. Gen. John M. Palmer's 14th Corps for a reconnaissance in force toward Dalton, Georgia. Hazen's brigade had served in Palmer's division in the battles of Stones River and Chickamauga, and during the Tullahoma campaign. *OR* 32, pt. 1, pp. 422–27.

5. Rentschler has the division designations reversed. The 2nd Division was at Loudon and the 3rd Division at New Market.

6. Capt. Henry Richards of the 93rd Ohio, Hazen's brigade, wrote in a letter to his sister: "Everything in this Department seems to be demoralized, and our division that had showed such good discipline is fast becoming contaminated." Richards added: "there was some satisfaction in being a soldier under [Rosecrans,] but I am fast becoming disgusted with the situation of things here." Richards felt there was a lack of organization in the department; that military affairs had been loosely managed, and those in command would not let the soldiers fight. (See note 4 in chapter 3.) The frequent change in the department's commander no doubt contributed to the problems. Henry Richards, *Letters of Captain Henry Richards of the Ninety-Third Ohio Infantry* (Cincinnati: Press of Wrightson, 1883), 29, 31.

7. The threat to Kentucky was real. During February 1864, Lt. Gen. James Longstreet proposed invading Kentucky in letters to Robert E. Lee (commander of the Army of Northern Virginia) and James A. Seddon (Confederate secretary of war). *OR* 32, pt. 2, pp. 653, 790, 809.

8. "Them" refers to the Army of the Ohio. Marcellus states in act 1, scene 4, of William Shakespeare's play *Hamlet:* "Something is rotten in the State of Denmarke."

9. Rentschler praises the Army of the Cumberland and predicts its victorious future once its component divisions are reunited. Maj. Gen. George H. Thomas was physically stout and Rentschler calls him "Fat George" here.

10. General Hazen was a tough disciplinarian and required more drill than most other commanders, which brought criticism from his troops, but the officers and men under his command knew he was a dedicated and competent leader who would not leave them if danger lurked.

11. Some officers returned to the army after their discharges and Rentschler cites some of the reasons.

12. Rentschler scolds those able-bodied men who remain safe at home rather than serving in the army for the Union cause, and the smell of the grocer's soul was probably that of pungent Limburger cheese. He used the German word *Kramer* for this theoretical person, which means small shopkeeper or grocer.

13. Many dishonest contractors, combined with significant corruption in the government's and the army's procurement and distribution systems, caused the soldiers much suffering by delivery of shoddy equipment, clothing, shoes, and rotten food. This situation endangered soldiers' lives and lowered morale.

14. Rentschler may have made up this story to illustrate his point.

15. The cattle suffered from lack of forage and starved to death on the march, so the butcher selected them first to feed the soldiers.

16. Sanitary goods included food, clothing, bandages, cordials, delicacies, and other items, that either supplemented or were not provided to the soldiers by the army. The United States Sanitary Commission was a relief organization operated by civilians. Boatner, *Civil War Dictionary,* 720.

17. The source of the saying Rentschler quotes is unknown.

18. The five German companies Rentschler mentions were Company E of the 5th Kentucky Infantry and Companies C, E, G, and I of the 6th Kentucky Infantry. The vast majority of the men in these companies were from Louisville. The 5th Kentucky was also known as the Louisville Legion.

19. Prejudice against foreigners (except possibly some from England, Scotland, and the Scotch-Irish) was common in the army and society in general at this time. In the mid-1850s a nativist movement aimed at keeping Catholics and foreigners from voting and holding political office swept many parts of the country. Although the American Party, whose members were called Know-Nothings, was virtually dead by 1861, prejudices remained. See Burton's *Melting Pot Soldiers: The Union's Ethnic Regiments* for additional information about prejudice against foreigners in the Union army.

20. The German word for a German is *Deutsch.* Many Americans used a corrupted form of this word and called Germans "Dutch" or "Dutchmen."

21. Rentschler points out that soldiers from the free states of the North appeared more prejudiced against the Germans than those from Kentucky (a slave state). Northern abolitionists who wanted to free the slaves did not view blacks or Germans (or Irish) as equal to native-born or old-stock Americans, even those who were risking their lives fighting for the Union cause.

22. The editor is not certain of the identity of the general, but he may have been Brig. Gen. August Willich.

23. While Gottfried Rentschler may have observed Union-loyal Kentuckians treating Negroes better than the Free States Americans did, his assertion that they did not call them Niggers is untrue. This derogatory term was in common use by Kentuckians, and Rentschler sometimes used it himself. See letter 11 in chapter 6 and letter 21 in chapter 11.

24. While tolerating prejudicial acts directed at them by native-born Americans and other ethnic groups, Germans had some prejudices of their own. They felt that they were products of a superior culture and were better soldiers than anyone else. Historian William L. Burton observed that Germans and members of other ethnic groups sometimes interpreted valid criticism and acts based on reasons other than ethnicity as being unjust and prejudiced. Biases and friction attributed to national origin were often based on political, religious, cultural, or other differences between the parties. Regardless of ethnic differences and prejudices, the native Germans in the 6th Kentucky and the vast majority elsewhere in the Federal army fought for their adopted country, hoping for better times. Burton, *Melting Pot Soldiers,* 200ff.

25. Despite Gottfried's belief that the mixing of Germans and Americans in the army would not be beneficial to either group, social and political gains were made by German Americans after the war. Germans were quick to point out that they had supported their adopted country in its time of need, and should be accepted as Americans. Germans also became more Americanized and many gave up the idea of creating a separate German society in America. Bruce Levine, *The Spirit of 1848: German Immigrants, Labor Conflict, and the Coming of the Civil War* (Urbana: Univ. of Illinois Press, 1992), 264–65.

26. Most operations performed by surgeons during the war were amputations. Three-fourths of the men wounded in the Civil War received a gunshot wound to the extremities, and about one out of six of these wounds required limb removal. A Minié bullet fired from a musket could not only fracture a bone, but the slug might also crush two or three inches of it making immediate amputation of the limb necessary. Infections also made some amputations necessary. Faye Lewellen, "Limbs Made and Unmade by War," *America's Civil War* (Sept. 1995): 38–39.

27. Rentschler uses sarcasm in his advice to women about their husbands.

28. Rentschler also provides advice to soldiers about women, followed by a quip.

29. The 3rd Division did not march to the Cumberland Gap.

30. Pvt. John Foerster of Louisville mustered in on December 24, 1861, and had been wounded at the battle of Shiloh on April 7, 1862. He mustered out at the end of his three-year enlistment.

31. No conscripts joined the regiment as a result of Lt. Amon's and Pvt. Foerster's mission to Louisville.

32. Knoxville resident Ellen House penned on December 1, 1863: "The city is completely ruined, scarcely a fence standing. The sidewalks are like a stable yard, and the stench is horrible." Sutherland, *Very Violent Rebel,* 57.

33. The members of Sheridan's and Wood's divisions of the Army of the Cumberland were proud of their army's stellar record of successes (Stones River, the Tullahoma campaign, and the battles around Chattanooga) and wanted to be reunited with it at Chattanooga. Rivalries between members of different organizations, including corps and armies, were strong and

202

NOTES TO PAGES 71–72

sometimes erupted into verbal and physical conflicts when they inter-mixed. See Bell Irwin Wiley's *Life of Billy Yank,* pages 320–27, for additional information regarding intra-service rivalries.

34. The Army of the Ohio consisted of only one corps (the 23rd) at this time, while the Army of the Cumberland contained three corps—the 4th, 14th and 20th. The Army of the Cumberland was successor to the original Army of the Ohio commanded by Maj. Gen. Don Carlos Buell. In a reorganiza-tion on October 24, 1862, Buell was replaced by Maj. Gen. William S. Rosecrans, and the Army of the Ohio was redesignated the 14th Army Corps, but soon became known as the Army of the Cumberland, because it was in a reconstituted Department of the Cumberland. The Department of the Ohio had ceased to exist on March 11, 1862, when it merged with the reorganized Federal Department of the Mississippi, but was revived on August 19, 1862, and included Illinois, Indiana, Ohio, Michigan, Wisconsin (until September 6), and Kentucky east of the Tennessee River, including the Cumberland Gap. The 23rd Army Corps was created on April 27, 1863, from regiments stationed in Kentucky and did not have a combat record to match the Army of the Cumberland. Most Cumberlanders loved Rosecrans, despite the defeat at Chickamauga. *OR* 16, pt. 2, pp. 641–42; *OR* 5, p. 54; *OR* 16, pt. 2, pp. 374–75. *OR* 23, pt. 2, p. 283.

35. Officers wore small rectangular pieces of material on the shoulders of their coats that displayed their rank. These were called shoulder straps. Rentschler makes fun of the transformation that seemed to take place when a soldier received his shoulder straps and believes the higher the rank, the more insecure and jealous an officer becomes.

36. The trestle bridge was completed on April 13, 1864. *OR* 32, pt. 2, p. 385; *OR,* series 3, pt. 5, p. 941.

37. The Tennessee and Georgia Railroad connected Chattanooga and Knoxville.

38. The 6th Kentucky and its brigade departed from Knoxville on February 24, 1864, and from February 27 until March 18 operated south of the Holston River between New Market and Morristown. Morristown lay fifteen miles northeast of New Market and about twenty-eight miles northeast of Strawberry Plains; these towns were located on the East Tennessee and Virginia Railroad. During this period the brigade marched about 150 miles without any contact with Longstreet's troops. The brigade returned to Strawberry Plains on March 19 and the next day began marching up into the Richland Valley. By March 29 the brigade had tramped at least eighty-five miles, reconnoitered Bean's Station (thirty-two miles northeast of Strawberry Plains) and had encamped at Powder Springs Gap fourteen miles north of Strawberry Plains. Reinhart, *A History of the 6th Kentucky,* 275.

39. The editor could not locate the March 8 order referred to by Rentschler. However, Maj. Gen. John M. Schofield wrote to General Thomas on

March 6: "I have no immediate use for Granger's Corps, and will order it to Cleveland if you so direct." Cleveland, Tennessee, was close to Chattanooga. *OR 32*, pt. 3, p. 26.

40. The 9th Corps was originally part of the Army of the Potomac and was ordered west on March 19, 1863. After two months in Kentucky, two divisions of the corps were ordered to Vicksburg, Mississippi, to take part in Grant's siege of that important Mississippi River city. Later, the 9th Corps was sent to Knoxville. In March 1864 the 9th Corps rejoined the Army of the Potomac. Boatner, *Civil War Dictionary*, 192.

41. The 6th Kentucky's veteran volunteers were not in this group of returning veterans. They did not return to the regiment until April 29, overstaying their authorized furloughs by about a month. General Hazen was furious over this matter but there is no evidence that the men were punished for their long unexcused absences. Reinhart, *A History of the 6th Kentucky*, 281.

42. Brig. Gen. Alpheus S. Williams, commander of the 1st Division of the 12th Corps, agreed with Private Rentschler about wartime corruption and wrote in a letter to his daughter: "It makes me sick, sometimes, to hear of the frauds and rascality that are practiced in all departments. Often to the suffering and misery of those exposed in the field. These things are found, from the miserable pasted shoes that men pay high prices for to the food they eat. In everything there is proof of contractors' and government agents' fraud and cheating. I think it was [the Duke of] Wellington who said that these things could be stopped only by hanging a contractor and inspector every Saturday night! I wish often it could be tried." Alpheus S. Williams, *From the Cannon's Mouth: The Civil War Letters of General Alpheus S. Williams*, ed. Milo M. Quaife (1959; rpt., introd. by Gary W. Gallagher, Lincoln: Univ. of Nebraska Press, 1995), 270.

43. See Bell Irwin Wiley's *Life of Billy Yank*, pages 212, 247, and 249–52, for additional information about gambling in the Federal army.

44. See note 42 above.

45. The Quartermaster Department was responsible for providing quarters, clothing, transportation, etc., to the troops. The Commissary Department provided food.

46. Sexual acts between white soldiers and black women did occur during the war. Some of the women were prostitutes, others camp followers; some did it to please the soldiers, while others were forced into it. See Thomas P. Lowry, M.D., *The Story the Soldiers Wouldn't Tell: Sex in the Civil War* (Mechanicsburg, Pa.: Stackpole Books, 1994), chapters 7, 12, and 13, for a discussion of sex between the races during the war.

47. The book Daeuble purchased may have been William D. Bickham's *Rosecrans' Campaign with the Fourteenth Army Corps, or the Army of the Cumberland: Narrative of Personal Observations with . . . Official Reports of the Battle of Stone River* (Cincinnati: Moore, Wilstach, Keys, 1863).

CHAPTER 6

1. While the 6th Kentucky and the rest of its brigade were tramping back and forth between various towns and villages in East Tennessee, several significant changes took place in the leadership of the Federal army. Ulysses S. Grant was commissioned a lieutenant general and given command of all United States armies. This promotion led Grant to move east, where he could control the vast Army of the Potomac and work on his plan to end the rebellion. Grant turned command of the Military Division of the Mississippi over to his protégé Maj. Gen. William T. Sherman, who in turn picked Maj. Gen. James B. McPherson as his replacement as head the Army of the Tennessee. Maj. Gen. Philip H. Sheridan was called to Washington and placed in command of the Cavalry Corps of the Army of the Potomac. Brig. Gen. John Newton replaced Sheridan as commander of the 2nd Division of the 4th Corps. The transfer of generals from the East into the Army of the Cumberland was an irritation to western officers, who were equally or better qualified but passed over for promotion. Ulysses S. Grant, *Personal Memoirs of U. S. Grant* (1885; rpt. ed. E. B. Long, 1952; rpt. unabridged with a new introd. by William S. McFeely, New York: DeCapo Press, 1982), 358; *OR* 32, pt. 3, p. 258; Boatner, *Civil War Dictionary*, 593, 747.
2. Harvey R. Wolfe of Shelby County mustered in on December 24, 1861, and was promoted from private (Company H) to quartermaster on March 28, 1862. He mustered out after three years.
3. The train Daeuble was expecting may have been Train No.1 that left Chattanooga at 10 A. M. on April 11 and was derailed three miles from Athens that same evening. Sabotage was initially suspected in this accident that severely injured about thirty officers and men of the 15th Ohio; however, the historian of the regiment reported years later that "the ties were rotten and the rails had parted and thrown the cars from the track." *Knoxville Whig and Rebel Ventilator*, Apr. 16, 1864; *The Fifteenth Ohio Volunteers and Its Campaigns, War of 1861–1865* (1916; rpt. Columbus, Ohio: The General's Books, n.d.), 421–22.
4. Parson Brownlow refused to take the Oath of Loyalty to the Confederacy and on November 5, 1861, fled to the mountains on the Tennessee–North Carolina border to avoid being arrested. He returned to Knoxville and was arrested on December 6, 1861—charged with treason for allegedly having a hand in burning railroad bridges in East Tennessee. Due to illness he was released from jail and allowed to return to his home, but he was kept under guard there. To prevent Brownlow from becoming a martyr, the outspoken Unionist was sent inside the Federal lines on March 3, 1862. He returned to Knoxville with Maj. Gen. Ambrose Burnside's army in the fall of 1863. Allen Johnson and Dumas Malone, *Dictionary of American Biography* (New York: Charles Scribner and Sons, 1958), 2:177–78.
5. Mrs. Brownlow was the former Eliza A. O'Brien.

6. William G. Brownlow and his wife had two sons and five daughters. Susan, the oldest daughter, was born in 1838, and the next oldest daughter, Mary, was born in 1849. The editor believes "Sun" was probably Susan but may have been Mary. The three younger daughters appear to have been too young to have a "full education" in 1864. Also, the handwritten German letter "e" at that time (as opposed to the Latin "e" used today) was similar to an "n" and the newspaper could have printed "Sun" instead of "Sue." Zella Armstrong, comp., *Notable Southern Families* (Baltimore: Genealogical Publishing, 1974), 44; 1860 Population Census, Knox County, Tennessee.

7. Col. Leonidas Houk of Anderson County, Tennessee, served in the 3rd Tennessee Infantry (U.S.), not the 3rd Tennessee Cavalry as Rentschler indicates. *OR,* series 3, pt. 1, p. 881; *OR* 16, series 1, pt. 1, p. 861.

8. The author was unable to determine whether any of Brownlow's property was destroyed by Union soldiers, but it is possible. Many Federal soldiers did not ask or care whether the property they were taking or destroying belonged to a Unionist or not. *OR* 31, pt. 3, p. 372.

9. Whether this marriage took place or not is uncertain.

10. The roster of the 41st Ohio does not show any demotions during 1864. The editor found no evidence to support Rentschler's claim regarding threats of demotion for members of the 41st Ohio who did not re-enlist, but it is possible. Robert L. Kimberly and Ephraim S. Holloway, *The Forty-first Ohio Veteran Volunteer Infantry in the War of the Rebellion, 1861–1865* (Cleveland: W. R. Smellie, 1897), 137–290.

11. Wilhelm Hauff (1802–1827) was a German writer, widely known for his macabre, vivid, and often amusing fairy tales. Black Forest (or Dutch) Michael appears in parts 1 and 2 of his fairy tale "The Cold Heart." Michael was a giant of a man who lived in the Black Forest (located in the Grand Duchy of Baden, which was bordered by the Rhine River in the west and the Kingdom of Württemberg in the east) and he corrupted men by giving them riches. In part 2 of "The Cold Heart," Dutch Michael trades riches and stone hearts to certain persons in exchange for their human hearts, thus depriving them of normal human feelings. *Fairy Tales of Wilhelm Hauff,* trans. Anthea Bell (London, New York, Toronto: Abelard-Schuman, 1969), part 2, pp. 194–219.

12. Circular 24 of the War Dept. dated March 17, 1864, revoked that portion of paragraph 5 of General Orders, No. 376 (1863), regarding the assignment of men not re-enlisting as veteran volunteers to duties in other companies and regiments until the expiration of their term of service. *OR,* series 3, pt. 4, p. 188.

13. Maj. Gen. Gordon Granger (1822–1876) took a leave of absence after being relieved from command of the 4th Corps, and later was sent to the Department of West Mississippi. He commanded the 13th Corps in the Mobile (Alabama) campaign. *OR* 31, pt. 3, p. 268.

14. Maj. Gen. Oliver O. Howard previously commanded the 11th Corps that came west in September 1863 to reinforce the Army of the Cumberland.

15. Hazen's brigade of the 3rd Division arrived within one and a half miles of Loudon on April 11, 1864, and encamped. The brigade departed on April 13 with its division for the march to McDonald's Station. The 2nd Division began its departure from Loudon on April 15, 1864. Reinhart, *A History of the 6th Kentucky,* 279–80; *OR* 32, pt. 1, p. 24.

16. The editor did not find any evidence to support Rentschler's claim that most of the work on the bridge was performed by Rebel deserters.

17. Fences protected crops from larger animals that might eat or trample them.

18. No one in the 6th Kentucky was captured on April 14, 1864.

19. Capt. Isaac N. Johnston of Pleasureville, Kentucky, mustered in on December 24, 1861, as captain of Company H. He was severely wounded in the battle of Shiloh on April 7, 1862. Johnston was captured on September 19, 1863, at the battle of Chickamauga. and sent to Libby Prison in Richmond, Virginia. He was one of the principals who dug a fifty-seven-foot-long tunnel through which 109 officers escaped on February 9, 1864. Forty-eight of the escapees were recaptured, but not Johnston. Two other escapees drowned. Johnston led the regiment through the Atlanta campaign and mustered out with his company on December 31, 1864. Reinhart, *A History of the 6th Kentucky,* 281–83.

20. Capt. Johnston's book *Four Months in Libby and the Campaign Against Atlanta* was published in 1864; however, no translations appeared in the *Louisville Anzeiger.*

21. President Abraham Lincoln signed an order creating the United States Sanitary Commission on June 9, 1861. This civilian organization coordinated local supply efforts, provided battlefield relief to soldiers, and offered medical advice to the army. Both men and women participated in its operations, which were funded by non-government sources. Wiley, *Life of Billy Yank,* 150.

22. John Dohn's epistle (letter) did not appear in the April 1, 1864, issue of the *Louisville Anzeiger* as Rentschler stated. However, the paper's editor disclosed in the April 2, 1864, issue, that John Dohn had sent the *Anzeiger* a letter stating that he was upset by Rentschler's letter, dated March 27, 1864, that reported many bakers and sutlers were overcharging soldiers and earning outrageous profits. The editor told Dohn that if he were not among those overcharging the soldiers, he should not take offense at Rentschler's statements. The editor also stated that Rentschler would respond to Dohn's letter, which he did, and the stinging response appeared in the April 15, 1864, issue of the *Anzeiger.* The *Report of the Adjutant General of the State of Illinois for the Civil War* does not list a John Dohn in the 24th Illinois regiment; however, there was a Pvt. John Dahm in Company A of this regiment. The *Anzeiger's* editor may have misread his signature. Pvt. John Dahm of Chicago mustered in on July 8, 1861, and mustered out on August 6, 1864. J. N. Reece,

Adj. Gen., *Report of the Adjutant General of the State of Illinois, 1861–1866,* vol. 2 (Springfield: Phillips Bro. State Printers, 1900), 302.

23. Capt. William Frank of Company E.

24. The editor was unable to locate a copy of the inspector general's report mentioned by Rentschler.

25. The editor could not locate the order that Rentschler stated the inspector general would issue.

26. The editor was not able to verify that John Dahm of the 24th Illinois was a baker, but it is possible.

27. The editor was unable to locate the general's letter quoted from by Rentschler.

28. Phillip Shaw Paludan stated in *"A People's Contest":* "Seamstresses in New York saw wages go from 17.5¢ per shirt in 1861 to 8¢ per shirt in 1864. Women who worked a fourteen-hour day at this job received on the average of $1.54 a week. The sewing women of Cincinnati wrote to President Lincoln in March 1865: 'We are unable to sustain life for the prices offered by contractors.'" Paludan, *"A Peoples Contest": The Union and Civil War 1861–1865,* 2nd ed. (Lawrence: Univ. of Kansas Press, 1996), 182–83.

29. Because John Dohn's [Dahm's?] letter is not available, the editor does not know what the "lance for veterans" was.

30. The *Louisville Volksblatt* was a Republican German-language newspaper.

31. General Hazen began his leave on March 18, 1864. Boatner, *Civil War Dictionary,* 390.

32. Company H comprised mostly men from Henry County and was led by Capt. Isaac N. Johnston.

33. Brig. Gen. John Newton replaced Maj. Gen. Philip H. Sheridan as commander of the 2nd Division on April 16, 1864, because of Sheridan's transfer to the Army of the Potomac. Boatner, *Civil War Dictionary,* 593.

34. Pvt. Henry Webert of Louisville mustered in on December 24, 1861, and was wounded at the battle of Chickamauga in 1863 and at Adairsville, Georgia, on May 17, 1864. He mustered out at the end of his three-year enlistment.

35. The *Louisville Anzeiger* published part of Rentschler's letter dated May 1, 1864, on May 4, and the remainder on May 5. The last three topics refer to matters discussed in the portion of the letter published on May 5.

36. Rentschler, at thirty-seven years old, was almost twice the age of many of the volunteers who had joined the Union army.

37. Rentschler was married, and may have been referring to his wife Paulina as the "old one."

38. May Day (May 1) was a day of celebration and various festivities including the crowning of a May queen and dancing around a Maypole.

39. A tremendous amount of equipment and supplies had to be assembled for an offensive by a huge army, and this took planning and time. In addition, Sherman's grand army was supposed to start its offensive at the same time

as the Federal armies in the East. Castel, *Decision in the West,* 91–92, 94, 118–19.

40. Rentschler's estimate of army strength was incorrect. By early May 1864, Maj. Gen. William T. Sherman had assembled most of his 110,000-man grand army in and near Chattanooga. The Federal force comprised Maj. Gen. George Thomas's Army of the Cumberland, consisting of the 4th, 14th, and 20th Corps—73,000 troops; Maj. Gen. James McPherson's Army of the Tennessee, consisting of the 15th Corps and two divisions from the 16th Corps—24,000 troops; and Maj. Gen. John Schofield's Army of the Ohio, consisting of the 23rd Corps—13,000 troops. Johnston's 54,000-man Confederate Army of Tennessee was massed at Dalton, Georgia, shielding the Confederacy's important railroad center, storehouses, and manufacturing facilities at Atlanta. Lt. Gens. William J. Hardee and John Bell Hood each commanded a corps. Johnston's army had 145 guns, just over half of Sherman's total. The numbers were clearly in the Federals' favor. Sherman's objectives required him to take the offensive. Joseph E. Johnston's strategy was to get his adversary to attack him in well-fortified positions, repel those attacks with great losses to the Federals, and then pursue the weakened Union army and crush or capture it. The result was the grueling Atlanta campaign that lasted over 100 days and cost both sides heavily. Castel, *Decision in the West,* 112, 115, 104.

41. Sherman's supply line stretched all the way back to Louisville, Kentucky, the largest Federal supply depot in the West. Equipment and supplies traveled from Louisville to Nashville, Tennessee, on the Louisville and Nashville Railroad, and then to Chattanooga on the Nashville and Chattanooga Railroad. The Western and Atlantic railroad ran south from Chattanooga to Atlanta, Georgia. Thousands of Union troops were required to protect the railroad between Louisville and Chattanooga from being severed by Confederate raids, and more would be needed to protect the Western and Atlantic Railroad as Sherman's army moved south. Sherman also needed troops to protect his flanks, so enemy forces could not turn them or get behind him.

42. Rentschler points out Sherman's problems in launching an offensive against Joseph E. Johnston's Confederates. As Sherman's army moved south, it would distance itself even further from its supply bases, while Johnston's army would move closer to its major supply base at Atlanta. While Sherman's army was spread out to protect its flanks, Johnston could concentrate his forces and attack a point of his choosing. Johnston could also move his army around, not giving the Federal army a target to hit, while stretching the latter's supply lines.

43. Voluntary enlistments were not sufficient to build the army to overwhelming strength, so Rentschler wonders why the Lincoln Administration had not acted to conscript more men for the army. The editor was unable to determine the meaning of *"von Semri kein Wessle."*

44. The 6th Kentucky, its division, and corps broke camp on May 3 (just two days after Rentschler predicts there will not be a spring campaign) and began moving south in conjunction with Sherman's other corps as the campaign to destroy the Army of Tennessee began. Reinhart, *A History of the 6th Kentucky*, 285.

45. Halleck had held the position of general-in-chief of the army before Grant was promoted to that position on March 12, 1864. Halleck became Chief of Staff of the Army under the direction of the secretary of war and Grant. Rentschler unfairly blames Halleck for the delay in the army's offensive, but praises Grant. *OR* 32, pt. 3, p. 58.

46. Rentschler obviously believes in Lt. Gen. Ulysses S. Grant's leadership.

47. Maj. Gen. Oliver O. Howard (who had lost his right arm at the battle of Seven Pines in Virginia) was appointed commander of the 4th Corps on April 10, 1864, replacing Maj. Gen. Gordon Granger. Rentschler's statement about not building a gold mountain on Howard reflects his belief that Howard was not a great general, but was better than Granger. Albert Castel wrote that Howard: "Not only allowed his troops to be surprised at Chancellorsville (Virginia); his performance at Gettysburg and Chattanooga had at best been mediocre. . . . Yet . . . [Howard] is intelligent . . . , brave, . . . and totally dedicated to duty." Granger was disliked and distrusted by Grant and Sherman. Castel, *Decision in the West*, 98.

48. On September 20, 1863, during the second day of the battle of Chickamauga, General Granger led his Reserve Corps to Horseshoe Ridge and determined fighting by his three brigades helped keep the Federals there from being overrun by Confederate forces. This deed won Granger command of the 4th Corps on October 10, 1863, when it was organized by consolidation of the 20th and 21st Corps. The editor believes that the reference to an acorn relates to a saying "that even a blind pig finds an acorn once in a while." Cozzens, *This Terrible Sound*, 439–77, 525.

49. There were times when many men were shirtless and shoeless. Men were instructed to repair their shoes with the hides of animals that had been slain for food, or to wrap their feet in the hides, if they had no shoes. *OR* 32, pt. 2, pp. 45, 46; Kimberly and Holloway, *Forty-first Ohio*, 75.

50. Ringgold, Georgia, lay southeast of Chattanooga on the Western and Atlantic Railroad which ran to Dalton, Georgia.

51. Capt. Richard C. Dawkins of La Grange in Oldham County mustered in with Company B on November 1, 1861, as a second lieutenant, and was promoted to first lieutenant on January 5, 1862; to captain on June 20, 1862; to major on May 25,1864; and to lieutenant colonel on September 16, 1864. Lt. Col. Dawkins mustered out with the regimental headquarters and final company of the 6th Kentucky on January 2, 1865. Because of illness he did not lead the regiment in the Atlanta campaign (May–August 1864), but assumed command of the regiment on August 22, 1864, at Chattanooga.

52. See note 19 above regarding Captain Johnston.
53. Capt. William Frank of Company E was very heavy and had a difficult time finding uniforms to fit his corpulent body.
54. Maj. Richard T. Whitaker commanded the 6th Kentucky. He was not a lieutenant colonel as Rentschler called him. See note 17 in chapter 1.
55. Capt. Henry C. Schmid of Louisville was a native of Marburg in Hesse and came to America in 1850. He mustered in on September 9, 1861, and was promoted from corporal to sergeant on November 14, 1861; to second lieutenant on May 29, 1862; and to captain on February 12, 1863. Schmid led Company C, which contained principally German-born men from Louisville. He was wounded on September 19, 1863, at the battle of Chickamauga. Schmid served his full three-year enlistment. Reinhart, *A History of the 6th Kentucky,* 180.
56. The 5th Kentucky was also known as the Louisville Legion. The original Louisville Legion dated back to 1839, and in 1846 the Legion served in the war with Mexico (officially designated as the 1st Regiment of Foot, Kentucky Volunteers). Many of the Legion's Mexican War veterans joined the Confederate army, but the Louisville Legion of 1861 to 1864 was strongly Union-loyal. David R. Deatrick, "Louisville Legion," in *The Encyclopedia of Louisville,* John E. Kleber, ed. in chief, (Lexington: Univ. Press of Kentucky, 2001), 557. *Report of the Adjutant General of the State of Kentucky, Civil War 1861–1865 (Union)* (Frankfort, 1866–76; rpt. Utica, Ky.: McDowell, 1988), 694.; Hazen, *Narrative of Military Service,* 249.
57. General Hazen graduated from the United States Military Academy at West Point, New York, in 1855. He was ranked twenty-eighth in a class of thirty-four. Boatner, *Civil War Dictionary,* 390.
58. See note 17 above regarding fences.
59. For an in-depth analysis of the tragic plight of the Union people of Tennessee during the Civil War see Noel C. Fisher's *War at Every Door,* 182–83.
60. War-weariness and staggering casualties, opposition to the Emancipation Proclamation, the conscription act (including draft riots), and other issues, led many Northerners to advocate ending the war other than by military means, and hostile feelings developed between peace advocates and those who wanted to vigorously prosecute the war. However, Lincoln and the Republicans were able to maintain control. Castel, *Decision in the West,* 4–8, 253–54.
61. A Gottfried was clerical garb.
62. Among the most zealous advocates for continuing the war until the North triumphed were the abolitionists. Thus, Rentschler's comment about throwing "a plantation full of niggers in their [the leaders in Washington] face."

CHAPTER 7

1. The 3rd Division assembled in a partly cultivated field for the review. The weather was pleasant but marching in the field created clouds of dust to the displeasure of the participants. John Daeuble's diary entry for April 29, 1864, in chapter 6.

2. Soldiers, including lower-level officers, were often not told of their destination.

3. Lt. Gen. Ulysses S. Grant, general-in-chief of the Federal armies, instructed Maj. Gen. William T. Sherman, Commander of the Military Division of the Mississippi, to "move against Johnston's Confederate army, to break it up and to get into the interior of the enemy's country as far as you can, inflicting all the damage you can against their resources." General Joseph E. Johnston's army was concentrated at Dalton, Georgia. OR 32, pt. 3, p. 246.

4. The terms weak and strong refer to the numerical strength of a regiment. A weak regiment probably had about three hundred or fewer officers and men. Sherman did not want his army slowed by large wagon trains with baggage, camp furniture and other nonessential items.

5. Soldiers carried food in a canvas bag called a haversack.

6. Officers' excess baggage was to be sent to Bridgeport in northeastern Alabama for storage.

7. The name of the poem and its author are unknown; Rentschler may have composed it himself.

8. Daeuble incorrectly referred to Rocky Face Ridge as Rocky Face Mountain and misspelled Buzzard Roost Gap. The Confederates had strongly fortified this ridge from its northern end, which began a little north of Tunnel Hill, to a point several miles southwest of Dalton, including at Mill Creek Gap and Dug Gap. Mill Creek Gap lay approximately three miles southeast of Tunnel Hill, and the Western and Atlantic Railroad ran through this gap on its way to Dalton and its terminus in Atlanta. The steeply ascending sides of this passage were called Buzzard Roost because of frequent sightings of that bird of prey perched there. Dug Gap was located about three miles south of Buzzard Roost. There was a third pass through the ridge about seven miles south of Dug Gap. This pass was known as Snake Creek Gap, and General Joseph E. Johnston left it unguarded. Hazen's brigade was posted on the left of its division on a ridge that faced down the valley toward Buzzard Roost Gap. Richard M. McMurry, *Atlanta 1864: Last Chance for the Confederacy* (Lincoln: Univ. of Nebraska Press, 2000), 42–43.

9. The 6th Kentucky suffered three, and possibly four casualties on May 9. Pvt. Charles Fischbach of Company G was mortally wounded, while Cpl. Engelbert Emig of Company E and Pvt. John C. Carroll Sr. of company K were wounded but survived. Pvt. Herman Flottman of Company I was wounded sometime between May 3–10. All these men had mustered in on

December 24, 1861. Emig was promoted to corporal on November 11, 1862, and mustered out on December 31, 1864. Carroll re-enlisted and transferred to the 4th Kentucky Mounted Infantry in early 1865. Flottman was wounded again near Peachtree Creek, Georgia, on July 21, 1864, and mustered out on December 31, 1864.

10. See note 9 above regarding Corporal Emig.

11. Lt. Gen. Ulysses S. Grant was accompanying the Army of the Potomac commanded by Maj. Gen. George Gordon Meade. Meade's army and General Robert E. Lee's Army of Northern Virginia fought to a standstill in the wilderness in Virginia on May 5 and 6, 1864. Federal casualties totaled approximately 17,700 and Lee's approximated 7,800. Grant then shifted his army toward Spotsylvania Courthouse where the two armies would clash again. Lee's army was not being pursued; instead Grant was trying to flank it. Castel, *Decision in the West,* 185–86; Boatner, *Civil War Dictionary,* 925.

12. The two men from the Louisville Legion mentioned by John Daeuble were Pvt. Joseph N. Parrish of Company C who was killed and Pvt. Johnson Todd of Company B who was wounded but survived. *Report of the Adjutant General of the State of Kentucky,* 1:690–91, 694–95.

13. Rentschler incorrectly refers to Mill Creek Gap as Tunnel Hill Gap.

14. The roar Rentschler mentions was probably only sniper fire.

15. Early in the war, a Federal brigade usually consisted of four regiments, and at full strength contained approximately 3,600–4,000 officers and men. A regiment was led by a colonel and a brigade was commanded by either a colonel or brigadier general. By October 1863, most regiments in the Army of the Cumberland had been depleted to 200–500 officers and men, so the number of regiments in a brigade was increased to more approximate normal brigade strength. Colonel Hazen consolidated two regiments into what he called a battalion. The senior officer in a battalion commanded that unit. Rentschler reported that on May 6 the brigade contained 2,356 soldiers. Hazen, therefore, reduced the number of officers reporting directly to him and created four combat teams rather than eight regiments operating as individual units. Technically, a battalion consists of two or more companies, but Hazen used the term for his two-regiment fighting units. Hazen numbered his battalions 1st, 2nd, 3rd, and 4th, and Rentschler lists them in numerical order.

16. The 6th Ohio mustered into service on June 18, 1861, at Camp Dennison, located approximately sixteen miles north of Cincinnati, and mustered out there on June 23, 1864. It lost eighty-six men killed or dead from wounds and fifty-eight men dead from diseases, illnesses, or other causes. Dyer, *Compendium,* 3:1498.

17. The buildings at the Catoosa Springs spa consisted of a three-story hotel and guesthouses. Reinhart, *A History of the 6th Kentucky,* 287.

18. A volley is the simultaneous firing of weapons and was considered the most efficient method while in line-of-battle formation.

19. The corps participating in the campaign at this time were: the 4th, 14th, and 20th Corps of the Army of the Cumberland; the 15th Corps and two divisions of the 16th Corps of the Army of the Tennessee; and the 23rd Corps, Army of the Ohio. Aggregate infantry troops were 93,000, a little higher than the 90,600 Rentschler reported. *OR* 38, pt. 1, p. 115.

20. The 23rd Kentucky was organized at Camp King near Covington in Kenton County, and commanded by Lt. Col. James C. Foy. Foy was mortally wounded on July 9, 1864, near Pace's Ferry (located at the Chattahoochee River). Maj. George W. Northup of the 23rd Kentucky replaced Foy as battalion commander. Reinhart, *A History of the 6th Kentucky*, 333.

21. General Thomas's order allowed one wagon each to corps, division, and brigade headquarters. A small supply train, sufficient for two days' forage (for the animals) and rations, ammunition train, and the wagons with the tools would constitute the train for the march. *OR* 38, pt. 4, p. 35.

22. Maj. Gen. David S. Stanley commanded the 1st Division of the 4th Army Corps.

23. In comparison to newly supplied Federal soldiers, the Rebels were poorly clothed and deficiently supplied. Thus, Rentschler's comment about their not having excess baggage.

24. One mile east of the village of Tunnel Hill stood a gravelish range of hills also called Tunnel Hill through which the almost 1,500-foot-long Western and Atlantic Railroad tunnel had been cut.

25. The mountain line containing the signal station was steep-sloped Rocky Face Ridge, which extended for twenty-five miles and had an elevation of 800 feet at its highest points. Reinhart, *A History of the 6th Kentucky*, 287–88.

26. Maj. Gen. John M. Palmer led a 25,000-man reconnaissance in force toward Dalton, Georgia, commencing on February 22, 1864. After three days of skirmishing with the Confederates positioned on Rocky Face Ridge, Palmer's force returned to Chattanooga. Major General Stanley's division of the 4th Corps participated with Palmer's 14th Corps in this reconnaissance. Castel, *Decision in the West*, 54; *OR* 32, pt. 1, pp. 419–21.

27. Harker's brigade of Newton's division moved up Rocky Face Ridge, drove off enemy skirmishers, and then cleared three-fourths of a mile south along the crest. Castel, *Decision in the West*, 131.

28. Stanley's division advanced toward Mill Creek Gap in the afternoon and drove enemy skirmishers from their rifle pits, but got no closer to the gap than one-half mile, not halfway into the Gap as Rentschler reported. Brig. Gen. John W. Geary's division, the 2nd Division of the 20th Corps, made a strong but failed attack at Dug Gap (south of Mill Creek Gap) in the late afternoon and lost almost four hundred men. Castel, *Decision in the West*, 131–35.

29. The Confederates knew that if Lincoln was re-elected president in November, he would not end the war without preserving the Union and

freeing the slaves, so the Rebels would continue their fight for the South's independence.

30. The cheering troops Rentschler mentions apparently assumed Maj. Gen. George Gordon Meade's Army of the Potomac (which Grant was accompanying) won the bloody battle in the wilderness in Virginia on May 5 and 6, 1864. See note 12 above.

31. General Sherman had sent the Army of the Tennessee south with orders to move through Snake Creek Gap (which the Rebels had left undefended) in order to get behind Johnston's army or destroy his railroad lifeline from Atlanta, while other units made diversionary attacks to keep the Rebels occupied. McPherson's troops made it through Snake Creek Gap, but retreated back to the Gap without carrying out their objective after meeting light resistance. Losses in Hazen's brigade were small, because their attack on Rocky Face Ridge was only diversionary and they did not try to force the enemy in their front off the ridge. McMurry, *Atlanta 1864,* 63–65.

32. The Army of Tennessee had acquired about one hundred British-made Whitworth rifles, which were more powerful and accurate at longer ranges than the arms normally carried by infantrymen. A good rifleman could hit a man as far away as a mile or even a mile and a half. Confederate sharpshooters continuously kept Sherman's men under dangerous fire, causing numerous casualties and much dread and anxiety. Union sharpshooters also had special rifles for long-range killing and took their toll of many unlucky Southerners. Castel, *Decision in the West,* 109; Paddy Griffith, *Battle Tactics of the Civil War,* U.S. edition (New Haven: Yale Univ. Press, 1989), 74.

33. Sherman expected McPherson to get behind Johnston and block his retreat, so the Federal army could defeat him. However, this did not happen. See note 31 above.

34. See note 9 above.

35. The 96th Illinois, commanded by Col. Thomas E. Champion of Warren County, Illinois, belonged to Brig. Gen. Walter C. Whitaker's brigade. There is no mention in Whitaker's official report of the incident Rentschler described; however, embarrassing events often went unreported. *OR* 38, pt. 1, p. 240.

36. The editor found no evidence to support the rumor that Schofield had been placed under arrest or his corps was delinquent in moving.

37. General Stanley's report for May 10 indicates that there was skirmishing on this day, and the enemy threw shells into the valley from howitzers they had dragged to the top of the ridge. *OR* 38, pt. 1, p. 220.

38. See note 12 above regarding casualties in the Louisville Legion on May 11, 1864.

39. Johnston's army retreated from Rocky Face Ridge on the night of May 12–13. Castel, *Decision in the West,* 149–50.

40. No report of the brigade's aggregate casualties to May 11, 1864, is available; however, the editor does not believe they were as high as the 100 to 125 that Rentschler estimated.

CHAPTER 8

1. Pvt. August Lamprecht of Louisville and Company E mustered in on December 24, 1861, and mustered out on December 31, 1864.
2. Johnston's army, now reinforced by Lt. Gen. Leonidas Polk's corps from Mississippi, fortified in front of Resaca (on the north bank of the Oostanaula River) and successfully repulsed attacks by the 14th and 23rd Corps on May 14, while the 15th Corps gained a bridgehead across Camp Creek. The 4th Corps arrived late in the afternoon but was not heavily engaged; however, troops from the 20th Corps sent to cover the 4th Corps' exposed left flank quashed an attack by Hood's corps, preventing a Federal disaster. McMurry, *Atlanta 1864*, 70.
3. Pvts. Deisinger and Zanger, and Sgt. Maas (who was promoted to sergeant on November 1, 1862) were from Louisville, and mustered in on December 24, 1861. Sgt. Maas mustered out on December 31, 1864.
4. The night attack Daeuble mentions did not amount to much. However, in the early afternoon, Hooker's 20th Corps, supported by the 23rd Corps, collided with Hood's corps on the Federal left and gained some nearby hills. Hazen's brigade made a charge but the brigades on its flanks unexpectedly remained behind their fortifications, allowing the enemy's infantry and artillery to concentrate their fire solely on the 6th Kentucky and Hazen's other regiments. Hazen lost over one hundred men in less than a minute and quickly recalled his brigade. The 6th Kentucky suffered fourteen killed and wounded in this ill-fated charge. *OR* 38, pt. 1, pp. 141, 422. Reinhart, *A History of the 6th Kentucky*, 299.
5. General Johnston ordered a retreat on the afternoon of the fifteenth because Brig. Gen. Thomas W. Sweeny's division had crossed the Oostanaula River at Lay's Ferry, threatening to isolate the Southern army from its supply line. Castel, *Decision in the West*, 179.
6. See Gottfried Rentschler's letter 13 dated May 11, 1864, in chapter 7, for more information on General Palmer's February reconnaissance toward Dalton.
7. The so-called "Grapevine" [telegraph rumor] was false.
8. Rentschler refers to the Confederacy as Mrs. Secesh (Secessionist). The Confederacy, however, was not close to taking its last breath, and almost a year of hard fighting lay ahead.
9. Germanic states (including Austria) fought the Turks in several wars during the seventeenth and eighteenth centuries. The Turks were known for their ferocity and cruelty. Turks to German children were like the bogeyman to Americans.
10. The Federals found large quantities of tobacco and peanuts in warehouses in Dalton. Castel, *Decision in the West*, 151.
11. The identity of the man from the Prussian Rhineland is unknown.
12. The Federal cavalry mentioned may have been from Brig. Gen. Hugh Judson Kilpatrick's division, who encountered Confederate infantry posted in a dense grove of thickets in the vicinity of the Dalton-Resaca crossroads

about two miles from Resaca. Kilpatrick was shot in the thigh in this fighting. Castel, *Decision in the West,* 151–52.

13. Troops of the 14th and 23rd Corps attacked fortified Confederate positions and were repulsed. Castel, *Decision in the West,* 159–61.

14. Losses in the brigade on May 14 were light, and probably were close to Rentschler's estimate.

15. Brig. Gen. Alpheus Williams's 20th Corps division arrived in time to stop a late evening attack on Stanley's exposed left flank. Brig. Gen John W. Geary's and Maj. Gen. Daniel Butterfield's divisions (also of Hooker's 20th Corps) were later placed between Stanley's and Williams's divisions, extending the Federal left. Castel, *Decision in the West,* 163–66, 169.

16. Lt. Col. Fullerton noted in his journal on the fourteenth that "Some confusion, caused by General Cox (who was on Schofield's left) being lost with two brigades." The country was heavily wooded. General Cox got into line around 1:00 A.M. on the fifteenth. *OR* 38, pt. 1, p. 853.

17. The rear of the captured enemy trenches faced the enemy, rather than the elevated front that would have provided more protection.

18. Some generals were reluctant to fight on Sunday, viewing it as a holy day. Major General Howard was known as a deeply religious man. Castel, *Decision in the West,* 98.

19. Brig. Gen. Mahlon D. Manson, an Ohio native, led the 2nd Brigade of the 3rd Division, 23rd Corps. He was severely wounded by the concussion of an exploding shell that landed near him around 3:00 P.M. on the fourteenth, while waiting for Brig. Charles G. Harker's brigade of Stanley's division to come and relieve his brigade on the front line. *OR* 38, pt. 2, p. 678.

20. Col. Samuel K. McSpadden of the 19th Alabama regiment mistook Hazen's line for his own, and was captured as he walked into it. Hazen, *Narrative of Military Service,* 252; *OR* 38, pt. 3, p. 640.

21. Berthold Auerbach, a popular nineteenth-century German-Jewish author, wrote the book *Schwarzwaelder Dorfgeschichten (Black Forest Village Stories),* containing the story "Der Lauterbacher," from which Rentschler appears to make a direct quote. However, Rentschler paraphrases rather than quotes Auerbach. Berthold Auerbach, *Saemptliche Schwarzwaelder Dorfgeschichten,* (Stuttgart and Berlin: J. G. Cotta'sche Buchhandlung Dachfolger, n.d.), 345.

22. Brig. Gen. John W. Geary's and Maj. Gen. Daniel Butterfield's divisions attacked Maj. Gen. Carter L. Stevenson's division of Hood's corps, and troops from Maj. Gen. William T. Ward's brigade of Butterfield's division captured Capt. Max Den Corput's four-gun "Cherokee Battery" (Georgia), but were unable to retain it. Union fire kept the Confederates from returning to their guns. That night, under the cover of darkness, some of Geary's men were able to move the guns to the Union line. Hooker lost about twelve hundred men in the attacks on Stevenson's division on May 15, but failed to dislodge it. Brig. Gen. Alpheus Williams's 20th Corps division repulsed attacks by Maj. Gen. Alexander P. Stewart's division. Williams lost

about four hundred men and Stewart lost about one thousand. Castel, *Decision in the West,* 174–80.

23. See note 4 above.

24. Brig. Gen. August Willich, commander of the 3rd Brigade of the 3rd Division, 4th Corps, was shot through his arm and side by a single bullet and never returned to field duty. Castel, *Decision in the West,* 173.

25. Brig. Gen. William T. Ward, a native Kentuckian and Mexican War veteran, led the 1st Brigade of the 3rd Division, 20th Corps. On June 29, 1864, he was appointed commander of the 3rd Division. Boatner, *Civil War Dictionary,* 889.

26. Rentschler's prediction about the timing of the army's arrival in front of Atlanta was greatly in error.

27. Eight members of the 6th Kentucky were killed or died from wounds and six were wounded but survived. Rentschler only listed the Germans. Reinhart, *A History of the 6th Kentucky,* 299.

28. See note 3 above.

29. Pvts. Wittich and Pape [not Pope] were from Louisville and mustered in on September 9, 1861. Pape completed his three-year enlistment.

30. Pvt. Reuther was from Louisville and mustered in on December 24, 1861. Pvt. Hetzel's place of residence is unknown; however, he mustered in on August 24, 1863, and mustered out on December 31, 1864.

31. Private Nolt [not Noll] of Louisville mustered in on December 24, 1861. He had been wounded on December 31, 1862, at the Battle of Stones River.

32. The fierce battle of Chickamauga took place on September 19–20, 1863, about eight or nine miles southeast of Chattanooga, Tennessee. Federal casualties were 16,170 and Confederate losses were 18,454. See note 1 in chapter 1.

33. The Rebels did not have the resources to supply their army with standard uniforms and many of them wore homemade clothing of differing styles and colors. Some wore captured Federal shirts, blouses, or pants.

34. The editor was unable to determine whether six brothers in the 51st Ohio were shot or not.

35. The retreating Southerners set the railroad and wagon bridges on fire after crossing the Oostanaula River. A footbridge was quickly constructed over the remains of the railroad bridge and the wagon bridge was also rapidly repaired by Sherman's men. Castel, *Decision in the West,* 180, 190.

36. The Rebel army was not demoralized as Rentschler thought. They did not feel beaten, but were retreating to a better position. Castel, *Decision in the West,* 180.

CHAPTER 9

1. Brig. Gen. John Newton's division led the way for the 4th Corps on May 17, skirmishing with the enemy's rearguard (Maj. Gen. Joseph Wheeler's cavalry). In front of Adairsville, Confederate infantry, cavalry, and artillery halted Brig. Gen. John Newton's advance. Maj. Gen. Oliver O. Howard

reported his corps' casualties at around two hundred for the day, somewhat less that the 250 reflected in John Daeuble's diary. *OR* 38, pt. 1, p. 191.

2. Daeuble incorrectly identified Adairsville as Cassville in his May 18 entry. The army reached Cassville late on May 19.

3. John Daeuble recorded for the first time that he was becoming depressed. He was not alone; the constant contact with the enemy and grueling conditions in the field were hard on the men. A large number were afflicted with sagging morale, and some were suffering from depression. Castel, *Decision in the West*, 262.

4. Brig. Gen. Charles G. Harker's brigade of Newton's division erected a foot-bridge over the remains of the railroad bridge and repaired the wagon bridge within three hours of entering Resaca. Col. George P. Buell's Pontoniers set up a floating bridge. Castel, *Decision in the West*, 190

5. See note 1 above.

6. The "little river" was really Oothkaloga Creek, a tributary of the Oostanaula River that began south of Adairsville, intersected the Western and Atlantic Railroad about two miles north of Adairsville, and then ran in a northerly direction until it veered west, crossed the railroad again and flowed into the Oostanaula northwest of Calhoun. *OR* 38, pt. 1, p. 376.

7. Wood's division followed the railroad, while Newton's and Stanley's followed the wagon road west of and parallel to the railroad. Johnston deployed his infantry, cavalry, and artillery about two miles north of Adairsville blocking the 4th Corps advance. A Confederate force began moving around Newton's left flank into the area on Wood's right flank, and Newton was hit with strong musketry and artillery fire. However, Stanley moved up to cover Newton's flank ending the threat to Newton's left and Wood's right. *OR* 38, pt. 1, p. 858.

8. The first time there was a possibility of capture was on May 13 when the division headed down a wrong road about one-half mile south of Calhoun. See letter 14 in chapter 8.

9. Rentschler's estimate of the number of shots fired at Hazen's brigade may have been exaggerated, but the fire was heavy and generally constant.

10. Pvt. Henry Webert of Louisville mustered in on December 24, 1861, and had previously been wounded on September 19, 1863, at the battle of Chickamauga. He mustered out on January 7, 1865.

11. Wheeler's cavalry performed effectively in slowing the 4th Corps advance on the seventeenth. Johnston decided to withdraw from Adairsville rather than making a stand there when he discovered that the valley was wider than shown on his maps, making it too difficult to defend his flanks. McMurry, *Atlanta 1864*, 77–79.

12. Troops advancing in line of battle trample crops and destroy fences in their path. Encamped troops take fences rails for their fires. Houses that were occupied by sharpshooters or just lay in the path of an army were often set on fire.

13. The filth on the woman would undoubtedly protect her from advances by amorous soldiers.

14. Johnston entrenched his army facing west, and stretching several miles from just north of Cassville to just south of Cass Station. Hazen's brigade was opposite the extreme left of the Confederate line. Johnston's army increased to more than seventy thousand men with the arrival on May 18 of Maj. Gen. Samuel French's division of Leonidas Polk's corps. Castel, *Decision in the West*, 198–99; Reinhart, *A History of the 6th Kentucky*, 303.

15. Rentschler's estimate of 200 to 300 casualties appears reasonable considering Hazen's brigade suffered 726 casualties for the month of May, of which 467 were incurred on May 27. Hazen, *Narrative of Military Service*, 262; *OR* 38, pt. 1, p. 387.

16. General Johnston had announced to his army that he intended to make a stand at Cassville; however, Lt. Gens. John Bell Hood and Leonidas Polk subsequently advised him that Federal artillery would enfilade their lines, making their positions untenable after a short time. Also, Federals had crossed the Etowah River a few miles downriver and his flank and line of retreat toward Atlanta were threatened, so he ordered another retreat. Castel, *Decision in the West*, 204–6.

17. Some bloody battles would be fought before Atlanta was captured by Sherman's army, but none would destroy the Confederacy's Army of Tennessee.

18. The 9th and 10th Ohio infantry regiments were organized at Camp Dennison during the first week in June 1861. The 9th Ohio was a German regiment from Cincinnati and among its original members was August Willich, who became the first colonel of the 32nd Indiana and later rose to brigadier general. Dyer, *Compendium*, 3:1500; Boatner, *Civil War Dictionary*, 929–30.

19. Capt. Isaac N. Johnston of Pleasureville in Henry County replaced Maj. Richard T. Whitaker who had resigned on May 11. Major Whitaker stated in his resignation letter that no one was available to care for his eighty-three-year-old father except for the old man's Negroes. He supported his request by stating that his only brother, Walter, was also in the service and that a capable officer was available to replace him in the 6th Kentucky. Although Captain Johnston was placed in command of the regiment, he was not promoted to a higher rank. Richard C. Dawkins of La Grange, who had been previously commissioned as a major, was ill and unable to undertake field service at this time. Reinhart, *A History of the 6th Kentucky*, 306.

20. John Daeuble's premonition of death grew stronger on May 24, and he wrote despairingly the pleading in this paragraph on another page of the leather-bound notebook that contained his diary entries.

21. General Joseph E. Johnston had sent his army to block Sherman's legions. Hooker found Hood's corps entrenched near New Hope Church on the afternoon of the twenty-fifth and ordered his three divisions to attack

Alexander P. Stewart's division of Hood's Corps (the center). The attack was soundly repulsed by Confederate infantry and artillery. Federal losses totaled 1,665 men and Confederate losses were around 300–400. Sherman's advance was temporarily stopped. *OR* 38, pt. 1, p. 143; *OR* 38, pt. 2, p. 14; *OR* 38, pt. 3, p. 818.

22. The Battle of Pickett's Mill ignited because General Sherman decided to turn the left flank of the Confederate line. General Wood's division of the 4th Corps (with Hazen's brigade in the lead) marched off about an hour before noon. Progress was painfully slow because the terrain consisted of dense forests and jungle-like thickets that concealed deep ravines, rugged ridges, and small streams. Units from the 14th and 23rd Corps were sent to support Wood's division. After Southern cavalry discovered the Federal movement, Maj. Gen. Patrick R. Cleburne's veteran division extended to its right to meet the threat. Hoping Wood's division was beyond the enemy's line, General Howard ordered an advance in line of battle. Cleburne's troops were waiting on the crest of a ridge (hidden by natural cover) for Hazen's men and poured a devastating fire into Hazen's center and right. Hazen's disciplined troops attacked courageously, but could not withstand the murderous fire of musketry and artillery poured on them from above and along their right flank. Hazen's brigade suffered 467 casualties. The 6th Kentucky was on the far left of the line and did not receive as much fire as those to its right, incurring only ten casualties. A subsequent attack by Col. William H. Gibson's brigade also failed and Col. Frederick Knefler's brigade was pushed back, too. Wood's casualties totaled about fifteen hundred men. The promised support from the 14th Corps and 23rd Corps units failed to materialize, causing great anger among Wood's troops. Reinhart, *A History of the 6th Kentucky,* 307–24.

23. Sherman rested his army near Cassville until May 23, while much-needed equipment, supplies, and thousands of troops (new regiments, recruits, veterans returning from furloughs, and soldiers recovered from wounds and illnesses) were brought forward. The red-bearded chieftain would have about eighty thousand men to send against the enemy when he made his next move. William T. Sherman, *War Is Hell: Personal Narrative of His March through Georgia,* ed. Mills Lane (Savannah, Ga.: Beehive Press, 1974), 37; *OR* 38, pt. 4, p. 274.

24. See Rentschler's letter 2 in chapter 2.

25. Wood's division was supposed to march directly to Gillem's bridge, located about eight miles southwest of Cassville. An error caused the 3rd Division to reach the Etowah River about three miles from the bridge and made it necessary to backtrack in scorching heat and choking dust. Rentschler's derogatory comment about General Wood indicates that the general and his staff were not subscribers to the *Louisville Anzeiger* or he feared no adverse consequences from his remark. Reinhart, *A History of the 6th Kentucky,* 307.

26. See note 22 above.

27. Rentschler erred in supposing that this was the last place the Confederates were capable of defending north of Atlanta.

28. Rentschler describes the battle of Pickett's Mill. The editor has not read any other accounts of the battle of Pickett's Mill that mention that the Rebels used the ploy that they wanted to surrender to lure Hazen's troops closer before opening fire.

29. Rentschler's statement that almost seventeen hundred casualties were suffered by Wood's division was somewhat in error. Hazen's attack lasted almost an hour, as did Gibson's. The exchange of fire lasted more than five hours. The final tally for the battle of Pickett's Mill shows General Wood's 3rd Division suffered 1,467 casualties. Official records indicate Hazen's command suffered 87 killed, 326 wounded, and 54 missing: total 467. However, some listed as wounded died after the official report was prepared, and some listed as missing were dead. See note 24 above.

30. Hazen gathered together the remnants of his shattered brigade near Little Pumpkin Vine Creek and led them to a new position to the right, pursuant to orders from General Howard. Hazen was heartbroken over the significant losses incurred by his brigade. One of his Ohioans later wrote that when a lieutenant asked Hazen: "General, where is our brigade? . . . The General looked at him a moment. The tears began to roll down his cheeks, and he said: 'Brigade, h—l, I have none. But what is left is over there in the woods.' He addressed us kindly, and told us to get all the rest we could. I was an eye-witness to this, and know he did shed tears about his brigade on that day." Silas Crowell, "The General Wept: Pathetic Incident of the Battle of New Hope Church," *National Tribune*, Dec. 31, 1896.

31. Col. William H. Gibson of the 49th Ohio succeeded Brig. Gen. August Willich as commander of the 1st Brigade, 3rd Division (Wood's) after the battle of Resaca, but Rentschler still referred to it as Willich's brigade. William F. Fox shows the 32nd Indiana suffered a total of twenty-two casualties for the battle on May 27. The *Report of the Adjutant General of the State of Indiana* lists fourteen members of the 32nd Indiana killed or mortally wounded on May 27, including Capt. Henry Seifert of Lawrenceburg and First Lt. Max Hupfauf. Rentschler mentions Max Hupfauf because he lived in Jeffersonville, Indiana, opposite Louisville. Fox, *Regimental Losses in the American Civil War*, 349. *Indiana War Records: Report of the Adjutant General of the State of Indiana, 1861–65* (Indianapolis: Samuel L. Douglas State Printer; 1866), 8:501–4.

32. The regiment's records indicate that two men of the 6th Kentucky were mortally wounded on May 27, eight men were wounded but survived, and one was captured. It was not unusual for men reported missing immediately after a battle to be found later.

33. Orderly sergeants were also called first sergeants.

34. Pvt. Conrad Seibel of Louisville had previously been wounded on November 23, 1863, at Orchard Knob, near Chattanooga. He had mustered in on December 24, 1861.

35. Sgt. Philipp Nocker [not Necker] of Louisville was promoted from corporal to sergeant on May 1, 1862. He had mustered in on December 24, 1861, and served his full three-year enlistment.

36. Cpl. Lorenz Ultsch of Louisville was promoted to corporal on November 8, 1862. He served his full three-year enlistment, which began on December 24, 1861.

37. Sergeant Daeuble was survived by his parents, his older brother, and his older sister. His father was a disabled wood sawyer.

38. There was a lot of fault to go around for the slaughter at Pickett's Mill. Sherman had ordered an attack on the enemy's flank but did not know where it was located. The attack was delayed over two hours after Wood's division arrived, which allowed the enemy time to move reinforcements to the point of attack. Howard originally ordered an attack in column, but the columns were sent almost one hour apart instead of the usual five minutes apart. Howard also did not use all the troops he had available. General Johnson, who was supposed to advance and support Hazen on the left, did not send a man forward until Gibson's brigade advanced, and the one brigade he sent was stopped by Kelly's cavalrymen and rendered ineffective. General McLean, who was supposed to advance on the right flank of Wood's division and keep Govan's brigade occupied and prevent an enfilading fire, neither showed his troops to the enemy nor ordered them to fire a shot. In fact, General Howard reported that McLean withdrew because "he [McLean] alleged in excuse his men were entirely without rations." One can understand why Ambrose Bierce called this tragedy "The Crime at Pickett's Mill." Reinhart, *A History of the 6th Kentucky*, 320.

39. Vincent Cronin, *Napoleon Bonaparte: An Intimate Biography* (New York: William Morrow, 1972), 128.

40. Castel estimated Confederate casualties in the battle of Dallas at between one thousand and fifteen hundred. Casualties of the 15th Corps totaled approximately four hundred, while the 16th Corps did not report any. Castel, *Decision in the West*, 246.

41. The attack against Newton's division occurred around 11:00 P.M. on May 29, 1864, and was in the nature of strong skirmish fire rather than a full-scale attack. *OR* 38, pt. 1, p. 195.

42. Maj. Gen. Francis P. Blair Jr. and his two 17th Corps divisions of the Army of the Tennessee arrived at the front June 8, 1864. Blair left two thousand men at Rome, Georgia, fifteen hundred men at Allatoona Pass, and brought the remaining nine thousand troops to Acworth. Castel, *Decision in the West*, 264–65.

43. Castel estimated that the Federal losses through May approximated twelve thousand men, while the Confederate losses were at least nine thousand. Castel, *Decision in the West*, 261–62.

44. General Johnston's Rebel army reached its peak strength in mid-May after the arrival on May 18 of Maj. Samuel French's division. The arrival of

twenty-five thousand more Confederate troops on May 29 mentioned by Rentschler did not occur. See note 15 above.

45. A call for 500,000 more troops was not made by the Federal Government until July 18, 1864. A total of 386,461 troops were eventually raised by this call. General Johnston's army increased during May, but Sherman's army still outnumbered it by about five to three at the end of May 1864. Frederick Phisterer, *Statistical Record of the Armies of the United States* (1883; rpt. Carlisle, Pa.: John Kallmann, 1996), 8; McMurry, *Atlanta 1864,* 194–95.

46. Rentschler's estimate of 8,000 wagons is overstated. Sherman began the campaign with 5,150 wagon and 860 ambulances (or about 50 wagons per one thousand men). Castel, *Decision in the West,* 117.

47. The officers and men in the ranks had done their jobs and fought hard. However, General Sherman has been criticized by some historians for his conduct of the campaign, such as not sending a significantly larger force to Snake Creek Gap to get behind Johnston's army at Dalton, and making uncoordinated frontal attacks at Resaca. McMurry, *Atlanta 1864,* 73–74; Castel, *Decision in the West,* 567; Philip L. Secrist, *The Battle of Resaca: Atlanta Campaign 1864* (Macon, Ga.: Mercer Univ. Press, 1998), 64.

48. See note 43 above. The editor was unable to verify whether more Confederates or Federals were captured during May; however, for the entire campaign many more Confederates were captured, especially after May. McMurry, *Atlanta 1864,* 196–97.

CHAPTER 10

1. The totals of the brigade's killed, wounded, missing, and the grand total agree with the numbers General Hazen published in his memoirs. Hazen, *Narrative of Military Service,* 262.

2. General Hazen states in his memoirs that two men of the 1st Ohio were killed by lightning on June 2, 1864, but that only two were disabled and sent to the hospital. *Narrative of Military Service,* 262.

3. *OR* 38, pt. 1, pp. 388–89.

4. See note 38 to letter 16 in chapter 9.

5. Rentschler again demonstrates his willingness to openly criticize generals.

6. The Confederate army took the supplies that it needed from the local farms.

7. Atlanta, indeed, was crowded with farmers and townspeople fleeing from the advancing Union army. An especially large influx of refugees occurred after the Confederate army began abandoning Marietta on May 21, 1864. Castel, *Decision in the West,* 212.

8. The editor was unable to locate any other reference to General Thomas's headquarters mail being captured by the enemy around this time.

9. Sherman decided to slide his army over to the railroad (east). This movement started on June 1 and the troops on the Federal right moved behind the other troops to get to their new positions. Johnston reacted to this change by moving his own army to the east. Ibid., 265–66.

10. Chapters 7–11 of Exodus, in the Old Testament, describe the twelve plagues and the exodus of the Jews from Egypt.

11. Earlier in the war military authorities ordered soldiers not to disturb civilians' property and possessions. This situation changed as the war wore on, and property and possessions of disloyal civilians were taken or destroyed (both under orders and without orders). Some soldiers were disheartened by actions they were ordered to take, especially those that could harm or endanger non-combatants—particularly women and children. Rentschler believed the negative effect on the Rebels' desire to continue the war was worth it. See Castel, *Decision in the West,* 263, regarding plundering and outrages committed against civilians by some of Sherman's men during June 1864.

12. See Genesis 25:24–29 and 28:10–22.

13. Diseases and illnesses afflicted a large number of men during the spring and summer. In the Army of the Cumberland alone, over forty-three thousand sick were received into hospitals during the Atlanta campaign. The Confederate army reported about 30,000 sick in their hospitals during the month of July alone. OR 38, pt. 1, pp. 181, 184; Thomas Lawrence Connelly, *Autumn of Glory; The Army of Tennessee, 1862–1865* (Baton Rouge: Louisiana State Univ. Press, 1971), 437.

14. Companies A and C of the 6th Kentucky and all the original enlistees of the 5th Kentucky (Louisville Legion) were mustered in on September 9, 1861, at Camp Joe Holt.

15. A private's pay was only $13.00 per month.

16. Johnston pulled his army back to Kennesaw Mountain on the night of June 18. Sherman assumed Johnston was retreating all the way back to the Chattahoochee River and advised General Halleck on the morning of the nineteenth that he was starting immediately for Marietta. That night he advised Halleck that the enemy had only moved his line back to Kennesaw Mountain, so his trip south was deferred. OR 38, pt. 4, p. 519.

17. Rentschler has the date wrong here. Sherman ordered strong assaults against the fortified Confederate position at Kennesaw Mountain on June 27, 1864. The principal attacks were made by the divisions of Morgan L. Smith (2nd Division of the 15th Corps), John Newton (2nd Division of the 4th Corps), and Jefferson C. Davis (2nd Division of the 14th Corps). It was a stunning defeat for Sherman, who has been criticized for ordering the attack against formidable entrenchments. Federal casualties of approximately three thousand were about triple those of the Confederates. OR 38, pt. 1, pp. 296–97, 633–34; OR 38, pt. 3, p. 317; McMurry, *Atlanta 1864,* 107–10.

18. The editor was unable to determine if the sutlers at Big Shanty were shut down by General Sherman as Rentschler stated.

19. On the evening of June 23 the skirmish line received orders to push back the enemy. The skirmishers forced the Rebels out of their rifle pits on the first crest of the hill, but their main line was too strong to be defeated by

skirmishers and the Federals had to retreat under a murderous fire. Hazen's brigade lost about eighty men in this action. Companies H and K of the 6th Kentucky were in this fight and suffered four killed and ten wounded. Capt. Friedrich Nierhoff of Company E, who was assisting Capt. Daniel W. Owens of Company K, was killed by a shot to the head. Captain Nierhoff of Louisville had been promoted from sergeant to first sergeant on March 10, 1862, and had been commissioned as a captain on May 31, 1864 (to date from May 11, 1864). Reinhart, *A History of the 6th Kentucky,* 329.

20. General Hazen noted in his diary that around 2:00 A.M. on June 30, Brig. Gen, Jefferson C. Davis's division was assaulted for a short time. However, Davis and his brigade commanders did not mention this in their reports. Hazen, *Narrative of Military Service,* 266.

21. An officer of the 6th Arkansas Regiment wrote to the *Atlanta Confederacy* on June 28, 1864, describing friendly mingling of pickets from each side and stated he had recently had a conversation with an unidentified officer of the 6th Kentucky on the picket line. Reinhart, *A History of the 6th Kentucky,* 330.

22. Johnston retreated from his Kennesaw Mountain line because he believed Sherman was going to move around his left flank. Castel, *Decision in the West,* 327–28.

23. Maj. Charles C. O'Neill (not O'Neal) of the 16th South Carolina Infantry was killed at Kennesaw Mountain on June 22, 1864. *Broken Fortunes: South Carolina Soldiers, Sailors and Citizens Who Died in the Service of their Country and State in the War for Southern Independence, 1861–1865,* Randolph W. Kirkland Jr. (Charleston: South Carolina Historical Society, 1995), 263.

24. Johnston ordered Brig. Gen. Francis A. Shoup, his chief artillery officer, to gather gangs of Negroes from plantations and use them to build extensive fortifications where the Western and Atlantic Railroad crossed the Chattahoochee River. About one thousand men worked on these fortifications. Maj. William B. Foster, chief engineer for Maj. Gen. William W. Loring's division, assisted Shoup. Castel, *Decision in the West,* 334.

25. The college building was the Georgia Military Institute.

26. Stanley's division drove the enemy out of their rifle pits, then Newton's and Wood's divisions moved abreast of Stanley and advanced about one mile, skirmishing with the retreating secessionists. Reinhart, *A History of the 6th Kentucky,* 332.

27. Hazen's brigade arrived at Pace's Ferry shortly after the Confederates cut the pontoon bridge loose and members of the 1st Ohio and 41st Ohio skirmished with Rebels on the south bank. Hazen, *Narrative of Military Service,* 267–68.

28. The Black Forest Cuckoo Clock, noted for its finely crafted housing, loud tick-tock, and cuckoo bird sound at periodic intervals, was invented by Franz Anton Ketterer in the village of Schoenwald near Triburg in the

Black Forest region of southwestern Germany. An industry quickly developed there as farmers produced large numbers of these clocks in the cold winter months. Eric Bruton, *The History of Clocks and Watches* (New York: Rizzoli International Publications, 1979), 79–83.

29. Rentschler included parts of the parable of the lost (prodigal) son. Luke 15:11–31.

30. Castel stated that in mid-July Sherman "has about 90,000 troops of all arms available for field duty, whereas he estimates Johnston's force (accurately enough) at no more than 60,000." The numbers for infantrymen and artillerymen are not separately disclosed. Rentschler stated in his letter dated July 6, 1864, that the number of cannon should have been 166 instead of 106. Official records indicate that as of June 30, 1864, General Joseph E. Johnston's army contained a total of 187 pieces of artillery, including 36 in the artillery reserve. Castel, *Decision in the West*, 359. *OR* 38, pt. 3, pp. 677–78.

31. The 4th Corps captured ninety Rebels on July 5 and 126 more on July 6, 1864. *OR* 38, pt. 1, pp. 893, 894.

32. Sherman's frequent shifting of his armies, corps, and divisions as they advanced contributed to this confusion with the army's wagon trains.

33. The editor does not know the source of the Jew/rifle story.

34. The brigade suffered 2 officers and 12 enlisted men killed during June, and 3 officers and 104 men wounded. Hazen, *Narrative of Military Service*, 266.

35. Rentschler was wrong about the Confederates abandoning Atlanta quickly. A lengthy siege and bombardment of the city took place before the Rebels abandoned the city in early September.

36. For a detailed critique of Sherman's and Johnston's strategies see McMurry, *Atlanta 1864*.

CHAPTER 11

1. Confederate desertions increased after the Southern army's withdrawal from Kennesaw Mountain and each retreat thereafter. Castel, *Decision in the West*, 351.

2. Schofield crossed one regiment on the afternoon of July 8, one-half mile upstream from Sope Creek (often called Soap Creek in contemporary records) at Isham's Ford (at a place the Confederates called Cavalry Ford), and then moved the rest of his corps across the Chattahoochee in pontoon boats and on pontoon bridges at Sope Creek. General Schofield's report indicates that one gun, not four, was captured. Castel, *Decision in the West*, 336, 339; *OR* 38, pt. 2, pp. 515–16.

3. Rentschler's description of General Sherman as a "slow-speaking man" does not seem accurate. Sherman was known for his nervous energy and rapid talking. William F. G. Shanks, *Personal Recollections of Distinguished Generals* (New York: Franklin Square, 1866), 24.

4. The editor was unable to verify the number of prisoners taken by the 14th Corps.

5. Sherman's original objectives were to destroy the Confederacy's main western army and to get into its interior and destroy its war-making resources. Although the capture of Atlanta was important in that it ensured Abraham Lincoln's reelection in 1864, it was not specifically listed by General Grant as the primary objective of the campaign.

6. The 1st Regiment Georgia Line belonged to the 1st Brigade of the 1st Division Georgia Militia and was assigned to the Army of Tennessee on June 1, 1864, by Governor Joseph E. Brown. The identity and fate of the wounded captain is unknown. William R. Scaife, *The Campaign for Atlanta* (Saline, Mich.: McNaughton and Gunn, 1993), 189.

7. General Hazen's provost marshal, Capt. Sherburn Easton, was wounded in the abdomen by a bullet that drove his belt into his abdomen. Hazen later wrote that "to save him from exposure to hospital diseases," he sent Easton "privately at night in an ambulance to the railroad . . . with orders to get on the train and make his way north as quickly as possible, exercising his own wits to avoid the doctors and hospitals." Easton was put in a hospital at Nashville, "where he at once became inoculated and came near death's door with gangrene." Hazen, *Narrative of Military Service*, 412.

8. Hazen's topographical officer, Lt. Ambrose G. Bierce of the 9th Indiana Regiment, was wounded in the head on June 23, 1864. The editor found no other references regarding the possibility that Bierce was shot by a fellow soldier. Bierce became a well-known author after the war and wrote several articles about his wartime experiences, including one entitled "The Crime at Pickett's Mill." Hazen, *Narrative of Military Service*, 264. See Ambrose Bierce, "The Crime at Pickett's Mill," in *The Collected Works of Ambrose Bierce*, vol. 1 (New York: Gordian Press, 1966).

9. Pvt. James B. Weyman of Independence, Kentucky, a member of Company A, was wounded in his leg on July 20, 1864, and died as a result of pyemia from amputation on September 27, 1864. He had mustered in on September 9, 1861.

10. On July 17, 1864, Lt. Gen. John Bell Hood was promoted to full general and replaced Gen. Joseph E. Johnston as commander of the Army of Tennessee, because President Jefferson Davis had lost confidence in Johnston. On July 20, Stewart's and Hardee's corps attacked Hooker's corps and Newton's division on the south side of Peachtree Creek. Hooker's troops had crossed the creek but had not entrenched at the time of the attack, while Newton's command had advanced a little beyond the creek and thrown up very light breastworks just before the assault. The Confederate attacks were furious for a while, but failed. About 20,000 Federals were engaged, and estimates of the size of the Confederate forces actually engaged range from about 13,000 to 20,000. Union troops suffered about 1,600–1,900 casualties, including a little over 100 in Newton's division. The Confederates' casualties totaled

about 2,500 or more. John Bell Hood's first attempt to defeat Sherman's army failed. Castel, *Decision in the West,* 365–83.

11. Rentschler's story about Atlanta being surrounded on July 20 was not true. Sherman intended to surround the city and cut off its supplies from outside but was not close to achieving that objective on the twentieth.

12. Capt. Isaac N. Johnston of the 6th later wrote that "several" of his men fell on July 21, 1864, before the defensive works were completed. Only two members of the 6th Kentucky appear as casualties in the regiment's records. Cpl. Alfred B. Carpenter (Company K) of Woodford County was killed by a gunshot wound in the abdomen, and Pvt. John Brown (Company D) of Shelby County was wounded. Both men had mustered in on December 24, 1861. Private Brown had previously been wounded and captured at LaVergne, Tennessee, on January 25, 1863, and exchanged sometime in March 1863. Brown recovered from his wound and completed his three-year enlistment. Johnston, *Four Months in Libby,* 183.

13. Shortly after Wood's division completed its advance and began entrenching, the so-called battle of Atlanta began on the Union left. Hood sent Cheatham's [formerly Hood's] and Hardee's corps to attack McPherson's army, which was approaching the city from the east. A fierce and costly eight-hour battle took place and, as in the previous battle at Peachtree Creek, the Confederates failed to win advantage while suffering significant casualties. Out of approximately 35,000 engaged, Hood lost about 5,500 men, which he could not replace. Sherman's losses amounted to approximately 3,800 out of about 30,000 engaged, including the Army of the Tennessee's commander, General McPherson, who was killed during the fighting. Brig. Gen. Manning F. Force was wounded but survived. Force was commander of the 1st Brigade, 3rd Division, 17th Army Corps. Scaife, *Campaign for Atlanta,* 164.

14. Cedar Bluffs was a low, east-west running ridge located about a mile north of Lovejoy Station. Scaife, *Campaign for Atlanta,* 530.

15. Maj. Gen. Lovell H. Rousseau of Louisville had returned from a successful mounted raid that destroyed the Montgomery and East Point railroad around Opelika, Alabama, severing Atlanta's ties to Alabama. Companies A and C of the 6th Kentucky served briefly under Rousseau before being consolidated into the 6th Kentucky Volunteer Infantry Regiment late in 1861. Scaife, *Campaign for Atlanta,* 348, 385.

16. Lt. Gen. William J. Hardee was not wounded in the July 22 battle of Atlanta as Rentschler reports. See note 13 regarding casualties.

17. The Confederates in front of Wood's division moved back to within about one and a half miles of Atlanta; Wood's troops advanced about a mile on July 22. Reinhart, *A History of the 6th Kentucky,* 337–39.

18. Pvt. Henry Flottmann of Jackson County, Indiana, mustered in on December 24, 1861, and was wounded in May 1864 at or near Rocky Face

Ridge and on July 21, 1864, near Peachtree Creek. He mustered out December 31, 1864. Pvt. Charles Stoesser of Louisville mustered in on December 24, 1861, and was wounded on November 25, 1863, at Missionary Ridge and on July 23, 1864, near Atlanta. Stoesser was discharged as disabled on December 29, 1864.

19. Confederate returns for July 31, 1864, show the Army of Tennessee had a total of 51,793 men present for duty, including Joseph Wheeler's cavalry of 8,388 men. In addition, the Georgia militia would aggregate about five thousand men. *OR* 38, pt. 3, p. 680; Castel, *Decision in the West*, 424.
20. President Lincoln had made a draft call for five hundred thousand men on July 18, 1864. Phisterer, *Statistical Record*, 8.
21. Maj. Gen. Lovell H. Rousseau was the organizer and first colonel of the 5th Kentucky Volunteer Infantry Regiment and at this time commanded the District of Tennessee. *OR* 38, pt. 1, p. 70.
22. *OR* 38, pt. 1, pp. 174–75.
23. General Sherman selected Maj. Gen. Oliver O. Howard to head the Army of the Tennessee after Maj. Gen. James McPherson was slain on July 22, 1864. Maj. Gen. David S. Stanley succeeded Howard as commander of the 4th Corps. *OR* 38, pt. 5, p. 272.
24. *OR* 38, pt. 5, p. 267.
25. Hooker was a competent corps commander and senior in rank to Howard, and believed he was entitled to command the Army of the Tennessee. However, Sherman disliked and distrusted Hooker, so he gladly accepted Hooker's resignation. Castel, *Decision in the West*, 419–22.
26. General Hazen's memoirs indicate that on July 28, the 41st Ohio and some other regiments "carried Rebel skirmish-pits in our front . . . captured three prisoners." Hazen, *Narrative of Military Service*, 274.
27. The battle of Ezra Church took place west of Atlanta and resulted in 632 Federal casualties, mostly in the 15th Corps. A. P. Stewart's and Stephen D. Lee's Confederate corps suffered close to three thousand casualties in their failed attacks. Initial Federal estimates of enemy casualties ranged between five and six thousand. Castel, *Decision in the West*, 434; Hazen, *Narrative of Military Service*, 274.
28. According to Jack W. Melton, co-author of *Melton & Pawl's Guide to Civil War Artillery Projectiles* (Kennesaw, Ga.: Kennesaw Mountain Press, 1996), the artillery shells Rentschler described were fired by a rifled and banded 32-pounder smoothbore with a bore diameter of 6.4 inches. A smoothbore 32-pounder fired a solid shot of that weight; however, a rifled bolt weighed twice that or 64 pounds. The Confederates converted many large caliber smoothbore cannon into rifled guns. E-mail to the editor from Jack W. Melton, Dec. 26, 2001. The editor was not able verify as to whether the 64-pounders came from Macon as Rentschler reported.
29. The Rebels had strong entrenchments and fortifications, so it is not likely that they suffered "considerable casualties" from the bombardment.

30. The usual Union fortification included an earthen parapet or wall more than ten feet thick, bombproof dugouts, and communication trenches covered with logs and earth for protection. Reinhart, *A History of the 6th Kentucky,* 340.
31. Officers purchased their food from the commissary, while non-officers were issued rations.
32. Rentschler makes fun of the shoes that are too large for the men in the regiment. The Germans were generally a couple inches shorter in height than the white native Kentuckians, so the shoes seemed even larger to him.
33. General Hazen's diary indicated that thirty-six men were wounded and missing, while Rentschler reports there were thirty-eight. Hazen, *Narrative of Military Service,* 274.
34. The 5th Kentucky and 1st Ohio did not veteranize, and their three-year enlistments were about to end.
35. The Chattahoochee bridge was opened by August 12, 1864. *OR* 38, pt. 5, p. 481.
36. Mars was the ancient Roman god of war and agriculture.

Chapter 12

1. The Union army used African Americans as cooks, teamsters, blacksmiths, hospital orderlies, laborers, and spies. The first black regiment was mustered into Federal service in September 1862. Boatner, *Civil War Dictionary,* 584.
2. Sow belly was salted pork, a staple in a soldier's field rations. Hardtack, also called crackers, was the hard bread issued in the field.
3. The editor could not locate any information about the Grass Devil mentioned by Rentschler, but it was surely a fearsome creature.
4. Frederick II (Frederick the Great) of Prussia, an accomplished military leader who ruled Prussia from 1740–1786, was sometimes called *der alte Fritz* (old Fritz). Giles MacDonogh, *Frederick the Great: A Life in Deeds and Letters* (New York: St. Martin's Press, 1999), 4, 131, 382–84.
5. Rentschler assumed that one regiment from each brigade served on picket each day, a regiment contains five hundred men, and each man fires one hundred shots. His estimate of a regiment's average strength on the picket line appears high.
6. The editor at the *Louisville Anzeiger* misread Rentschler's writing or there was a typesetting error. Rentschler was obviously referring to the 6th Indiana of Hazen's brigade, not the 6th Maryland regiment.
7. Col. William H. Gibson's 1st Brigade of the 3rd Division, 4th Corps, did not advance on Hazen's right, allowing the 6th Indiana to be flanked by the enemy. General Hazen noted that one man from the 23rd Kentucky was killed by grapeshot on August 3 while in reserve. This may have been the slain soldier Rentschler mentioned. Hazen, *Narrative of Military Service,* 275.
8. The Arch Rebel was Confederate President Jefferson Davis.

9. General Thomas believed Schofield was heavily engaged with the enemy during the morning and early afternoon of August 5 and ordered a demonstration to prevent reinforcements from being sent from his front to the Confederate left. However, there was only heavy skirmishing in Schofield's front. *OR* 38, pt. 1, pp. 915, 916; pt. 2, p. 517.

10. Grigori Aleksandrovich Potemkin, governor of the Crimea and former lover of Catherine II (the Great), organized a fabulous tour of the Crimea for the Russian Empress in 1787, and successfully disguised all the weak points in his administration, giving rise to the spurious tale of his building artificial villages for her to see. "Potemkin village" came to denote any pretentious facade designed to cover up a shabby or undesirable condition. David Warnes, *Chronicle of the Russian Tsars: The Reign-by-Reign Record of the Rulers of Imperial Russia* (London: Thames and Hudson, 1999), 137, 140.

11. Rentschler's source was wrong. Schofield did not suffer significant casualties on August 4 or 5.

12. Camp Sumter at Andersonville, Georgia, was a poorly supplied, disease-ridden prison camp in which over 13,000 Union soldiers died while in captivity. The chances of dying at Andersonville were much greater than being killed in battle. Boatner, *Civil War Dictionary,* 15.

13. Maj. Gen. George Stoneman led his cavalry division directly to Macon, Georgia, instead of meeting Brig. Gen. Edward M. McCook's cavalry division at Lovejoy Station south of Atlanta as originally planned. Stoneman destroyed some of the Georgia Central Railroad east of Macon, but upon arrival at Macon on July 30, found Georgia Militia and Home Guards supported by artillery. Gen. Joseph E. Johnston and his wife were living in Macon at this time, and Johnston was offered command of these forces, but he declined because he preferred to act only in an advisory capacity. Stoneman abandoned the plan to break up the railroad at Macon, and decided to attempt to free approximately thirty thousand Federals at the Andersonville prison camp. However, he quickly changed his mind and when he headed north encountered Brig. Gen. Alfred Iverson's Southern cavalry division. Stoneman attacked Iverson and was defeated. Then Iverson counterattacked, and Stoneman, Col. James Biddle, and Biddle's brigade (about six hundred officers and men) were captured. Two other Federal brigades escaped. This engagement is called the battle of Sunshine Church. Scaife, *Atlanta,* 115–18; Gilbert E. Govan and James W. Livingood, *A Different Valor: The Story of General Joseph E. Johnston, CSA* (Indianapolis: Bobbs-Merrill, 1956), 323–24.

14. James P. Brownlow, colonel of the 1st Tennessee Cavalry (U.S.) and youngest son of Tennessee Unionist William G. "Parson" Brownlow, led the 1st Tennessee Cavalry and 4th Kentucky Mounted Infantry (both of Brig. Gen. John T. Croxton's brigade of Brig. Gen. Edward M. McCook's 1st Cavalry Division) through an enemy encirclement during the division's disastrous raid to Lovejoy Station, south of Atlanta. Confederate cavalry

had learned of the raid and descended on McCook's command, causing the Federals to flee for their lives. McCook reported heavy losses and lack of cooperation from General Stoneman, who was supposed to meet him at Lovejoy Station. David Evans, *Sherman's Horsemen; Union Cavalry Operations in the Atlanta Campaign* (Bloomington: Indiana Univ. Press, 1996), 17; Scaife, *Campaign for Atlanta*, 111–16.

15. The battle of Utoy Creek took place on the Federal right on August 6. Most of the fighting was done by Brig. Gen. James W. Reilly's brigade of Brig. Gen. Jacob D. Cox's 23rd Corps division. Reilly suffered 306 casualties. Major General Bate's entrenched Confederates suffered no more than twenty casualties. Sherman initially thought his casualties were about a thousand. Castel, *Decision in the West*, 457–58.

16. The Kingdom of Bavaria bordered Rentschler's native Kingdom of Württemberg in the east.

17. Atlanta was too strongly fortified to take by direct attack, so Sherman would have to tighten the siege by further cutting off its line of communication.

18. Grant's offensive in Virginia had stalled at Petersburg, and his army had been besieging Lee's Army of Northern Virginia there since mid-June. Catton, *The Civil War* (New York: Fairfax Press, 1980), 211–13.

19. Capt. William Frank of Company E believed Decherd was a desolate place.

20. Capt. Isaac N. Johnston of Company D succeeded Major Richard T. Whitaker as commander of the 6th Kentucky after the major resigned on May 11. See note 19 in chapter 9.

21. The reports were never published in the *Louisville Anzeiger*.

22. Maj. Gen. Lovell H. Rousseau commanded the District of Tennessee and the 4th Division of the 20th Corps. *OR* 38, pt. 5, p. 636.

23. The stretch of railroad running between Anderson, Tennessee, and Stevenson, Alabama, covered approximately eleven miles. In mid-September, a fourteen-mile stretch of the railroad running between Anderson and the tunnel at Cowan, Tennessee, was added to the 6th Kentucky's responsibility. Reinhart, *A History of the 6th Kentucky*, 345.

24. Companies A and C mustered out on September 23, 1864, at Louisville; Company B mustered out on November 2, 1864, at Louisville; Companies D through I mustered out on December 31, 1864, at Nashville; and Company K and the regimental headquarters mustered out on January 2, 1865, at Nashville. Reinhart, *A History of the 6th Kentucky*, 346–48.

EPILOGUE

1. Reinhart, *A History of the 6th Kentucky*, 344, 347–49; Thomas Speed, R. M. Kelly, and Alfred Pirtle, *Union Regiments of Kentucky* (Louisville, Ky.: Courier-Journal, 1897), 332.

2. Reinhart, *A History of the 6th Kentucky*, 348–49; William F. Fox, *Regimental Losses of the American Civil War 1861–65* (Albany, N.Y.: Albany Publishing, 1889), 337.

3. John Daeuble Pension File No. 173731.
4. Gottfried Rentschler Pension File No. 605075; Pauline Rentschler v. Gottfried Rentschler, Louisville Chancery Court, Case No. 19740, June 1866; "Gottfried Rentschler," *Highland (Illinois) Journal,* Nov. 25, 1897; Arndt, *German-American Newspapers and Periodicals,* 160–61.
5. Gould, *Investigations,* 27.
6. Burton, *Melting Pot Soldiers,* 110.
7. Gary Cross, "The XI Corps at Gettysburg July 1, 1863," *Blue & Gray Magazine* 19, no. 2 (holiday 2001): 68; Stephen W. Sears, *Chancellorsville* (Boston and New York: Houghton Mifflin, 1996), 432–37.
8. Stierlin, *Der Staat Kentucky,* 193; Rippley, *German-Americans,* 71; Burton, *Melting Pot Soldiers,* 110.
9. Yater, *Two Hundred Years at the Falls of the Ohio,* 92, 93.
10. U. S. Census, Population, Kentucky, 1860, 1870, 1880.
11. Arndt, *German-American Newspapers,* 169.
12. Tapp and Klotter, *Kentucky: Decades of Discord,* 1–15.

APPENDIX B

1. Reinhart, *A History of the 6th Kentucky,* 21, 29–40; *OR* 7, p. 529.
2. Reinhart, *A History of the 6th Kentucky,* 42–45; *OR* 10, pt. 2, pp. 329–30, 108, 292–93; Livermore, *Numbers and Losses,* 80.
3. Van Horne, *Army of the Cumberland,* 99–100; *OR* 10, pt. 1, pp. 108, 326; Livermore, *Numbers and Losses,* 80. For additional information see Stacy D. Allen, "Shiloh! The First Day's Battle" *Blue & Gray Magazine* 14, no. 3 (winter 1997); Stacy D. Allen, "Shiloh!: The Second Day's Battle and Aftermath," *Blue & Gray Magazine* 14, no. 4 (spring 1997); and James D. McDonough, *Shiloh: In Hell Before Night* (Knoxville: Univ. of Tennessee Press, 1977).
4. *OR* 10, pt. 1, pp. 672–77; Reinhart, *A History of the 6th Kentucky,* 80–87.
5. Reinhart, *A History of the 6th Kentucky,* 90–95.
6. Ibid., 96, 98–102.
7. Ibid. 110–11; For further information about the march to Louisville see Kenneth A. Hafendorfer, *Perryville: Battle for Kentucky* (Louisville: KH Press, 1991), 66–86; and Kenneth W. Noe, *Perryville: The Grand Havoc of Battle* (Lexington: Univ. Press of Kentucky, 2001), 58–79; *OR* 16, pt. 2, pp. 873–75.
8. For a detailed account of the battle of Perryville see the works by Hafendorfer and Noe cited in the previous note; Reinhart, *A History of the 6th Kentucky,* 122–24.
9. Reinhart, *A History of the 6th Kentucky,* 124–36.
10. See Peter Cozzens, *No Better Place to Die: The Battle of Stones River* (Urbana: Univ. of Illinois Press, 1990), for an excellent description of the battle of Stones River.
11. Reinhart, *A History of the 6th Kentucky,* 144–53; *OR* 20, pt. 1, p. 557.
12. Ibid., 159–63.
13. Ibid., 163; *OR* 20, pt. 1, pp. 545–46.

14. Reinhart, *A History of the 6th Kentucky,* 173, 177, 179, 192; Warner, *Generals in Blue,* 226.

15. Van Horne, *Army of the Cumberland,* 302–8.

16. Reinhart, *A History of the 6th Kentucky,* 195–96.

17. See Cozzens, *This Terrible Sound,* for an excellent description of this battle.

18. Reinhart, *A History of the 6th Kentucky,* 212–27.

19. Van Horne, *Army of the Cumberland,* 386–87, 392, 394–95.

20. *OR* 30, pt. 4, pp. 209–11; Hazen, *Narrative of Military Service,* 156.

21. Reinhart, *A History of the 6th Kentucky,* 231–62. See Cozzens, *Shipwreck of Their Hopes,* for an excellent description of the battles around Chattanooga.

22. Reinhart, *A History of the 6th Kentucky,* 263–83.

23. Ibid., 284–342, 348–49. See Castel, *Decision in the West,* and McMurry, *Atlanta 1864,* for descriptions of the Atlanta campaign.

24. Reinhart, *A History of the 6th Kentucky,* 343–48.

Index

Party (Know Nothings) xxii–xxiii; on
Washington's birthday, 196n4
Louisville and Nashville Railroad, 208n41.
Louisville Volksblatt, 85, 180–81n45,
207n30.

Maas, Sgt. Franz, 111, 115, 215n3.
Macon, Ga., 151, 158, 231n13.
Manchester, Tenn., 173.
Manson, Brig. Gen. Mahlon D., 114,
216n19.
Marietta, Ga., 134, 136, 158, 165.
Maryville, Tenn., 22, 44, 45, 51.
McCook, Brig. Gen. Edward M., 155, 158,
231–32n13, 231–32n14.
McDonald's Station, Tenn., 86, 95.
McLean, Brig. Gen. Nathaniel C. 222n38.
McPherson, Maj. Gen. James B., 126, 145,
150, 228n13.
McSpadden, Col. Samuel K., 216n20.
Melcher, Lt. Valentine, 13, 186n31.
*Melting Pot Soldiers: The Union's Ethnic
Regiments*, xx.
*Memoirs of the Confederate War for
Independence*, xx.
Mill Creek Gap. See Buzzard Roost Gap.
Missionary Ridge, xxx, 1, 12, 15, 56, 175.
Missionary Ridge, battle of, 13–15, 68,
174, 186n32.
Missouri Regt., 15th, 10, 185n21.
Moccasin Point, 2, 182n5.
Morganton, Tenn., 22.
Morrison, Tenn., 55, 63.
Mossville, Tenn., 80.
Mühlheim am Bach in Württemberg,
xxiii, xxvi.
Murfreesboro, Tenn., 172, 173.

Nashville, Tenn., 50, 61, 160, 165, 172.
Nashville and Chattanooga Railroad, 172,
175, 191n4, 208n41.
Nativism, xxiv, xxx, 200n19.
Negroes: See African Americans.
Nelson, Brig. Gen., William, 171.

New Hope Church, Ga., battle of, 122–23,
219–20n21.
New Market, Tenn., 63, 64.
Newton, Brig. Gen. John, 119, 127, 143,
144, 204n1, 207n33.
Newton's division, 89, 104, 143.
Nierhoff, Capt. Friedrich, 135, 224–25n19.
Necker [Nocker], Sgt. Philipp, 126, 225n35.
19th Brigade, 4th Div, Army of the Ohio,
171, 174.
Noll [Nolt], Pvt. August, 115, 217n31.

Ohio, Department of the, 65, 70.
Ohio Regts: 1st, 1, 46, 102, 130, 148, 153,
223n2; 6th, 20, 46, 102, 212n16; 9th,
xxxvi, 122, 219n18; 10th, 122, 219n18;
41st, 1, 10, 12, 33, 37, 69, 82, 102, 130,
191n43; 71st Ohio, 160; 93rd, 1, 8, 102,
123, 130; 100th, 63, 82; 104th, 63;
124th, 1, 10, 46, 102, 113, 130.
Orchard Knob, battle of, 175, 185n27.
O'Neal [O'Neill], Maj. Charles C., 136,
225n23.
Oostanaula River, 109, 113, 114, 217n35.
Oothkaloga Creek, 119, 218n6.

Palmer, Maj. Gen. John M., 65, 104,
184n19, 213n26.
Patrick, Charles, 169.
Payne, Col. Oliver. H., 102.
Peachtree Creek, 143, 144, 147, 150, battle
of, 227–28n10.
Perryville, Ky., battle of, 172.
Philadelphia, Tenn., 49, 80.
Pickett's Mill, Ga., battle of, 121, 123,
124–26, 175, 220n22, 221–22n28–38.
Pirtle, Maj. John, xxviii.
Pittsburg Landing, Tenn., 171–72.
Pope [Pape], Heinrich, 115, 217n29.
Potemkin, Grigori Aleksandrovich,
157–58, 231n10.
Powder Springs Gap, Tenn., 74, 77, 78.
Prejudice, xxii, xxiv, xxxii, xxix–xxx,
67–68, 166–67, 200n19, 201n24.

Two Germans in the Civil War was designed and typeset on a Macintosh computer system using QuarkXPress software. The body text and display type are set in Minion. This book was designed and typeset by Barbara Karwhite and manufactured by Thomson-Shore, Inc.